# THE
# PEOPLE
# INSIDE

THE
# PEOPLE
## INSIDE

by

Ray Fawkes

*Edited by*
James Lucas Jones

*Book design by*
Jason Storey

*For Baron*
*A promise is a promise*

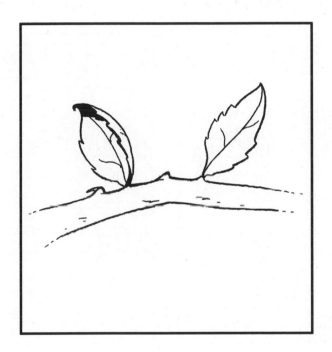

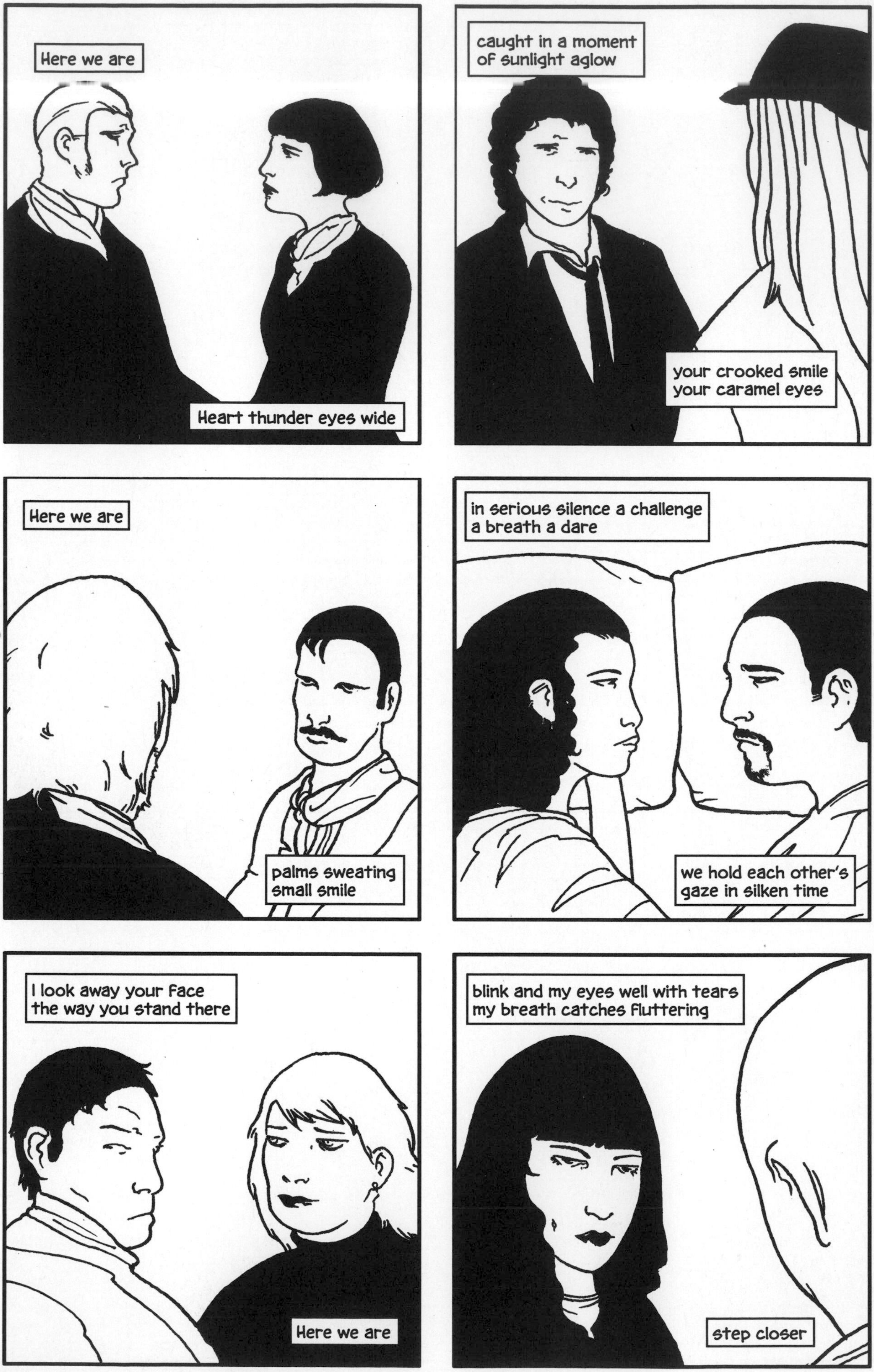
Here we are
Heart thunder eyes wide
caught in a moment
of sunlight aglow
your crooked smile
your caramel eyes
Here we are
palms sweating
small smile
in serious silence a challenge
a breath a dare
we hold each other's
gaze in silken time
I look away your face
the way you stand there
Here we are
blink and my eyes well with tears
my breath catches fluttering
step closer

Here we are

I don't deserve to be this happy I've never felt so right

never done this before

smile church music were you ready for this all along it seems so

Here we are

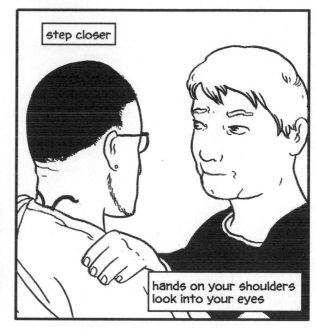

step closer

hands on your shoulders look into your eyes

sigh

the sky opens up above me

raise my glass and grin

Here

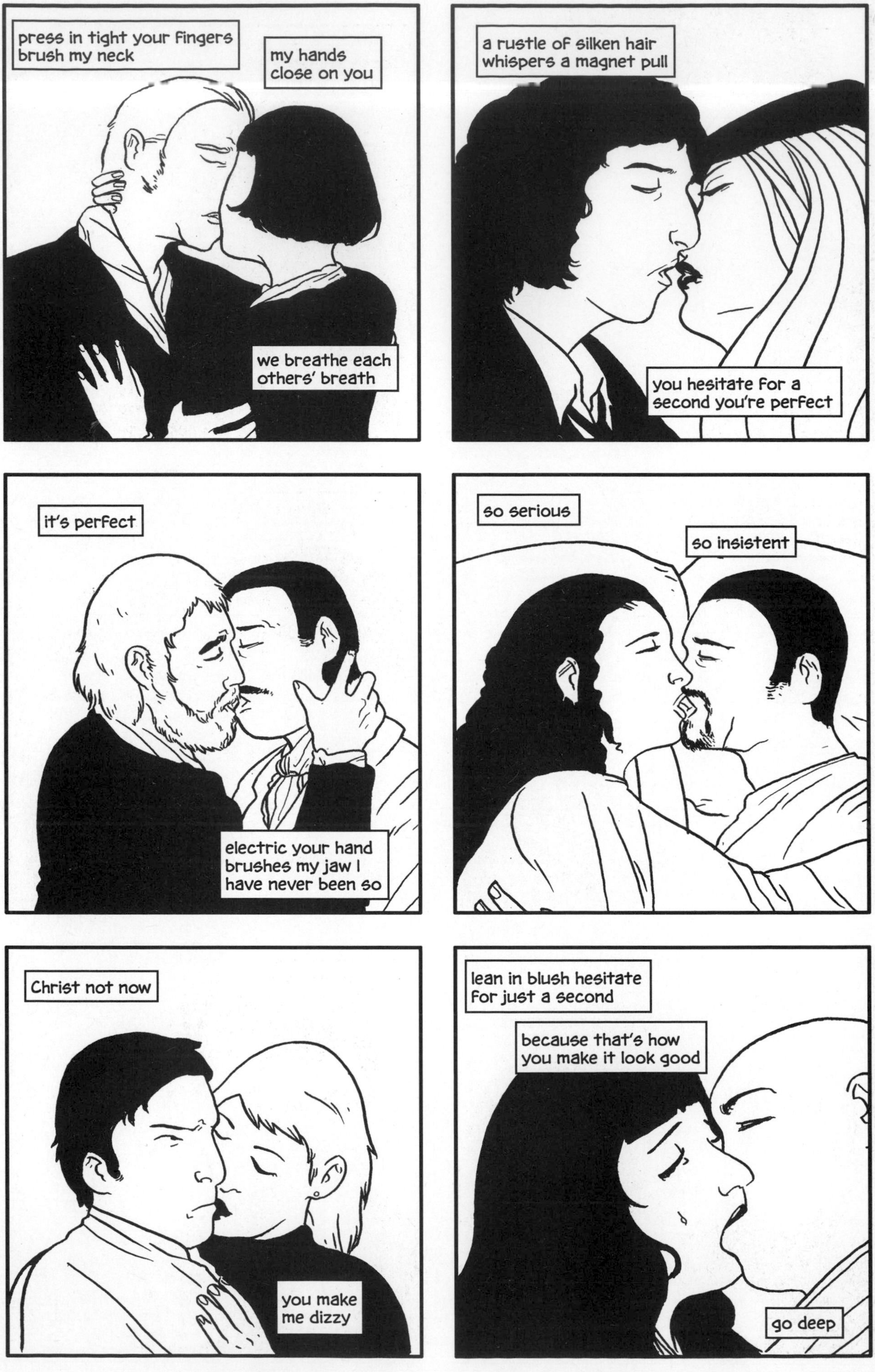
press in tight your fingers brush my neck
my hands close on you
we breathe each others' breath
a rustle of silken hair whispers a magnet pull
you hesitate for a second you're perfect
it's perfect
electric your hand brushes my jaw I have never been so
so serious
so insistent
Christ not now
you make me dizzy
lean in blush hesitate for just a second
because that's how you make it look good
go deep

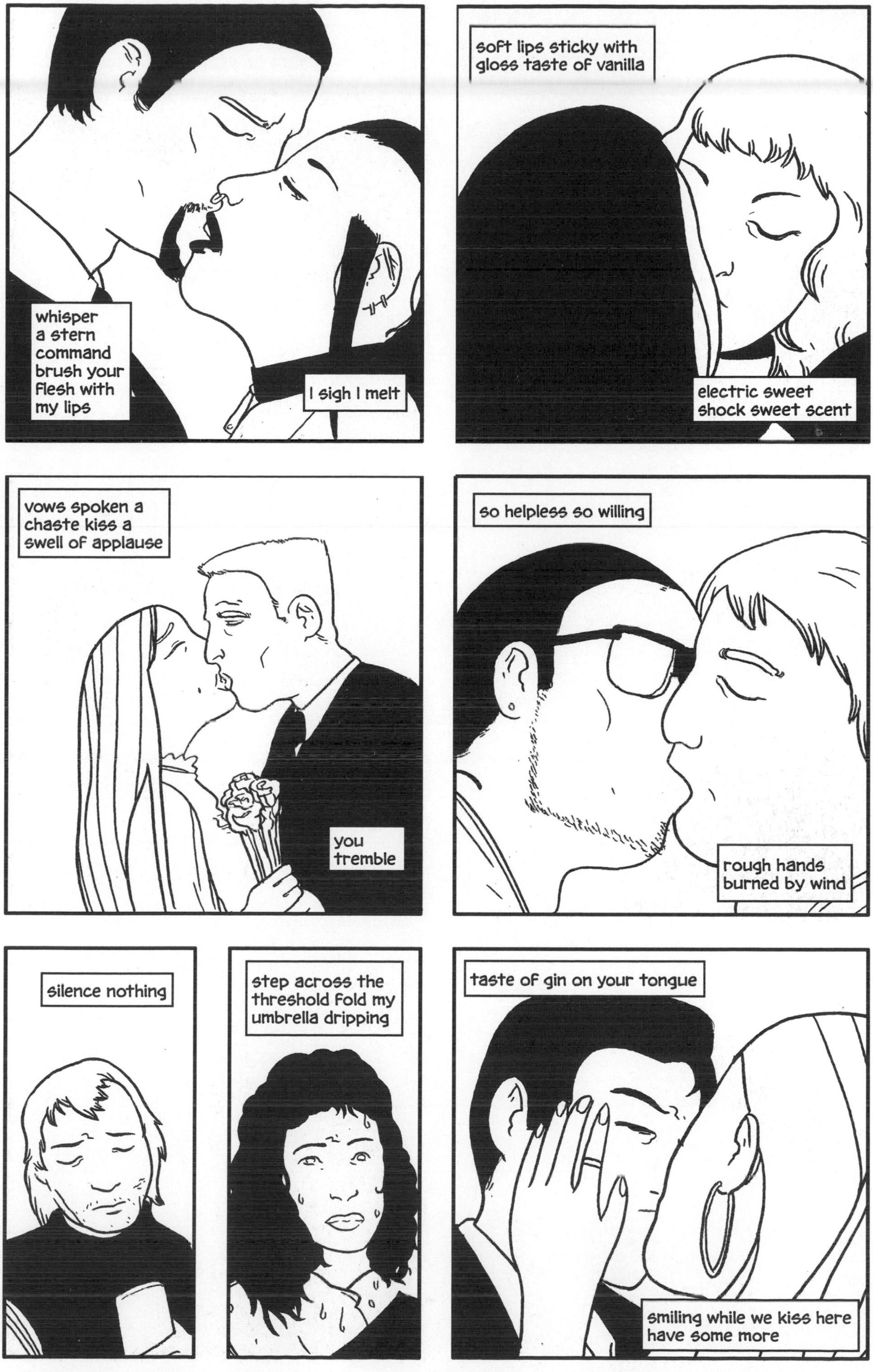
whisper a stern command brush your flesh with my lips
I sigh I melt
soft lips sticky with gloss taste of vanilla
electric sweet shock sweet scent
vows spoken a chaste kiss a swell of applause
you tremble
so helpless so willing
rough hands burned by wind
silence nothing
step across the threshold fold my umbrella dripping
taste of gin on your tongue
smiling while we kiss here have some more

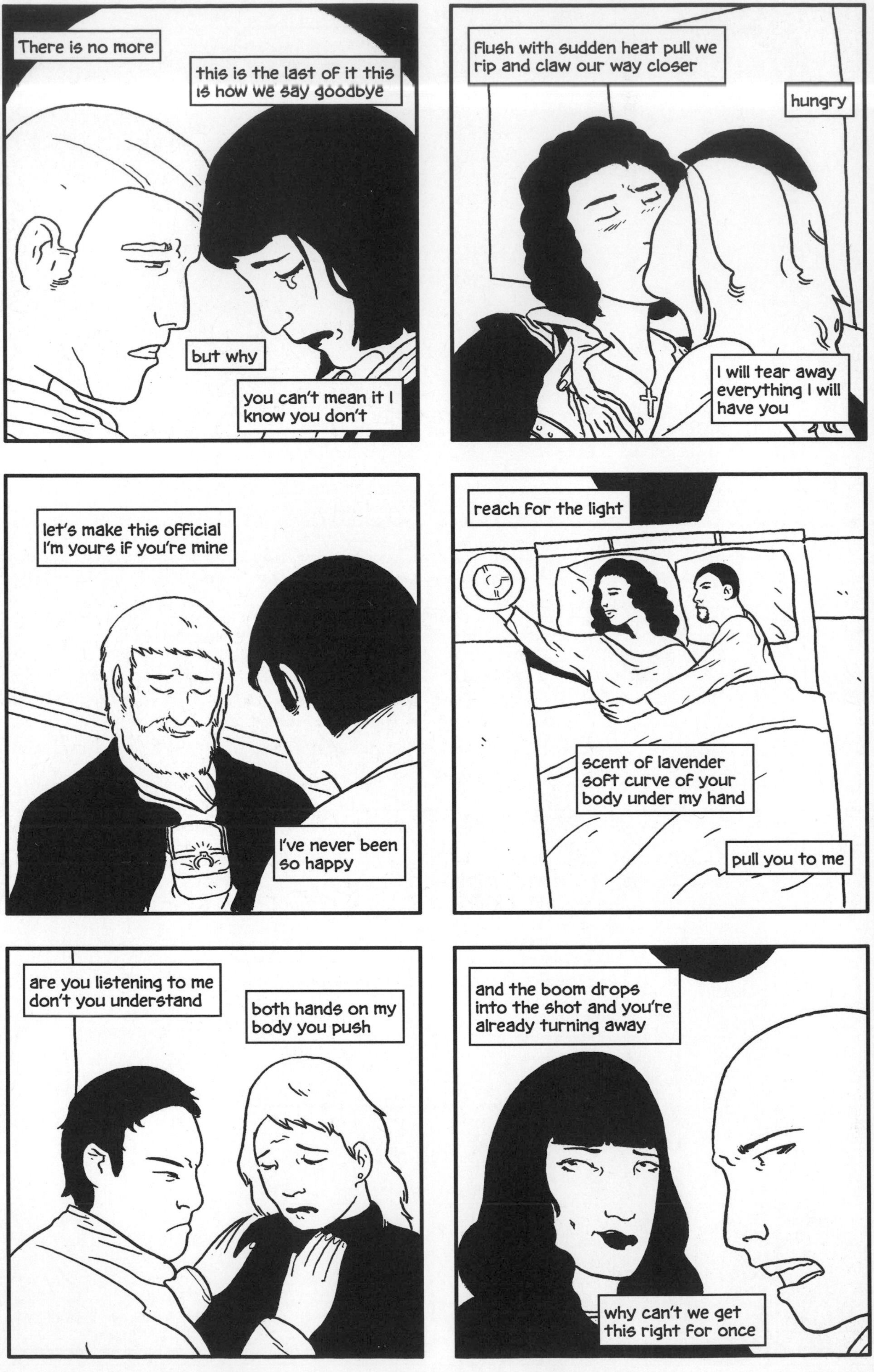
There is no more
this is the last of it this is how we say goodbye
but why
you can't mean it I know you don't
Flush with sudden heat pull we rip and claw our way closer
hungry
I will tear away everything I will have you
let's make this official I'm yours if you're mine
I've never been so happy
reach for the light
scent of lavender soft curve of your body under my hand
pull you to me
are you listening to me don't you understand
both hands on my body you push
and the boom drops into the shot and you're already turning away
why can't we get this right for once

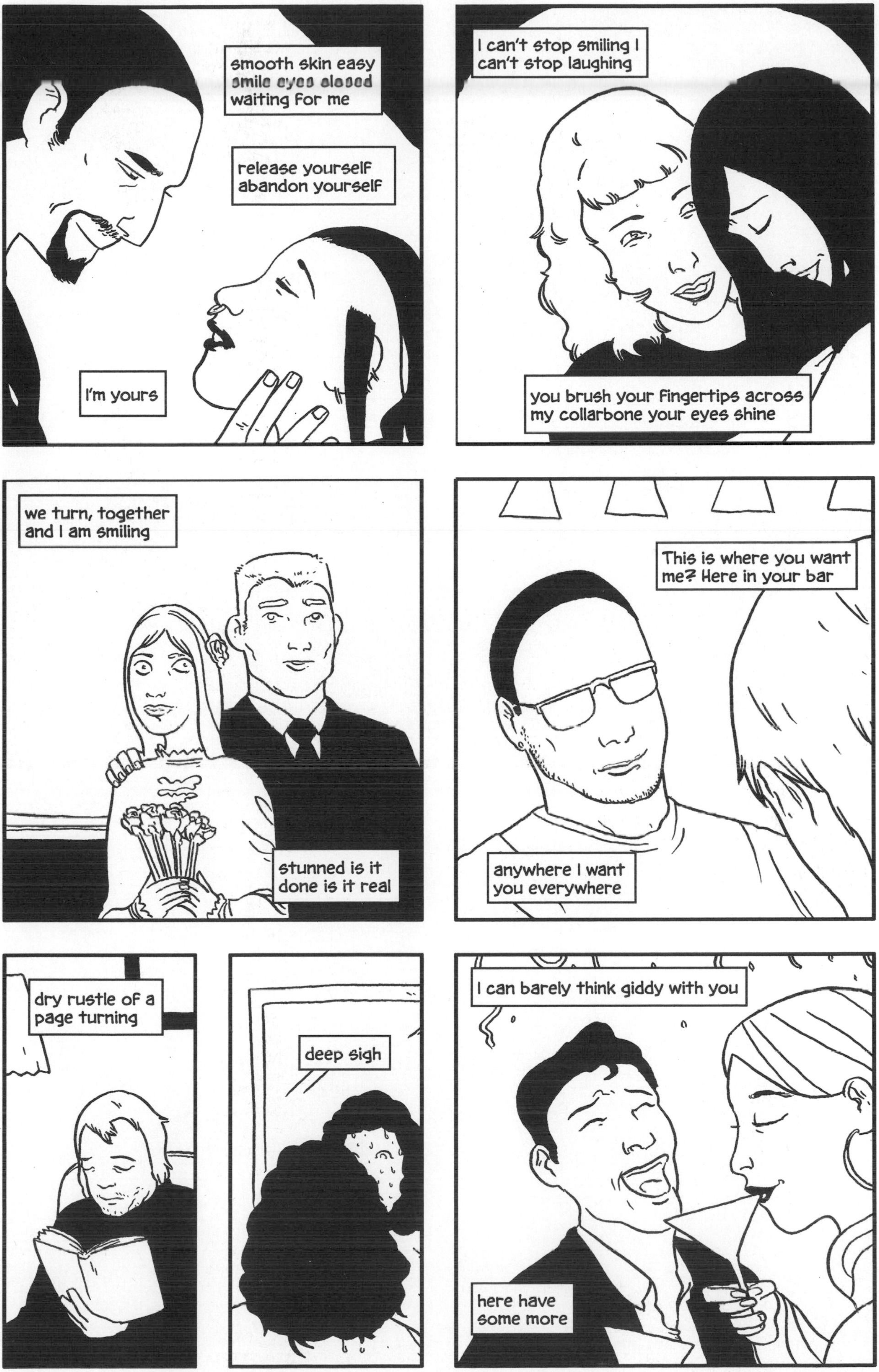
smooth skin easy smile eyes closed waiting for me
release yourself abandon yourself
I'm yours
I can't stop smiling I can't stop laughing
you brush your fingertips across my collarbone your eyes shine
we turn, together and I am smiling
stunned is it done is it real
This is where you want me? Here in your bar
anywhere I want you everywhere
dry rustle of a page turning
deep sigh
I can barely think giddy with you
here have some more

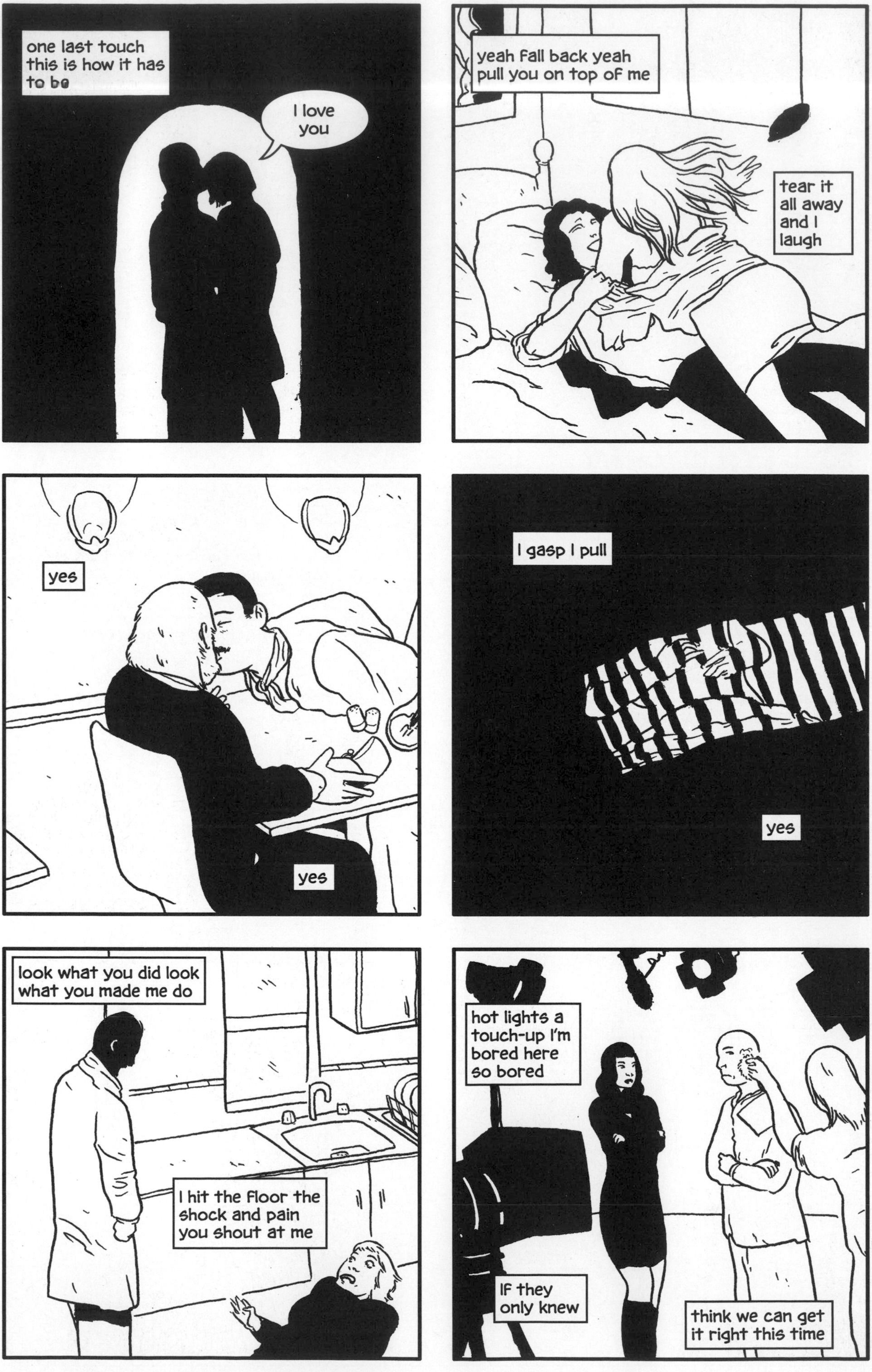
one last touch this is how it has to be
I love you
yeah fall back yeah pull you on top of me
tear it all away and I laugh
yes
yes
I gasp I pull
yes
look what you did look what you made me do
I hit the floor the shock and pain you shout at me
hot lights a touch-up I'm bored here so bored
If they only knew
think we can get it right this time

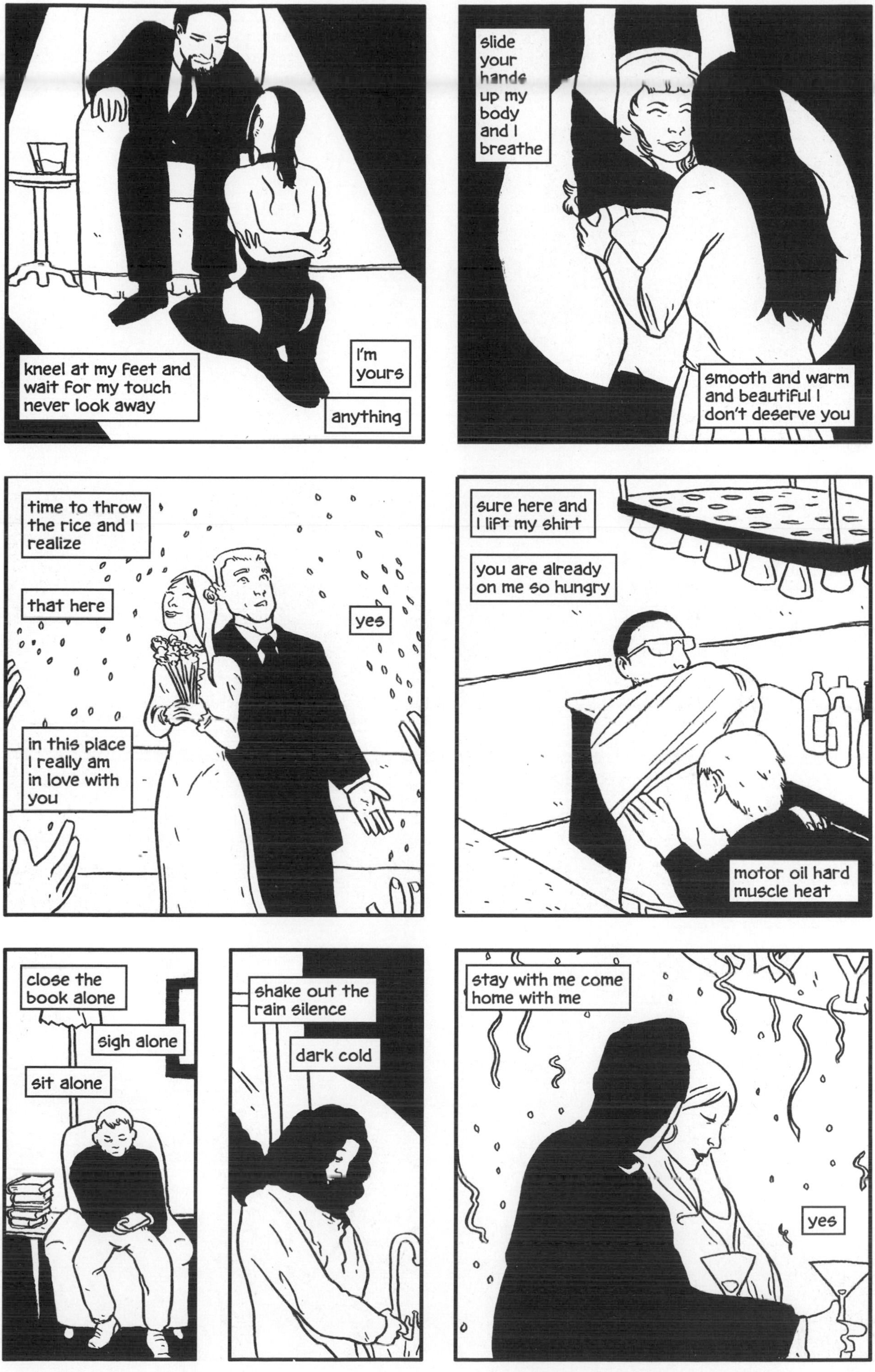
kneel at my feet and wait for my touch never look away
I'm yours
anything
slide your hands up my body and I breathe
smooth and warm and beautiful I don't deserve you
time to throw the rice and I realize
that here
yes
in this place I really am in love with you
sure here and I lift my shirt
you are already on me so hungry
motor oil hard muscle heat
close the book alone
sigh alone
sit alone
shake out the rain silence
dark cold
stay with me come home with me
yes

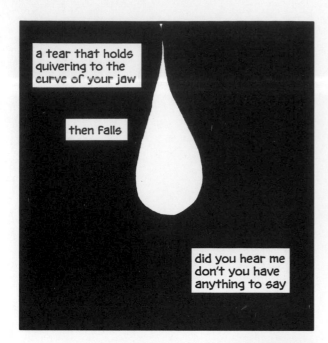

a tear that holds quivering to the curve of your jaw

then falls

did you hear me don't you have anything to say

hot and close

sweat and sigh

sheer cloth lies where it was dropped where it was flung in giddy haste

just us here us now together nothing between us

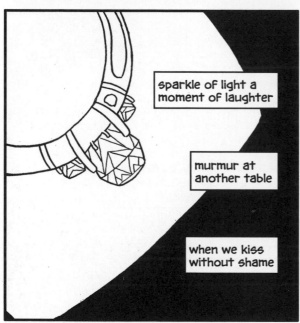

sparkle of light a moment of laughter

murmur at another table

when we kiss without shame

a thoughtless moment

shouting you make me so angry you want a piece of me is that what you want

take a piece of me I'll take a piece of you

please stop

wires and cameras and wheels and cables and tracks

mumbling behind the lights angle aperture

exposure

are we ready

I will leash you I will claim you for my own
I will have you plunder you violate you
creak and snap of leather steel clip
tell me
tell me what you'll do to me
breathing each others' breath
opened up wet and warm and flushed
flowers on the car seat
shedding petals
we will leave together we will start together
I push you down and look up
a rack of glasses hanging above all in their rows so orderly
grab you hold you
press into you
pressed into leather
a faded cross
are we alone
no we're not alone
kitty
are we
yes you say yes
lightheaded blood pumping
yes

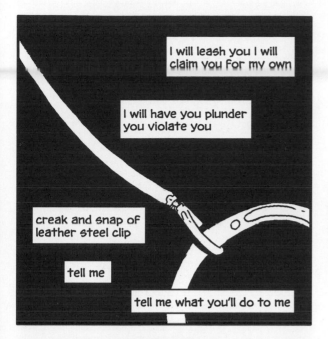

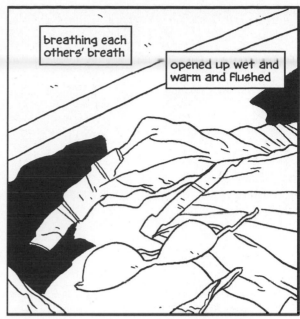

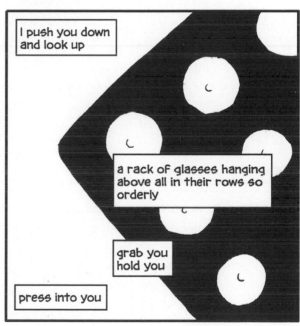

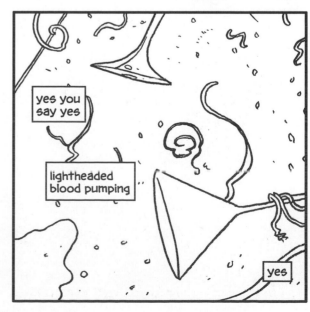

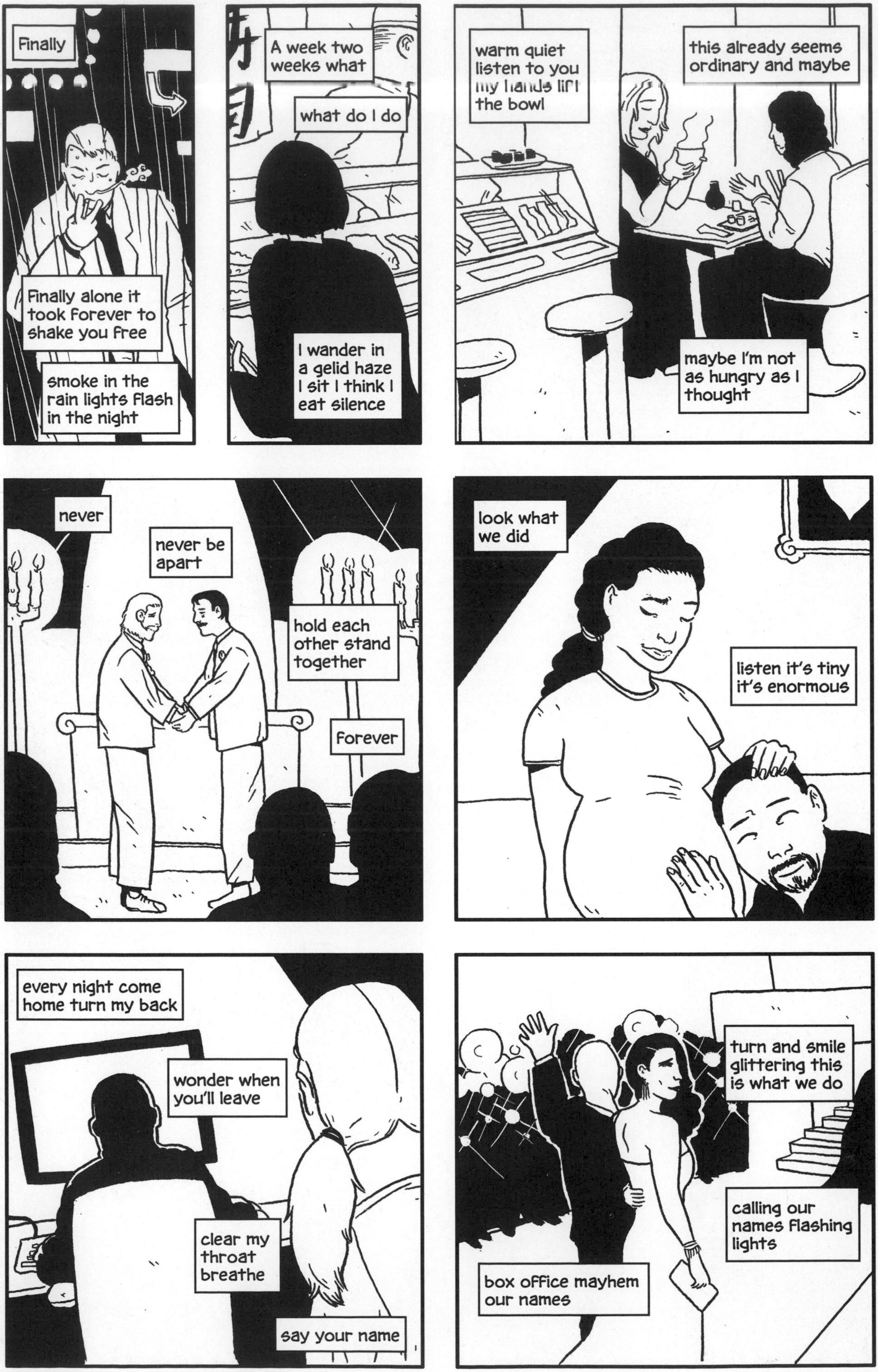
Finally
Finally alone it took forever to shake you free
smoke in the rain lights flash in the night
A week two weeks what
what do I do
I wander in a gelid haze I sit I think I eat silence
warm quiet listen to you my hands lift the bowl
this already seems ordinary and maybe
maybe I'm not as hungry as I thought
never
never be apart
hold each other stand together
forever
look what we did
listen it's tiny it's enormous
every night come home turn my back
wonder when you'll leave
clear my throat breathe
say your name
turn and smile glittering this is what we do
calling our names flashing lights
box office mayhem our names

carve yourself into the shape I choose cut away

who you used to be wear the collar never

never take it off

let's see where this goes

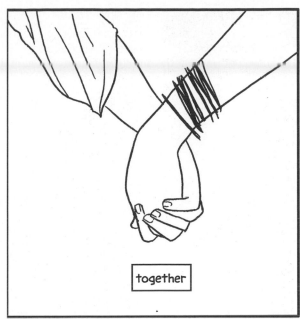

together

the threshold tradition

you lift me hold me you are so strong

our house now mine and yours together

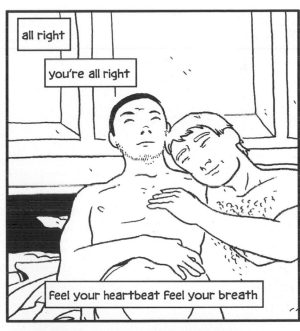

all right

you're all right

feel your heartbeat feel your breath

in tentative rain leaves hiss and fall

we're not alone

are we

am I

where am I

oh

but time alone

does mean time to think

smoke curling away behind

I feel someone looking at me

I turn

thinking about us how much do I say how much do I show

eyes slide sideways am I hungry

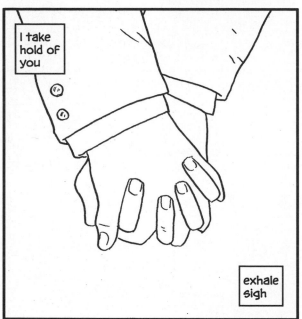

I take hold of you

exhale sigh

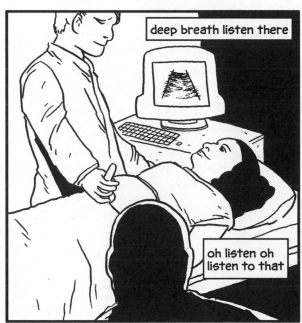

deep breath listen there

oh listen oh listen to that

I want to make you happy

cotton whispers as I pull it aside

what is this

what a pack of lies

they cry for us

perfect even smile

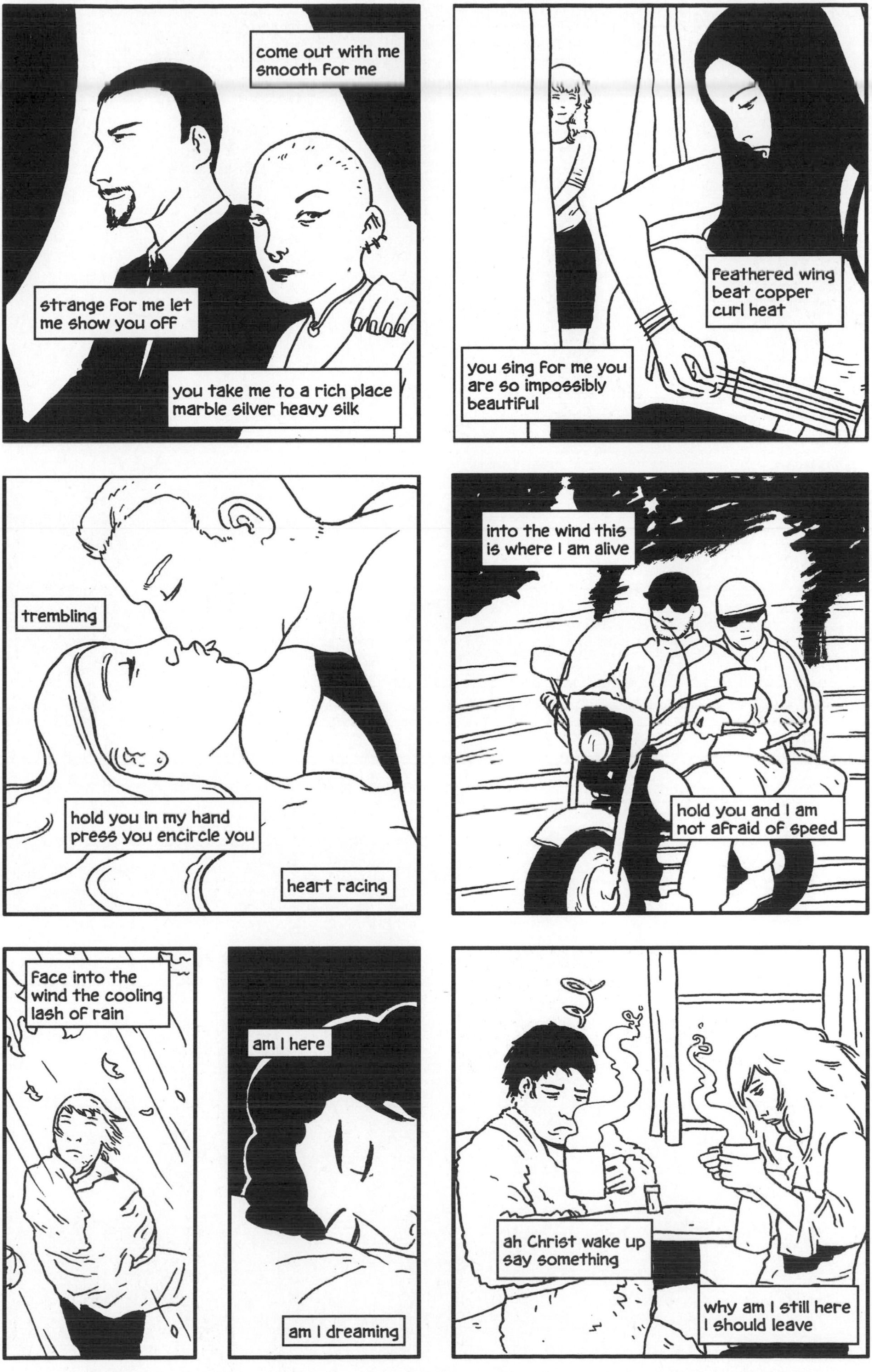
come out with me smooth for me
strange for me let me show you off
you take me to a rich place marble silver heavy silk
feathered wing beat copper curl heat
you sing for me you are so impossibly beautiful
trembling
hold you in my hand press you encircle you
heart racing
into the wind this is where I am alive
hold you and I am not afraid of speed
face into the wind the cooling lash of rain
am I here
am I dreaming
ah Christ wake up say something
why am I still here I should leave

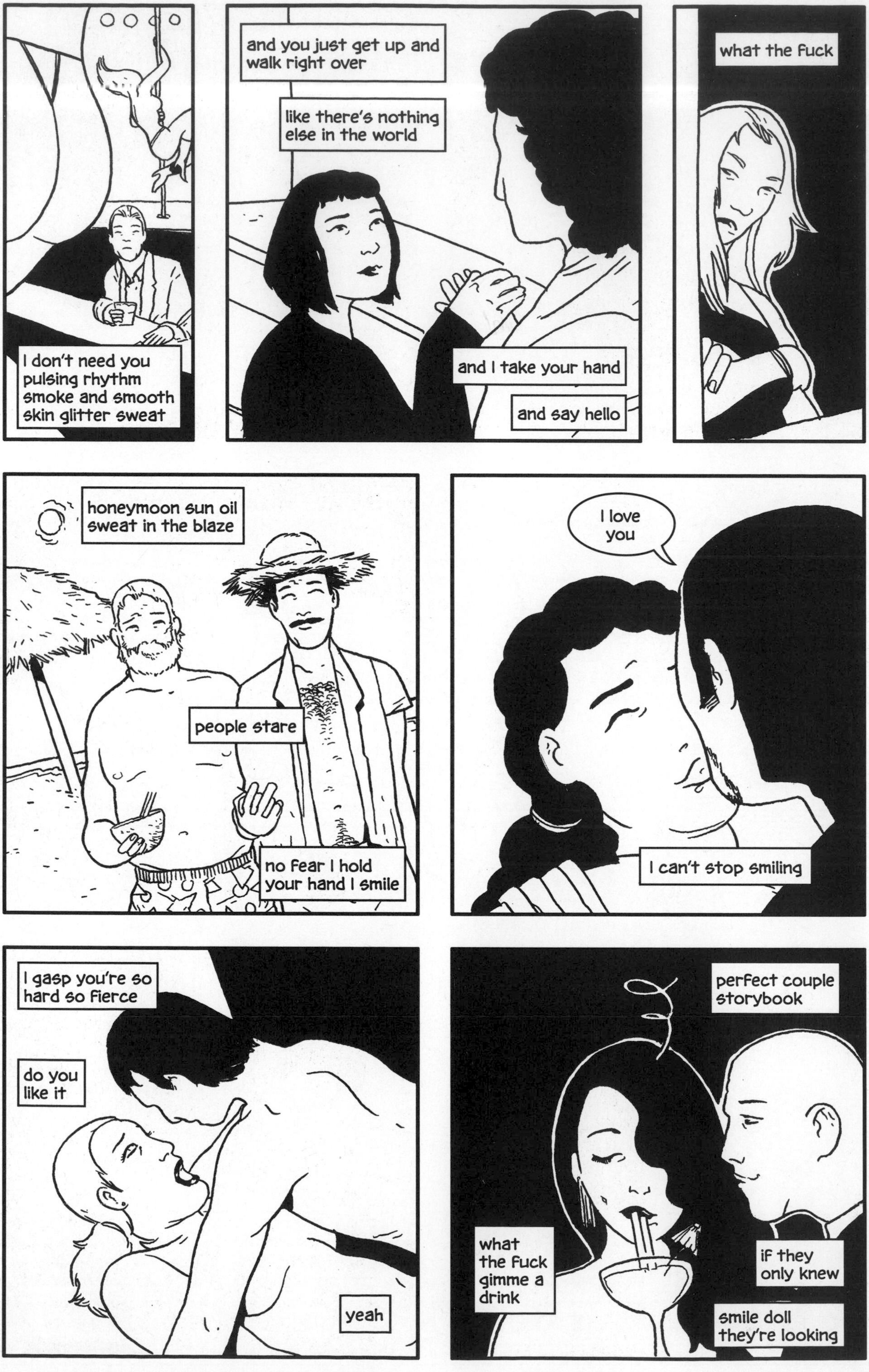
I don't need you pulsing rhythm smoke and smooth skin glitter sweat
and you just get up and walk right over
like there's nothing else in the world
and I take your hand
and say hello
what the fuck
honeymoon sun oil sweat in the blaze
people stare
no fear I hold your hand I smile
I love you
I can't stop smiling
I gasp you're so hard so fierce
do you like it
yeah
perfect couple storybook
what the fuck gimme a drink
if they only knew
smile doll they're looking

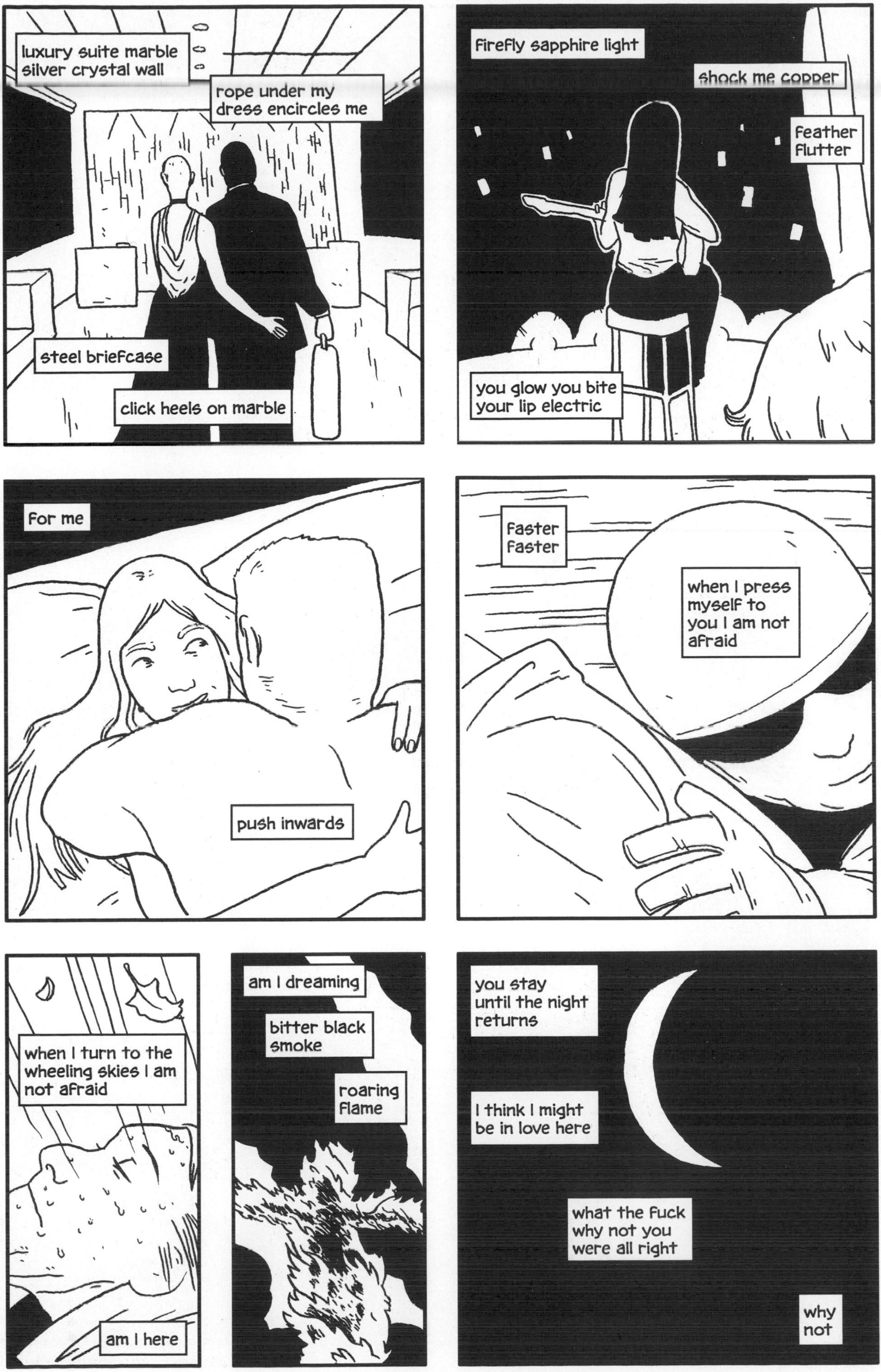
luxury suite marble silver crystal wall
rope under my dress encircles me
steel briefcase
click heels on marble
firefly sapphire light
shock me copper
feather flutter
you glow you bite your lip electric
for me
push inwards
faster faster
when I press myself to you I am not afraid
when I turn to the wheeling skies I am not afraid
am I here
am I dreaming
bitter black smoke
roaring flame
you stay until the night returns
I think I might be in love here
what the fuck why not you were all right
why not

who cares

the fire the electric need to tell you who I am to draw a smile

I'm possessed

I smile

that did not just happen

wind chime sound

a rocking bamboo fountain knocks

everything in its place and you are happy to let me point the way

to make the choices

cardboard and dust our footsteps echo in empty rooms

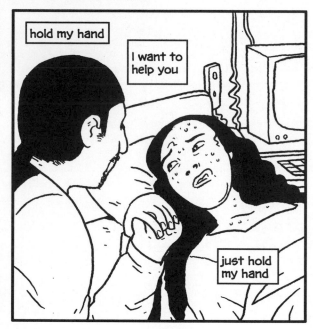

hold my hand

I want to help you

just hold my hand

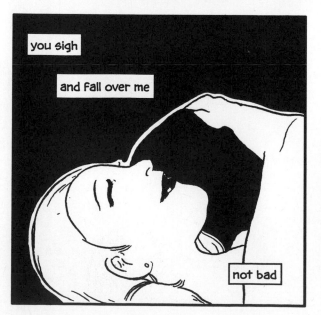

you sigh

and fall over me

not bad

our little castle fairy tale couple if they only knew

heh fairy tale

smile babe hold my hand you never know

when someone's looking

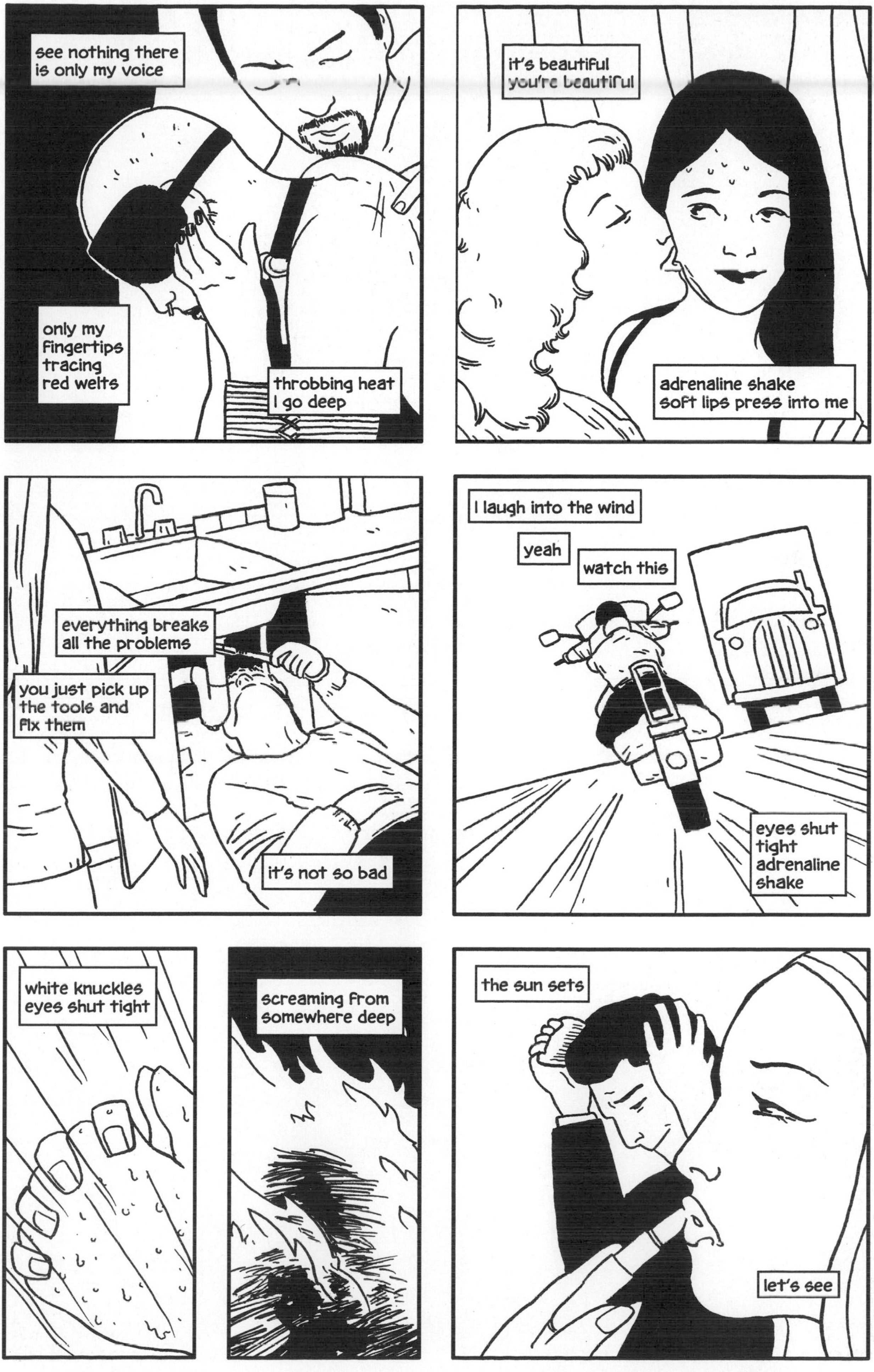
see nothing there
is only my voice
only my fingertips tracing red welts
throbbing heat
I go deep
it's beautiful
you're beautiful
adrenaline shake
soft lips press into me
everything breaks
all the problems
you just pick up the tools and fix them
it's not so bad
I laugh into the wind
yeah
watch this
eyes shut tight adrenaline shake
white knuckles
eyes shut tight
screaming from
somewhere deep
the sun sets
let's see

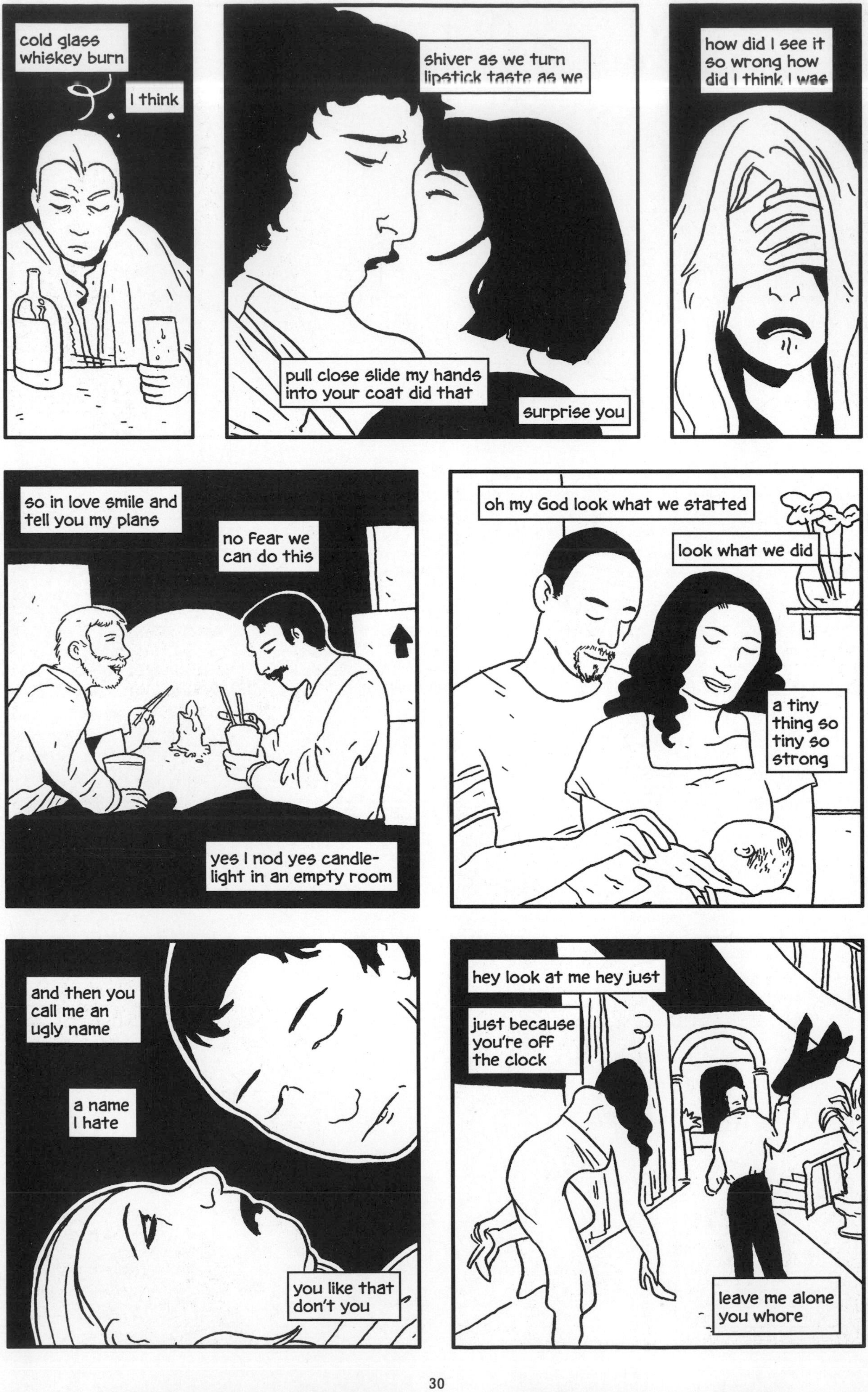
cold glass
whiskey burn
I think
shiver as we turn
lipstick taste as we
pull close slide my hands
into your coat did that
surprise you
how did I see it
so wrong how
did I think I was
so in love smile and
tell you my plans
no fear we
can do this
yes I nod yes candle-
light in an empty room
oh my God look what we started
look what we did
a tiny
thing so
tiny so
strong
and then you
call me an
ugly name
a name
I hate
you like that
don't you
hey look at me hey just
just because
you're off
the clock
leave me alone
you whore

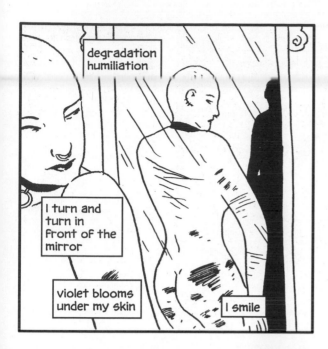

degradation humiliation

I turn and turn in front of the mirror

violet blooms under my skin

I smile

I don't pretend to understand

sapphire light from the stage still on you in your eyes

I look away

shake

sweat cold glass

gimme a kiss

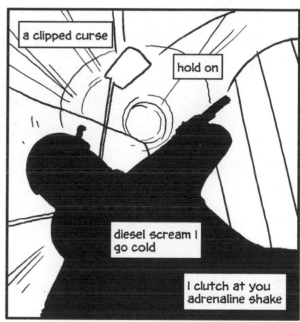

a clipped curse

hold on

diesel scream I go cold

I clutch at you adrenaline shake

a ragged leaf traces its descent

eyes snap open

inhale hiss

eyes slide over

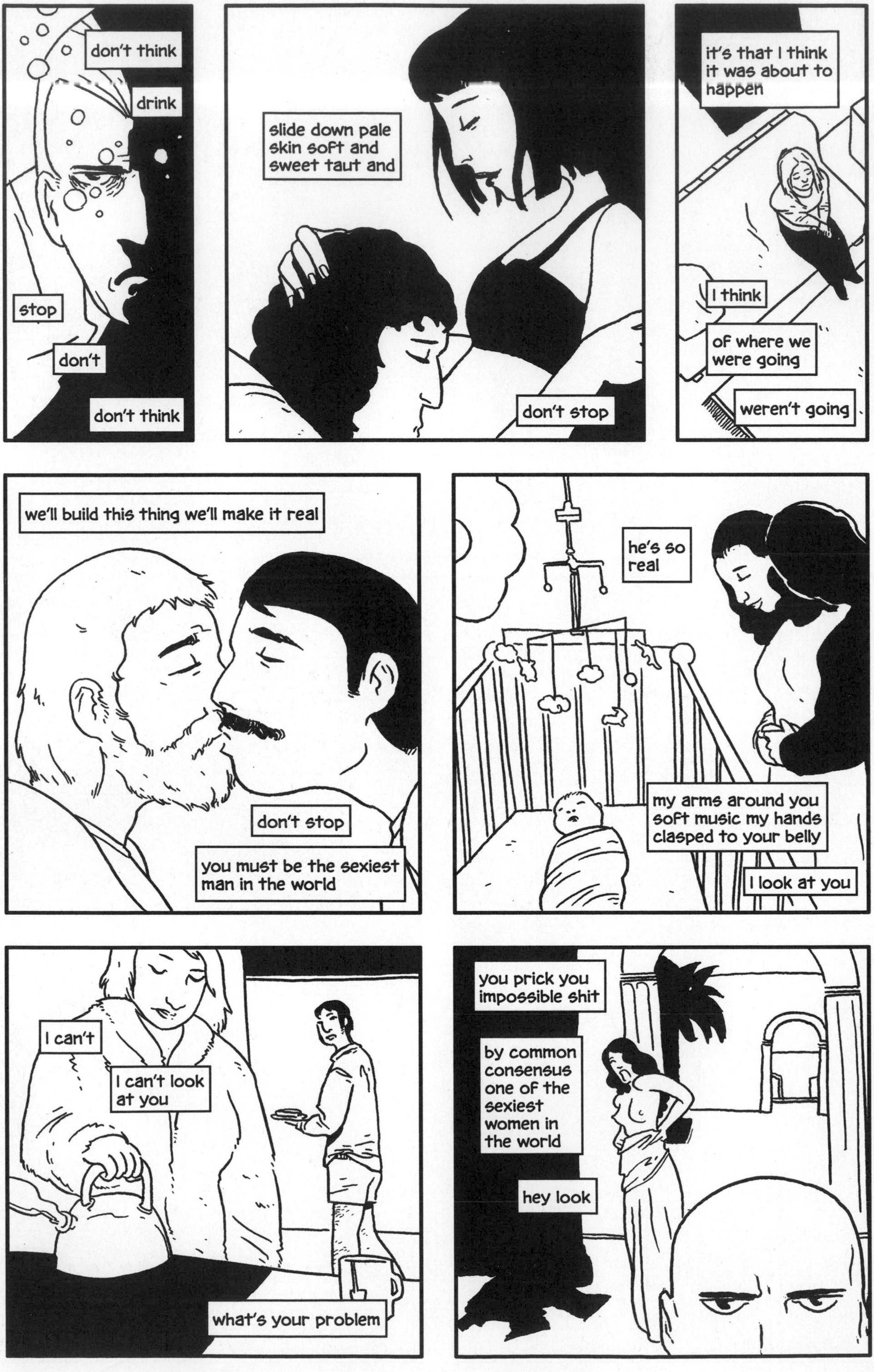
don't think
drink
stop
don't
don't think
slide down pale skin soft and sweet taut and
don't stop
it's that I think it was about to happen
I think
of where we were going
weren't going
we'll build this thing we'll make it real
don't stop
you must be the sexiest man in the world
he's so real
my arms around you soft music my hands clasped to your belly
I look at you
I can't
I can't look at you
what's your problem
you prick you impossible shit
by common consensus one of the sexiest women in the world
hey look

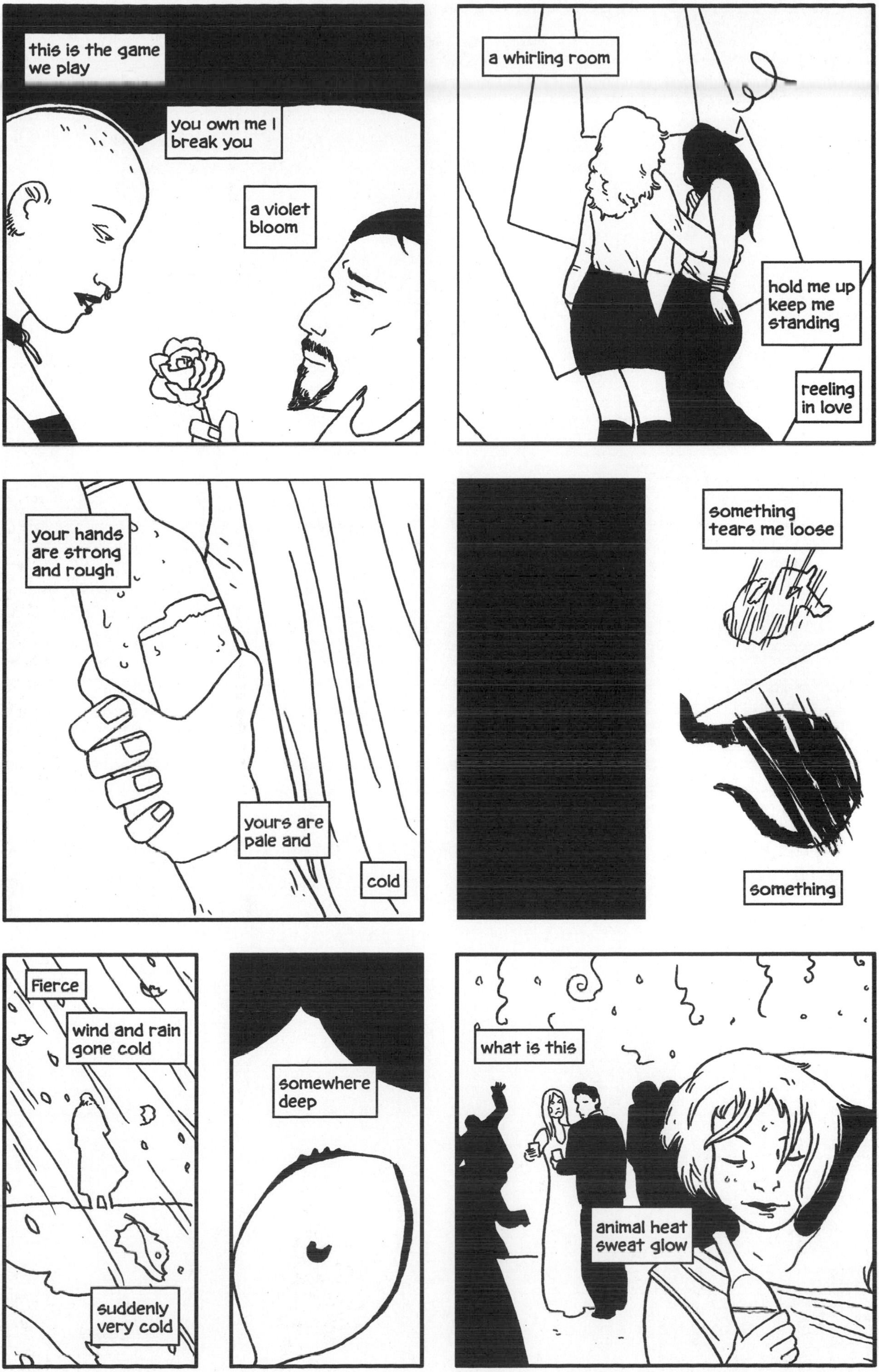
this is the game we play
you own me I break you
a violet bloom
a whirling room
hold me up keep me standing
reeling in love
your hands are strong and rough
yours are pale and
cold
something tears me loose
something
Fierce
wind and rain gone cold
suddenly very cold
somewhere deep
what is this
animal heat sweat glow

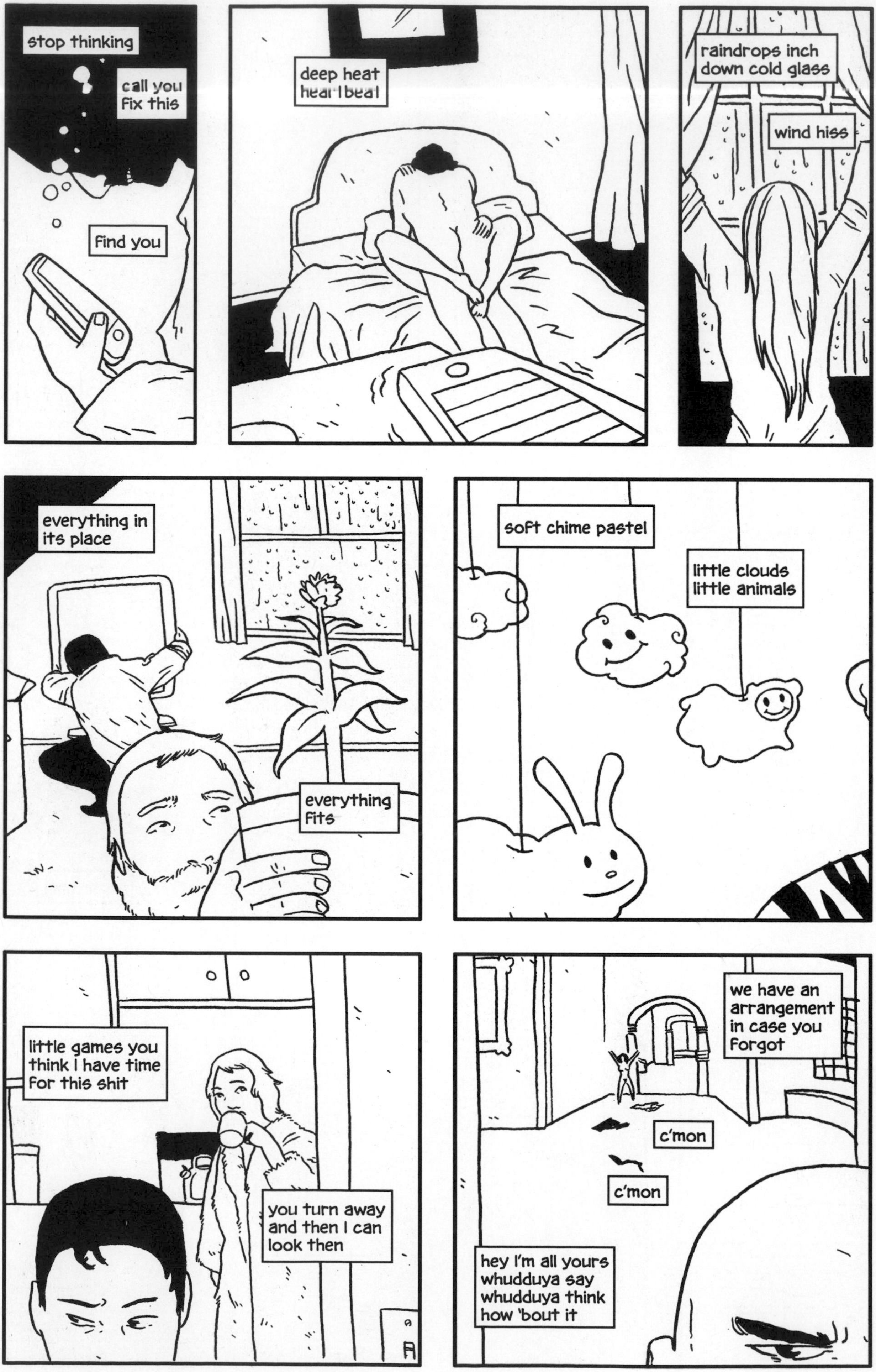
stop thinking
call you
fix this
find you
deep heat
heart beat
raindrops inch
down cold glass
wind hiss
everything in
its place
everything
fits
soft chime pastel
little clouds
little animals
little games you
think I have time
for this shit
you turn away
and then I can
look then
we have an
arrangement
in case you
forgot
c'mon
c'mon
hey I'm all yours
whudduya say
whudduya think
how 'bout it

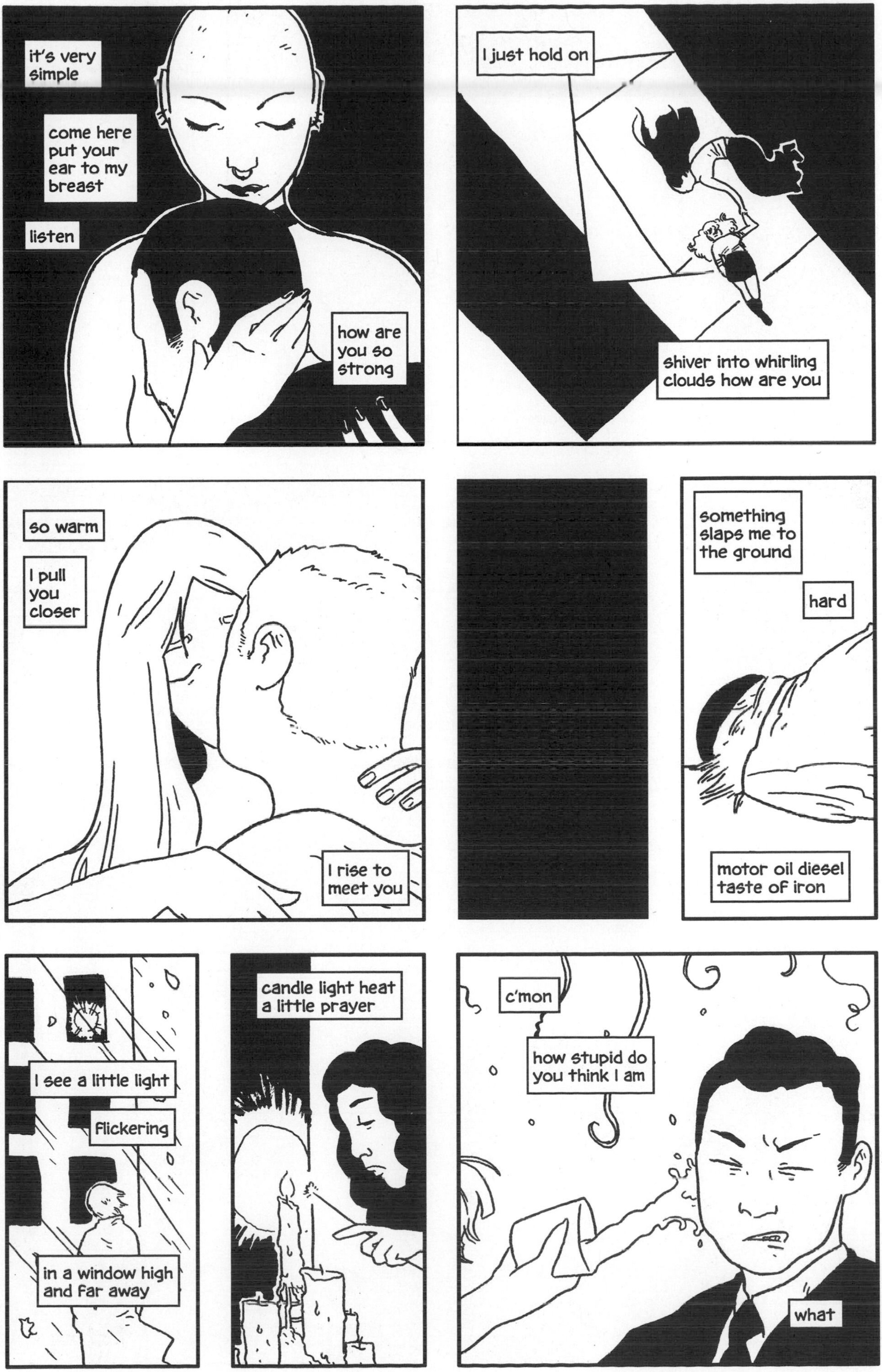
it's very simple
come here put your ear to my breast
listen
how are you so strong
I just hold on
shiver into whirling clouds how are you
so warm
I pull you closer
I rise to meet you
something slaps me to the ground
hard
motor oil diesel taste of iron
I see a little light
flickering
in a window high and far away
candle light heat a little prayer
c'mon
how stupid do you think I am
what

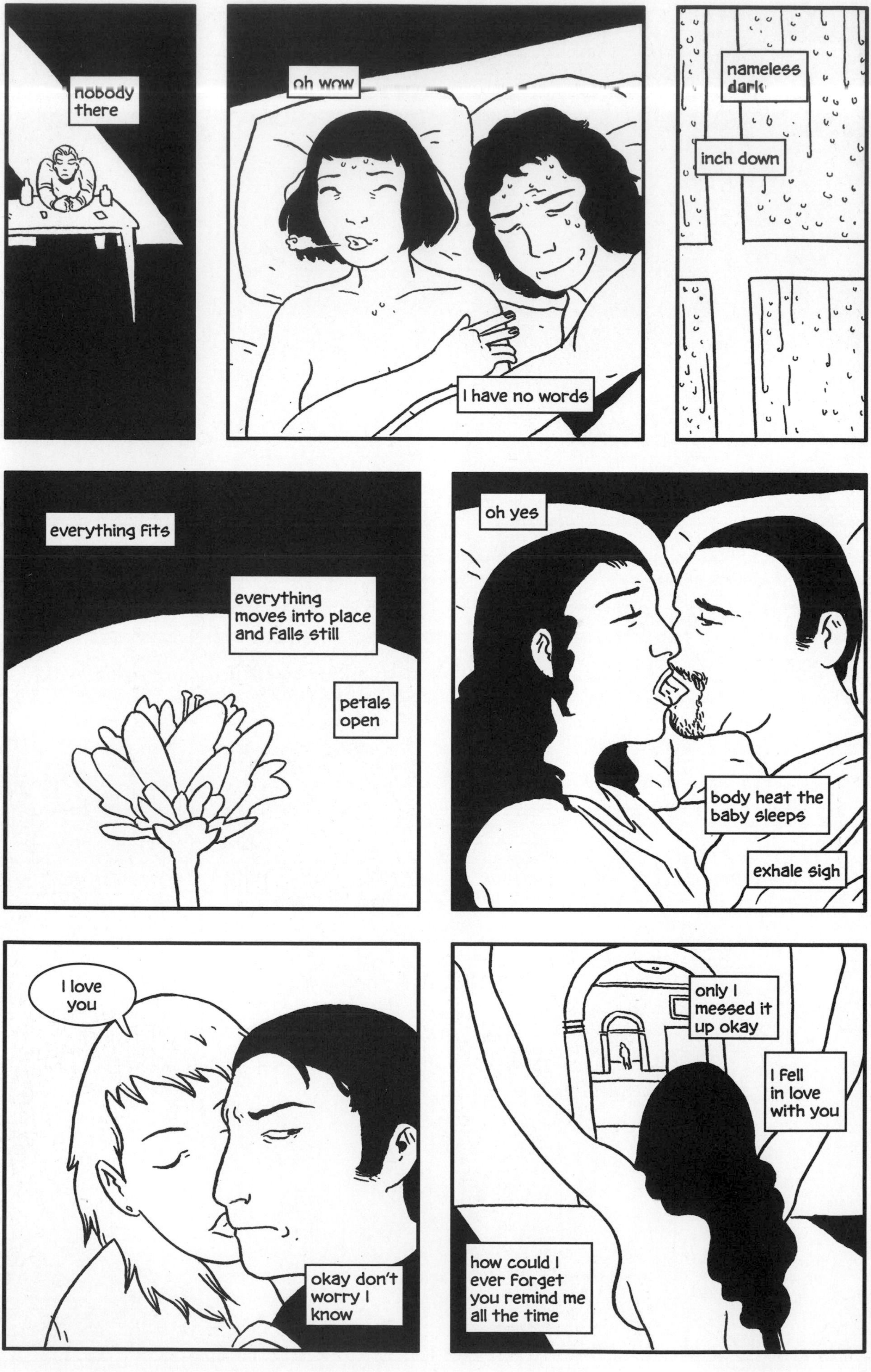
nobody there
oh wow
I have no words
nameless dark
inch down
everything fits
everything moves into place and falls still
petals open
oh yes
body heat the baby sleeps
exhale sigh
I love you
okay don't worry I know
only I messed it up okay
I fell in love with you
how could I ever forget you remind me all the time

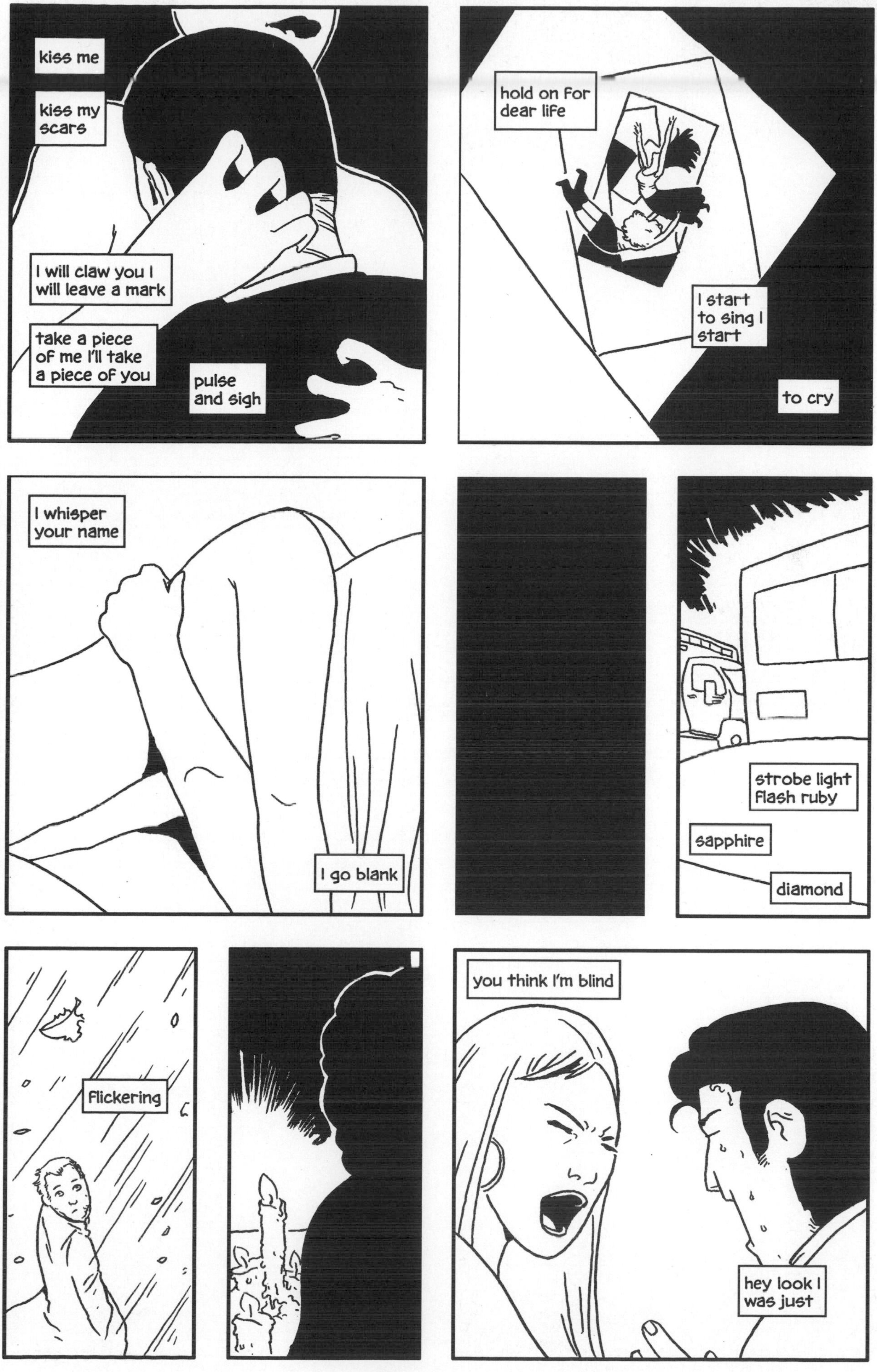
kiss me
kiss my scars
I will claw you I will leave a mark
take a piece of me I'll take a piece of you
pulse and sigh
hold on for dear life
I start to sing I start
to cry
I whisper your name
I go blank
strobe light flash ruby
sapphire
diamond
flickering
you think I'm blind
hey look I was just

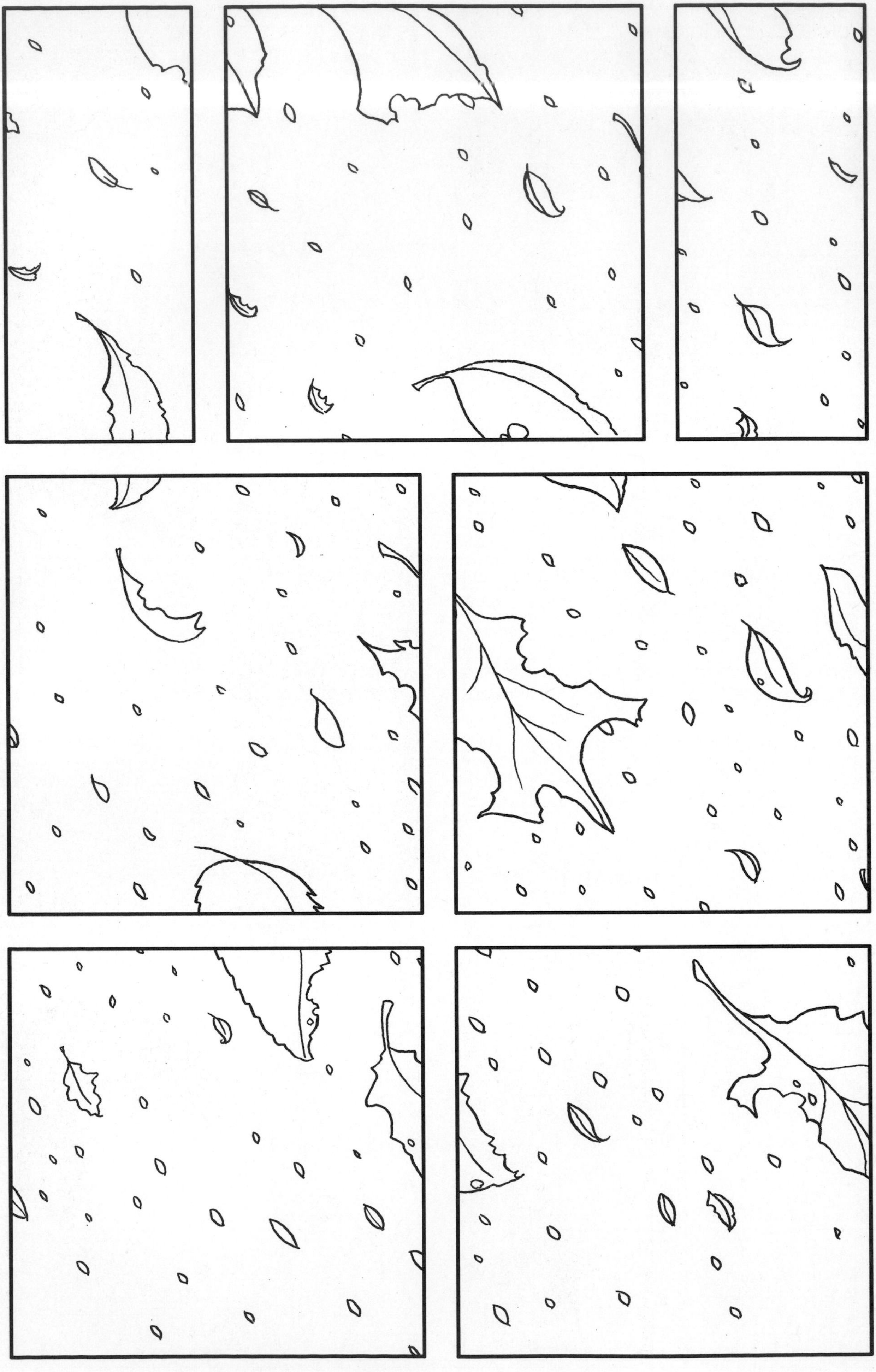

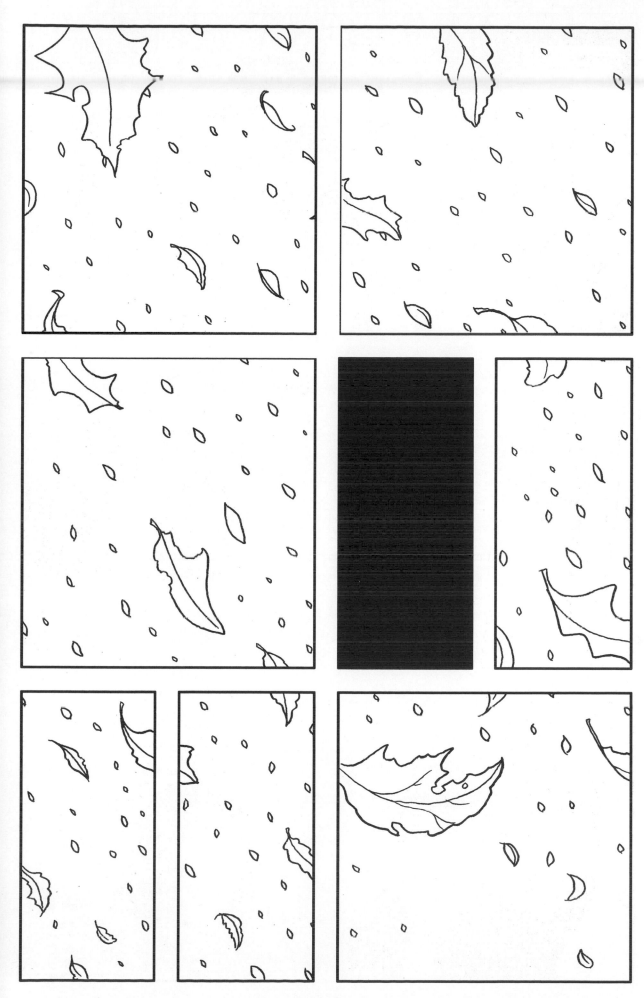

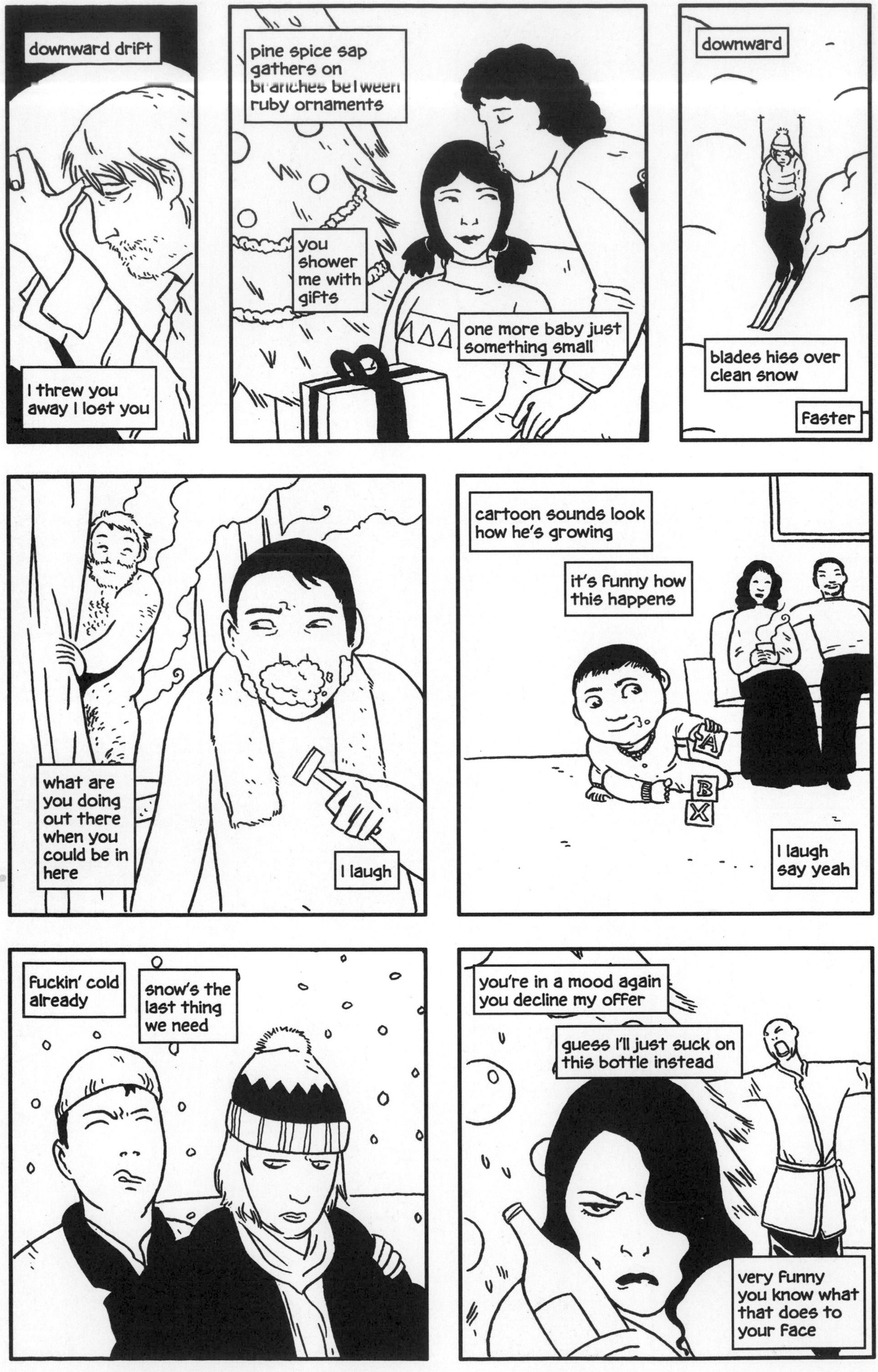
downward drift
I threw you away I lost you
pine spice sap gathers on branches between ruby ornaments
you shower me with gifts
one more baby just something small
downward
blades hiss over clean snow
faster
what are you doing out there when you could be in here
I laugh
cartoon sounds look how he's growing
it's funny how this happens
I laugh say yeah
fuckin' cold already
snow's the last thing we need
you're in a mood again you decline my offer
guess I'll just suck on this bottle instead
very funny you know what that does to your face

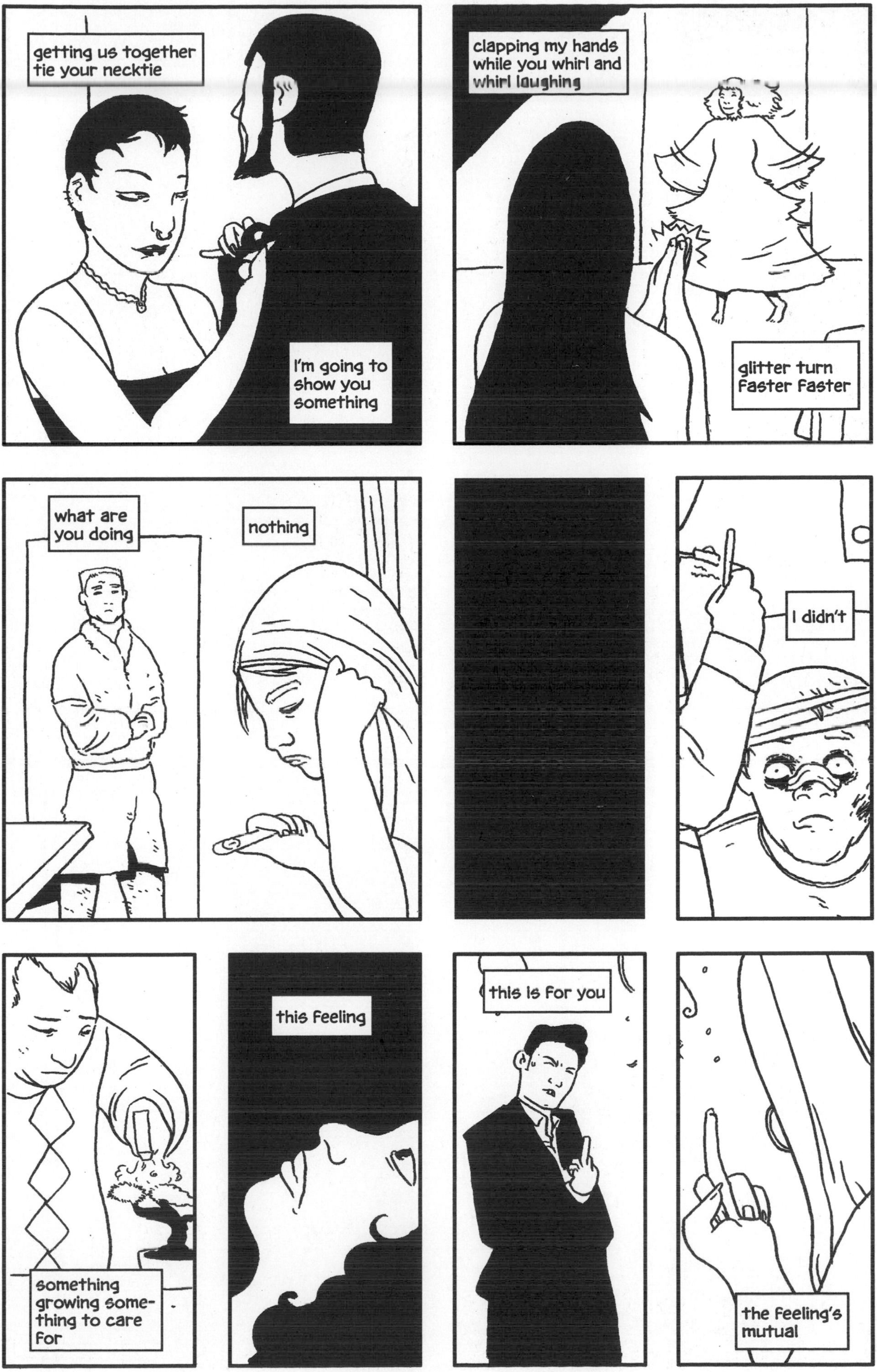
getting us together
tie your necktie
I'm going to show you something
clapping my hands while you whirl and whirl laughing
glitter turn faster faster
what are you doing
nothing
I didn't
something growing some-thing to care for
this feeling
this is for you
the feeling's mutual

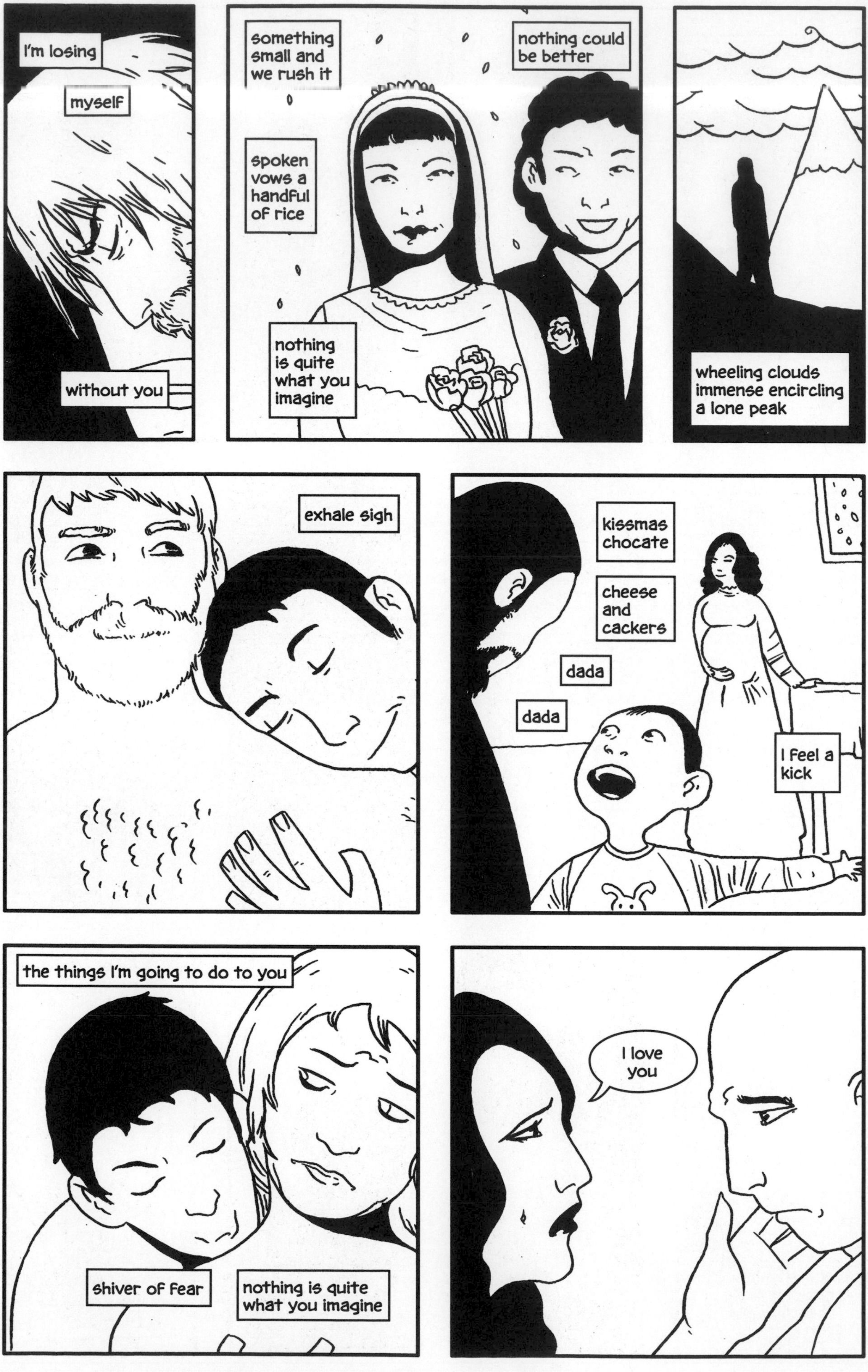
I'm losing
myself
without you
something small and we rush it
nothing could be better
spoken vows a handful of rice
nothing is quite what you imagine
wheeling clouds immense encircling a lone peak
exhale sigh
kissmas chocate
cheese and cackers
dada
dada
I feel a kick
the things I'm going to do to you
shiver of fear
nothing is quite what you imagine
I love you

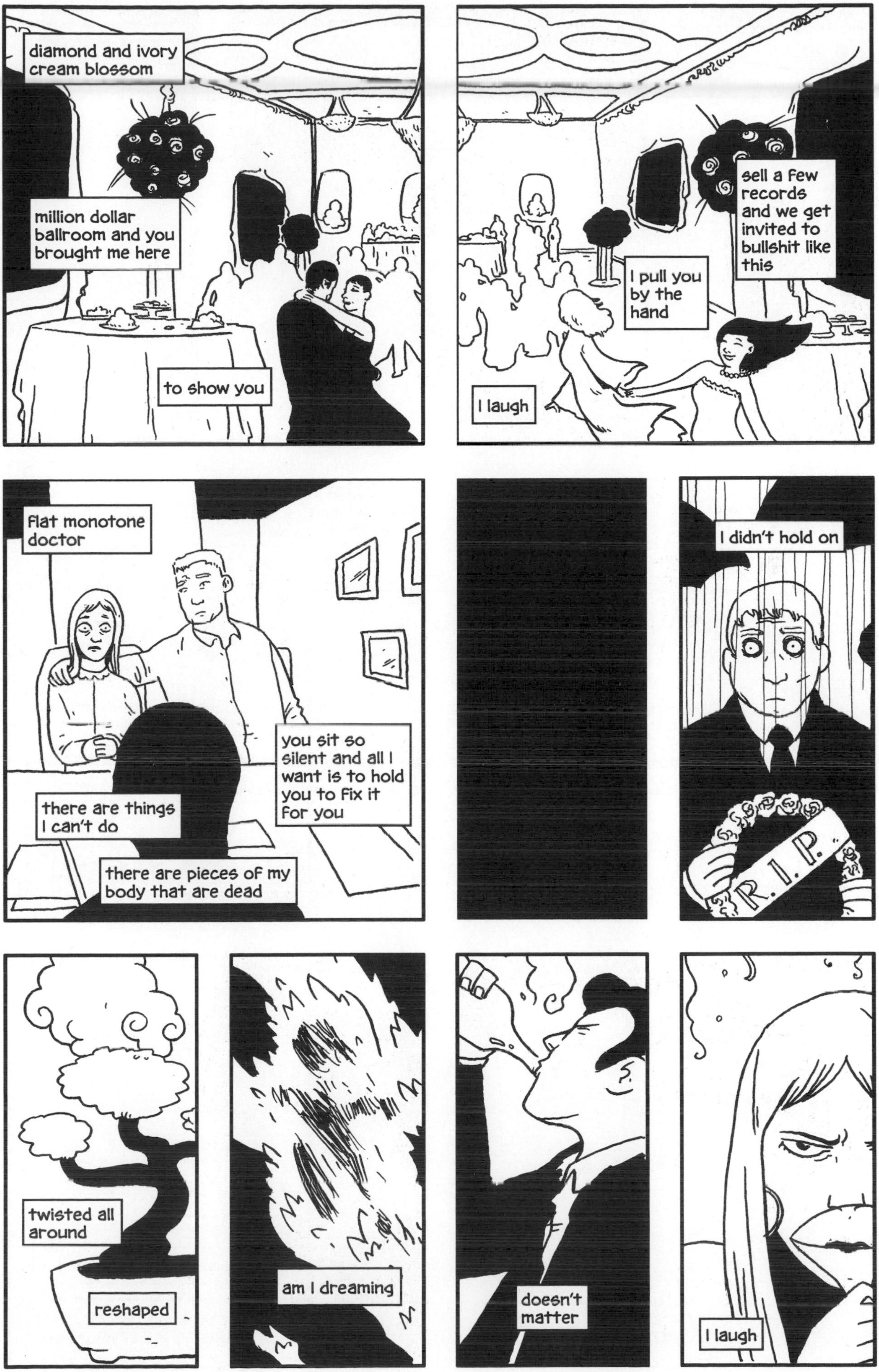
diamond and ivory cream blossom
million dollar ballroom and you brought me here
to show you
sell a few records and we get invited to bullshit like this
I pull you by the hand
I laugh
flat monotone doctor
you sit so silent and all I want is to hold you to fix it for you
there are things I can't do
there are pieces of my body that are dead
I didn't hold on
R.I.P.
twisted all around
reshaped
am I dreaming
doesn't matter
I laugh

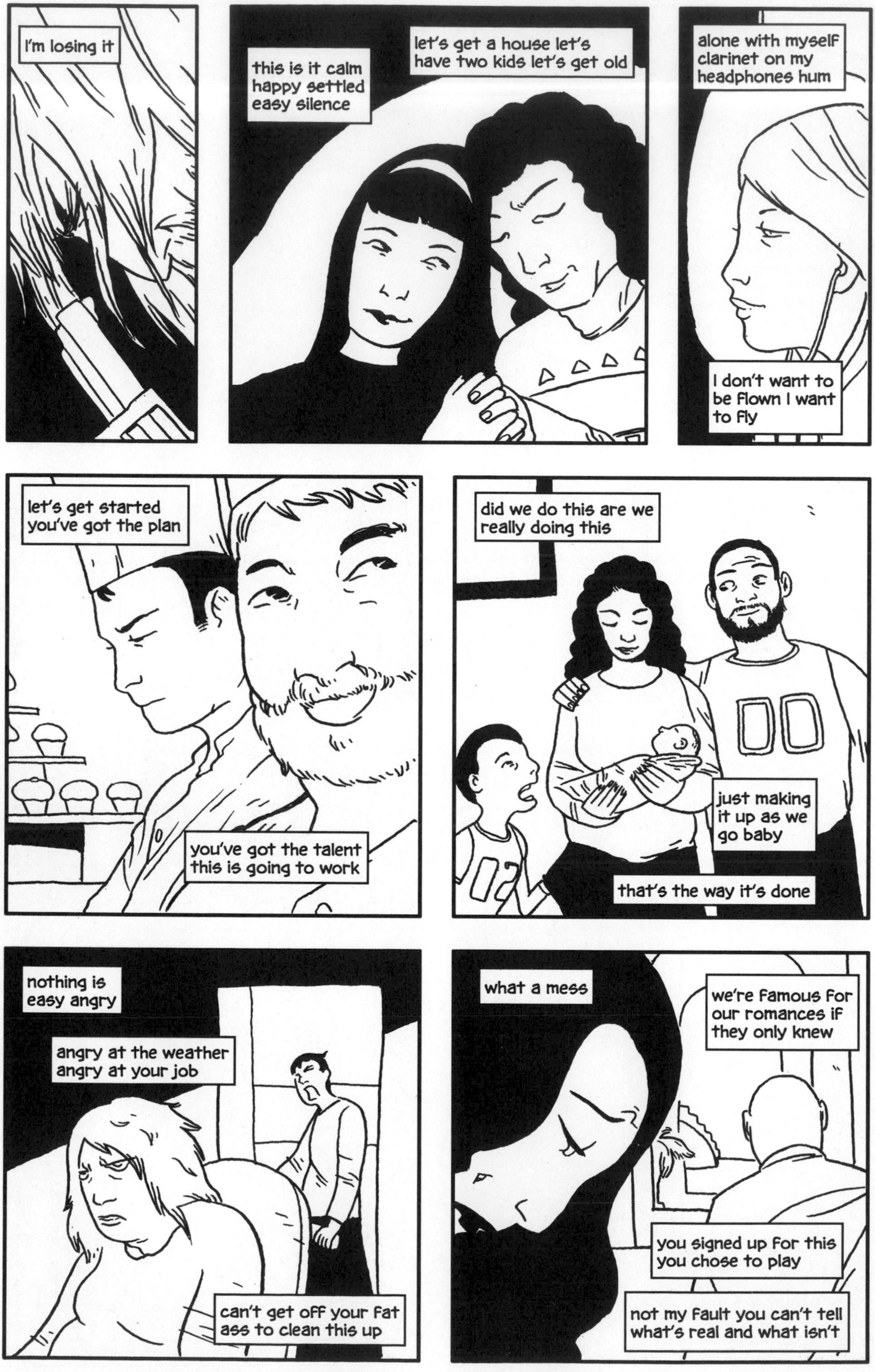
I'm losing it
this is it calm happy settled easy silence
let's get a house let's have two kids let's get old
alone with myself clarinet on my headphones hum
I don't want to be flown I want to fly
let's get started you've got the plan
you've got the talent this is going to work
did we do this are we really doing this
just making it up as we go baby
that's the way it's done
nothing is easy angry
angry at the weather angry at your job
can't get off your fat ass to clean this up
what a mess
we're famous for our romances if they only knew
you signed up for this you chose to play
not my fault you can't tell what's real and what isn't

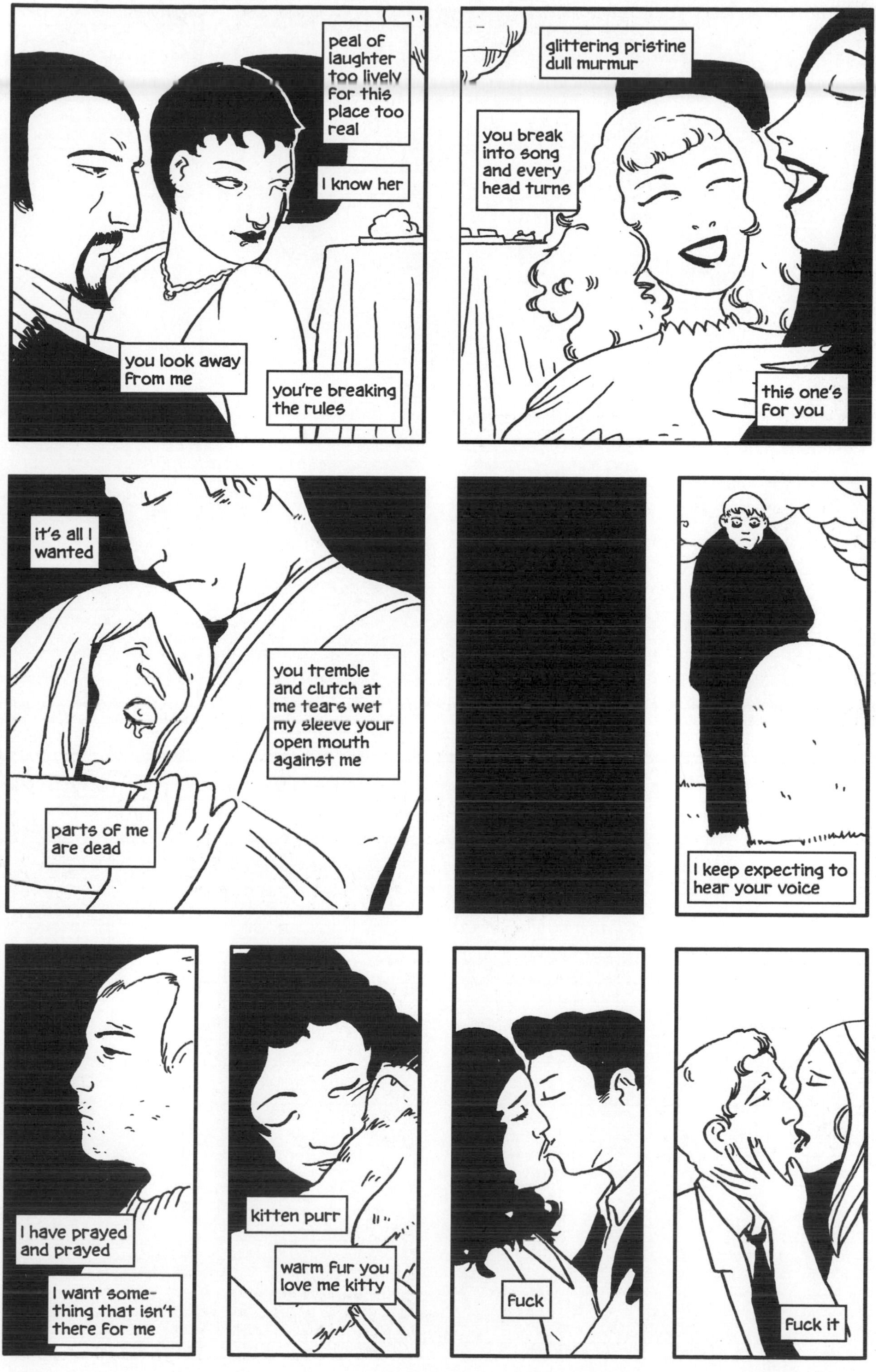
peal of laughter too lively for this place too real
I know her
you look away from me
you're breaking the rules
glittering pristine dull murmur
you break into song and every head turns
this one's for you
it's all I wanted
you tremble and clutch at me tears wet my sleeve your open mouth against me
parts of me are dead
I keep expecting to hear your voice
I have prayed and prayed
I want some-thing that isn't there for me
kitten purr
warm fur you love me kitty
fuck
fuck it

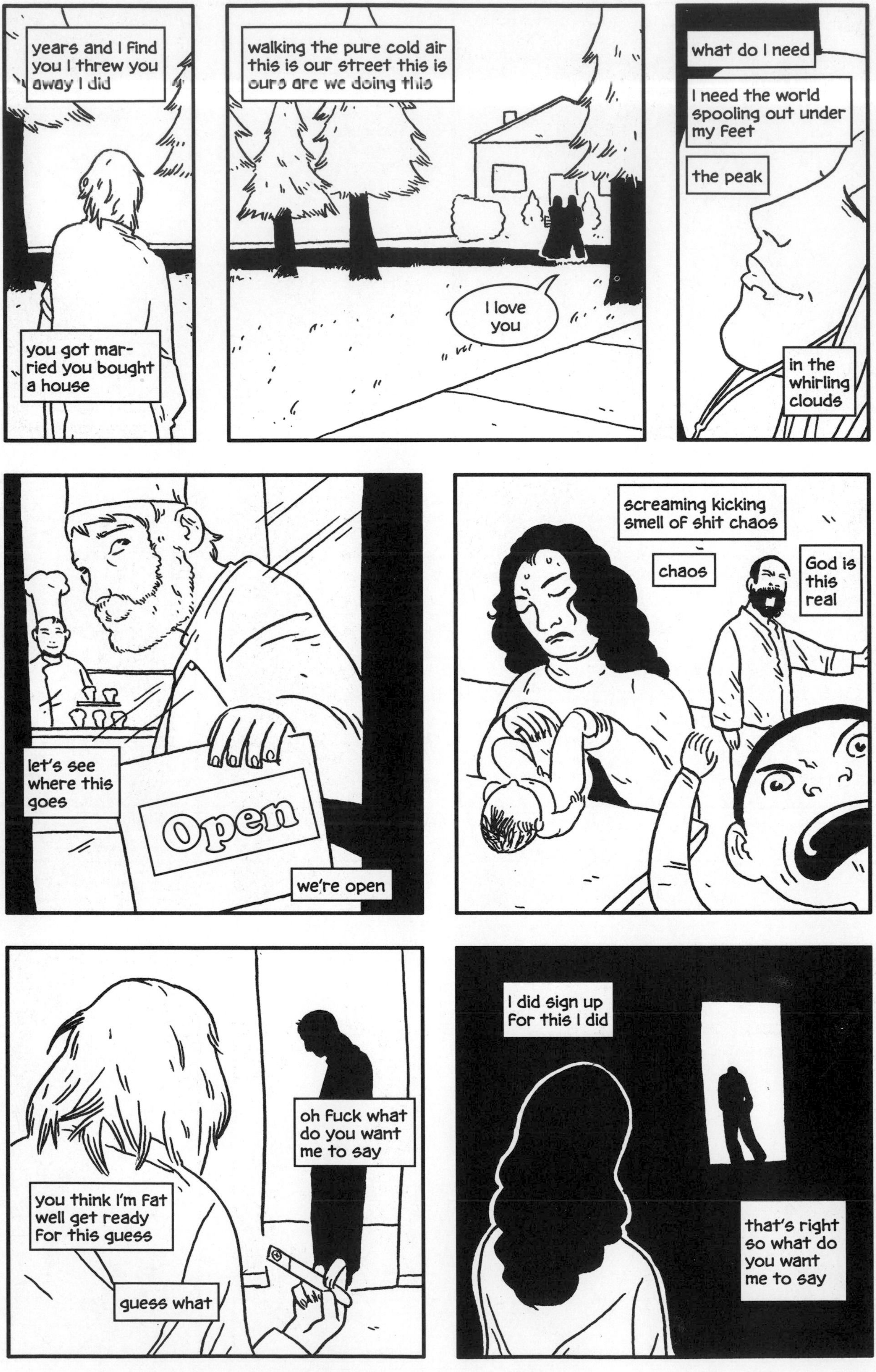
years and I find you I threw you away I did
you got mar-ried you bought a house
walking the pure cold air this is our street this is ours are we doing this
I love you
what do I need
I need the world spooling out under my feet
the peak
in the whirling clouds
let's see where this goes
Open
we're open
screaming kicking smell of shit chaos
chaos
God is this real
you think I'm fat well get ready for this guess
guess what
oh fuck what do you want me to say
I did sign up for this I did
that's right so what do you want me to say

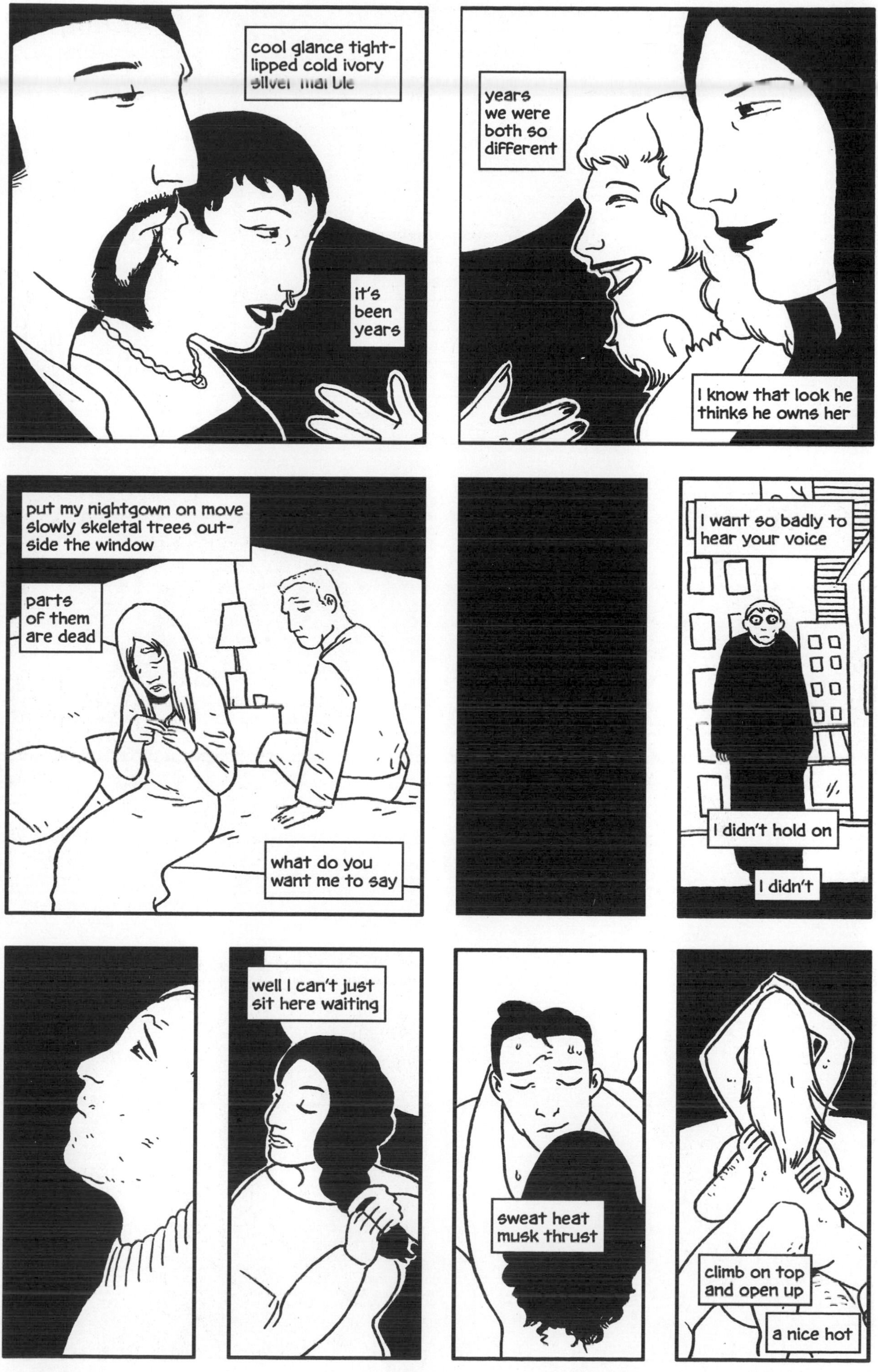
cool glance tight-lipped cold ivory silver marble
it's been years
years we were both so different
I know that look he thinks he owns her
put my nightgown on move slowly skeletal trees outside the window
parts of them are dead
what do you want me to say
I want so badly to hear your voice
I didn't hold on
I didn't
well I can't just sit here waiting
sweat heat musk thrust
climb on top and open up
a nice hot

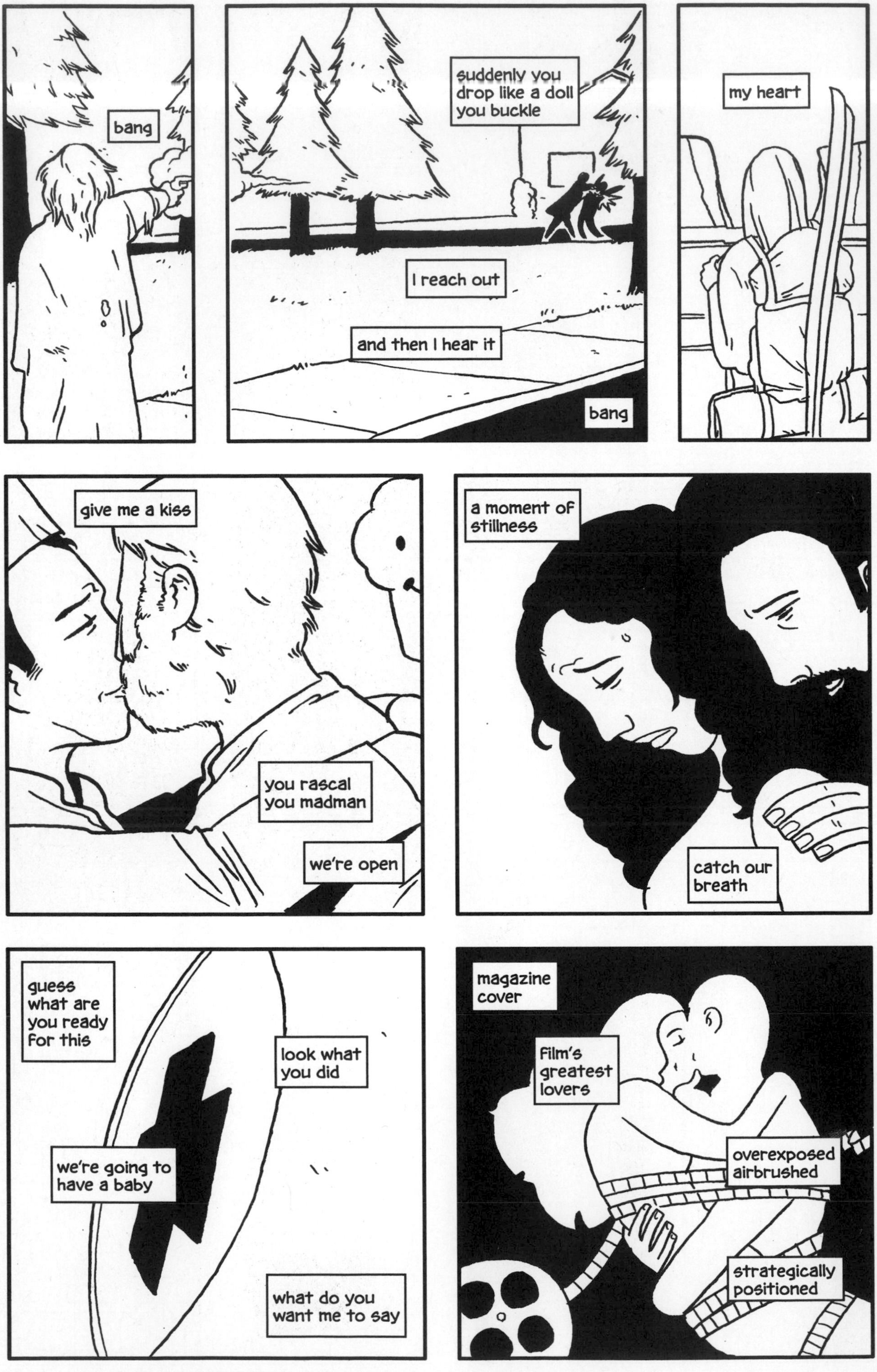
bang
suddenly you drop like a doll you buckle
I reach out
and then I hear it
bang
my heart
give me a kiss
you rascal you madman
we're open
a moment of stillness
catch our breath
guess what are you ready for this
look what you did
we're going to have a baby
what do you want me to say
magazine cover
Film's greatest lovers
overexposed airbrushed
strategically positioned

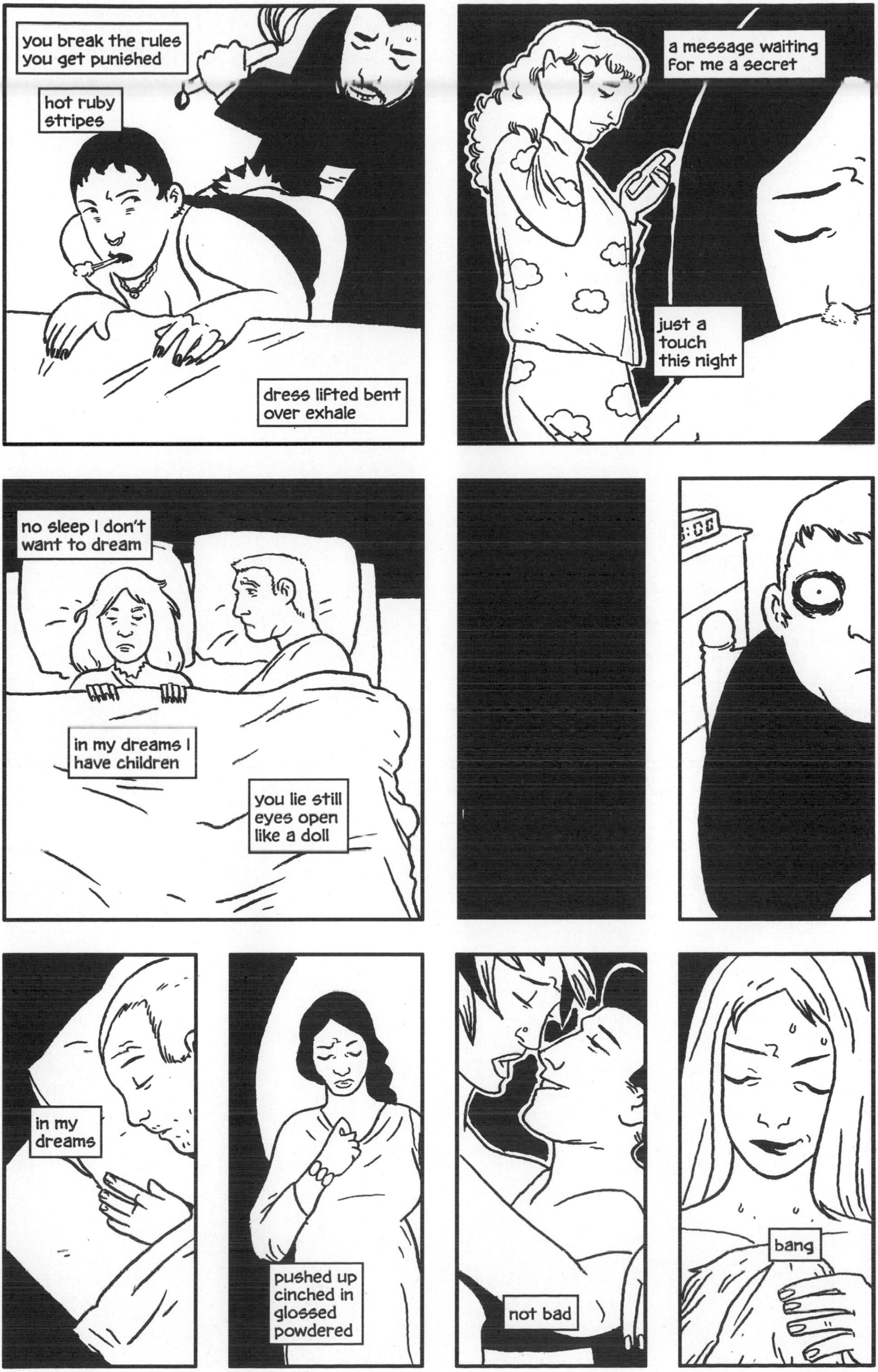
you break the rules you get punished
hot ruby stripes
dress lifted bent over exhale
a message waiting for me a secret
just a touch this night
no sleep I don't want to dream
in my dreams I have children
you lie still eyes open like a doll
in my dreams
pushed up cinched in glossed powdered
not bad
bang

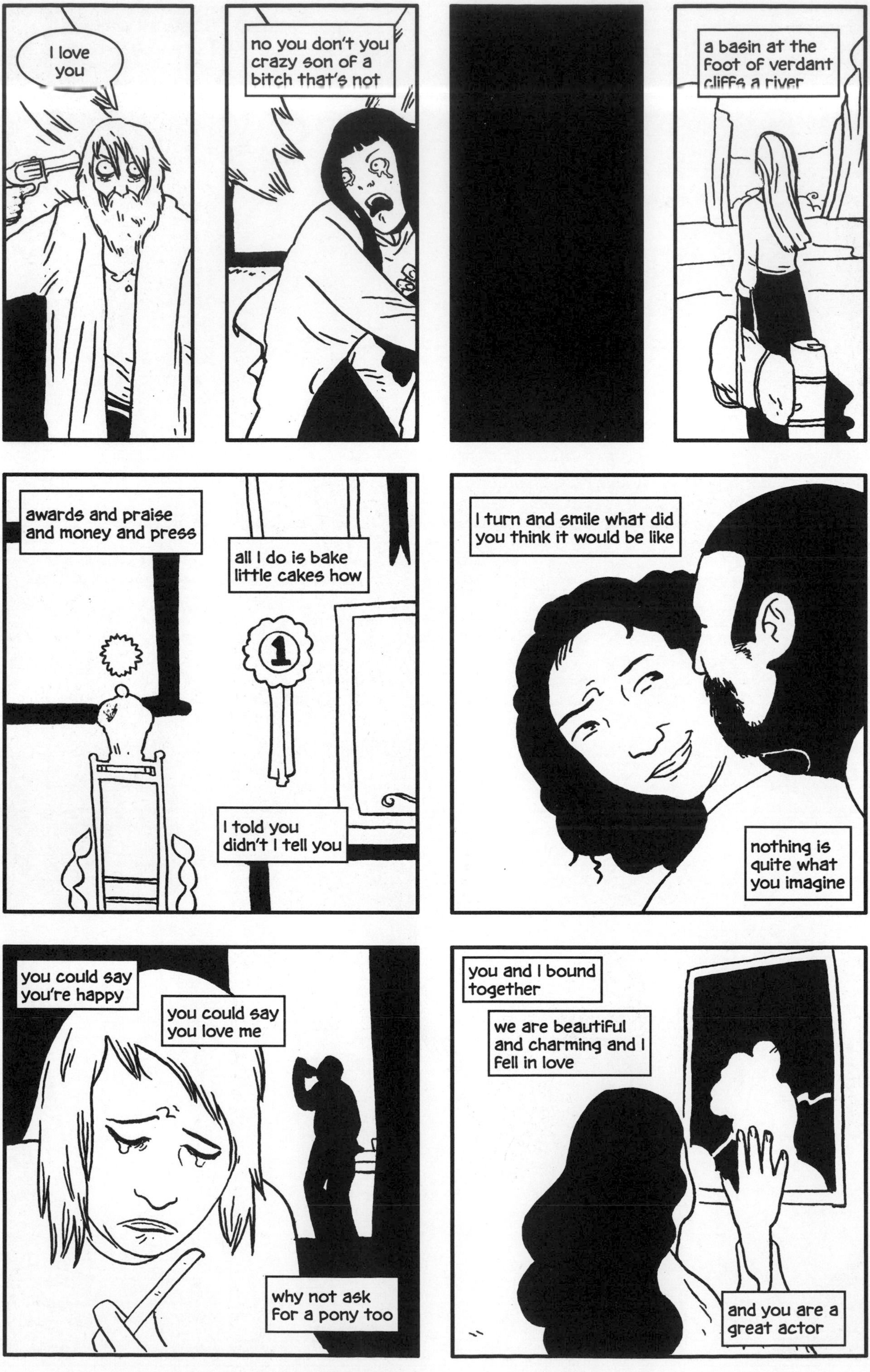
I love you
no you don't you crazy son of a bitch that's not
a basin at the foot of verdant cliffs a river
awards and praise and money and press
all I do is bake little cakes how
I told you didn't I tell you
I turn and smile what did you think it would be like
nothing is quite what you imagine
you could say you're happy
you could say you love me
why not ask for a pony too
you and I bound together
we are beautiful and charming and I fell in love
and you are a great actor

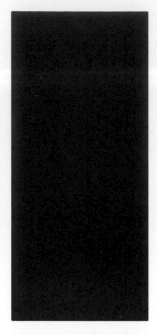

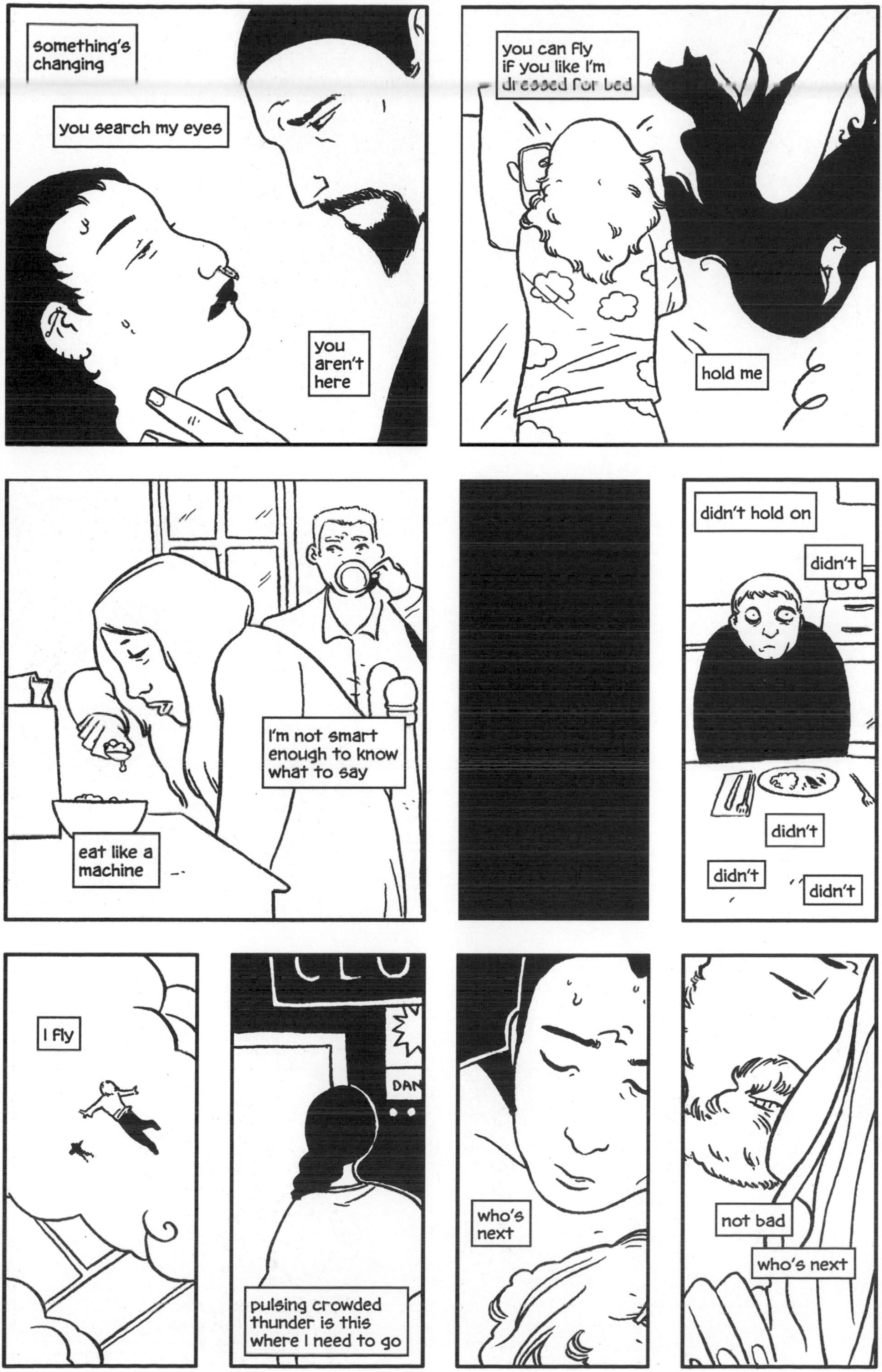
something's changing
you search my eyes
you aren't here
you can fly if you like I'm dressed for bed
hold me
I'm not smart enough to know what to say
eat like a machine
didn't hold on
didn't
didn't
didn't
didn't
I fly
pulsing crowded thunder is this where I need to go
who's next
not bad
who's next

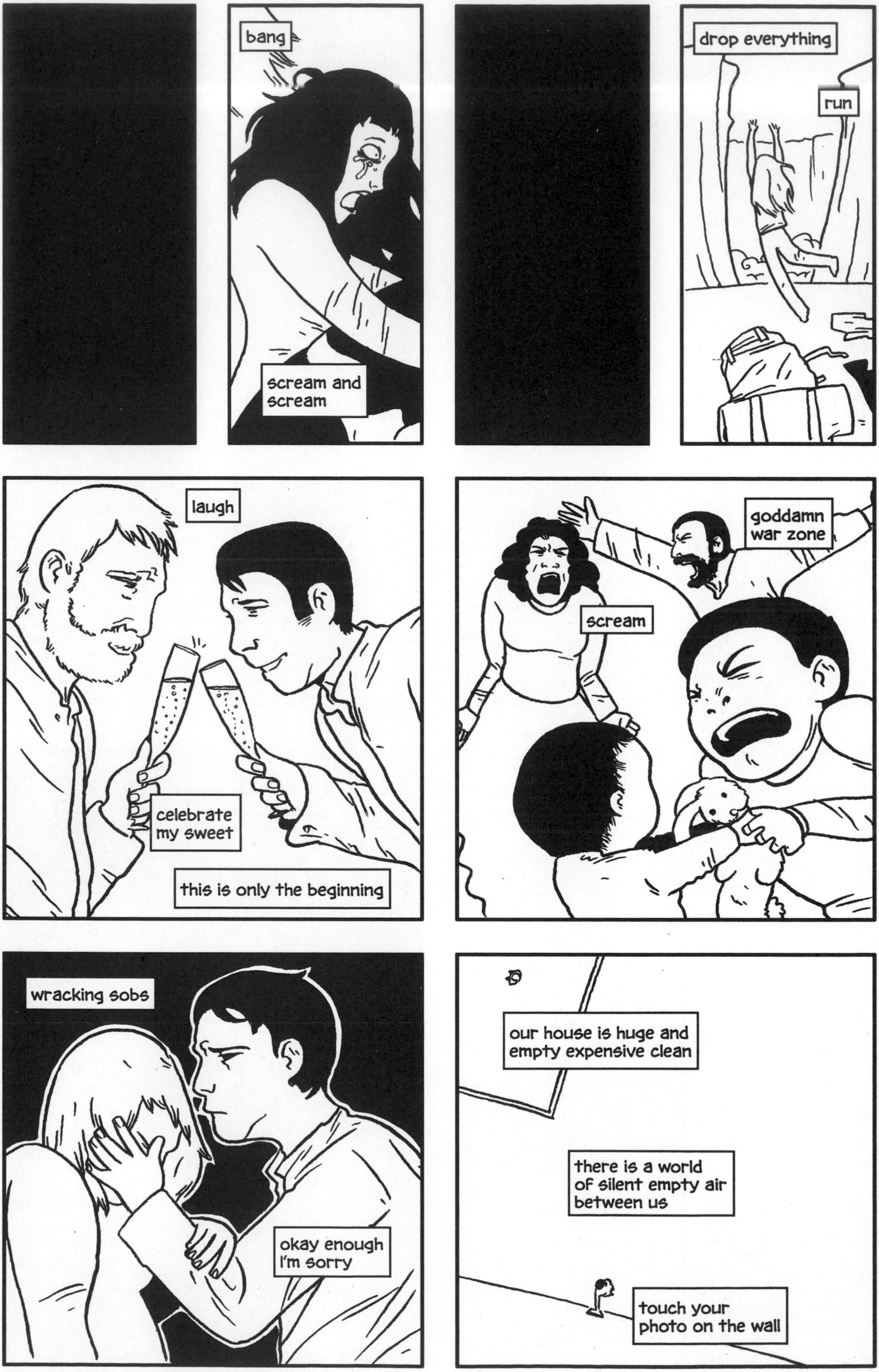
bang
scream and scream
drop everything
run
laugh
celebrate my sweet
this is only the beginning
goddamn war zone
scream
wracking sobs
okay enough I'm sorry
our house is huge and empty expensive clean
there is a world of silent empty air between us
touch your photo on the wall

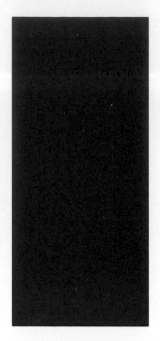

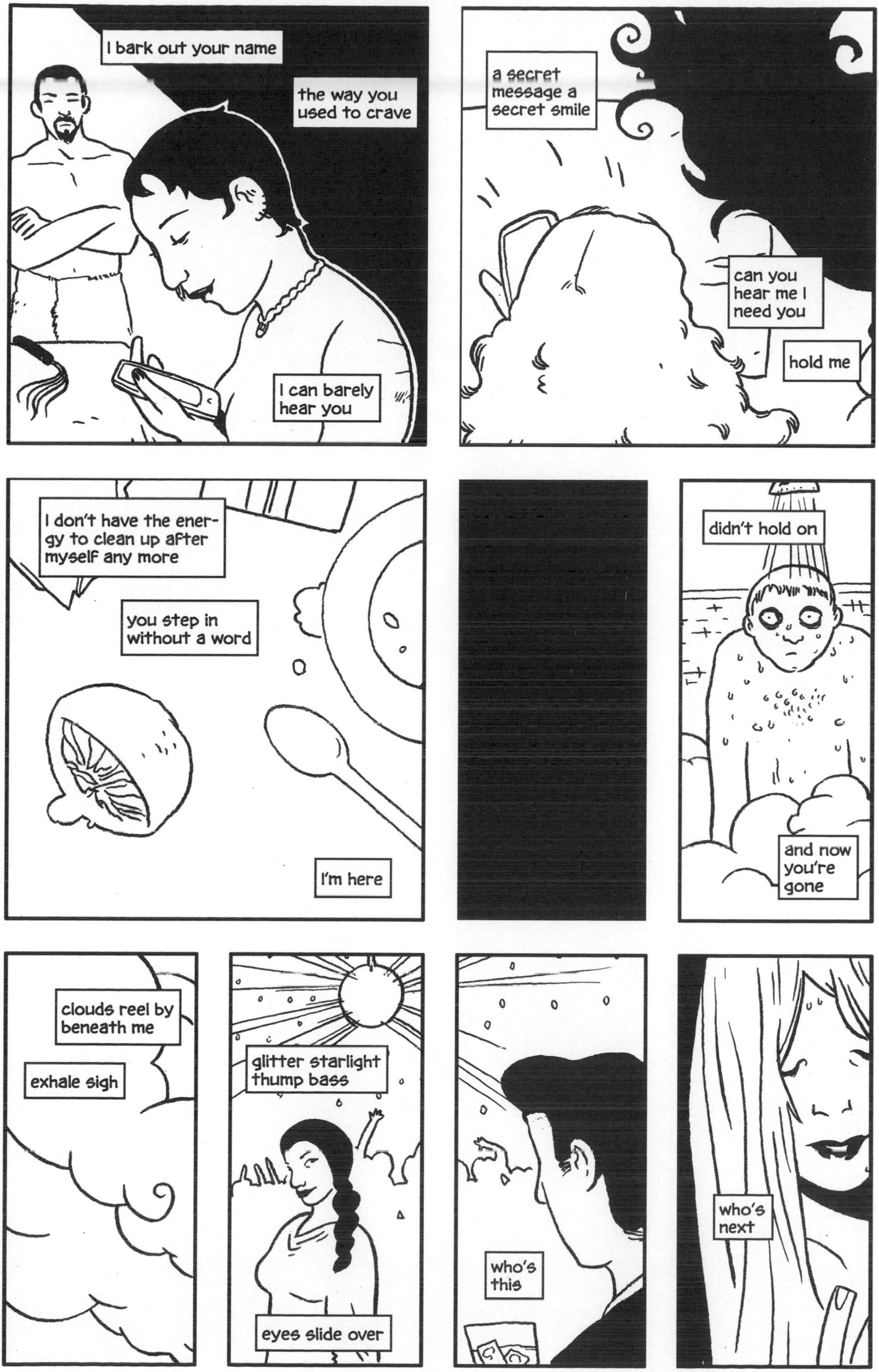
I bark out your name
the way you used to crave
I can barely hear you
a secret message a secret smile
can you hear me I need you
hold me
I don't have the ener-gy to clean up after myself any more
you step in without a word
I'm here
didn't hold on
and now you're gone
clouds reel by beneath me
exhale sigh
glitter starlight thump bass
eyes slide over
who's this
who's next

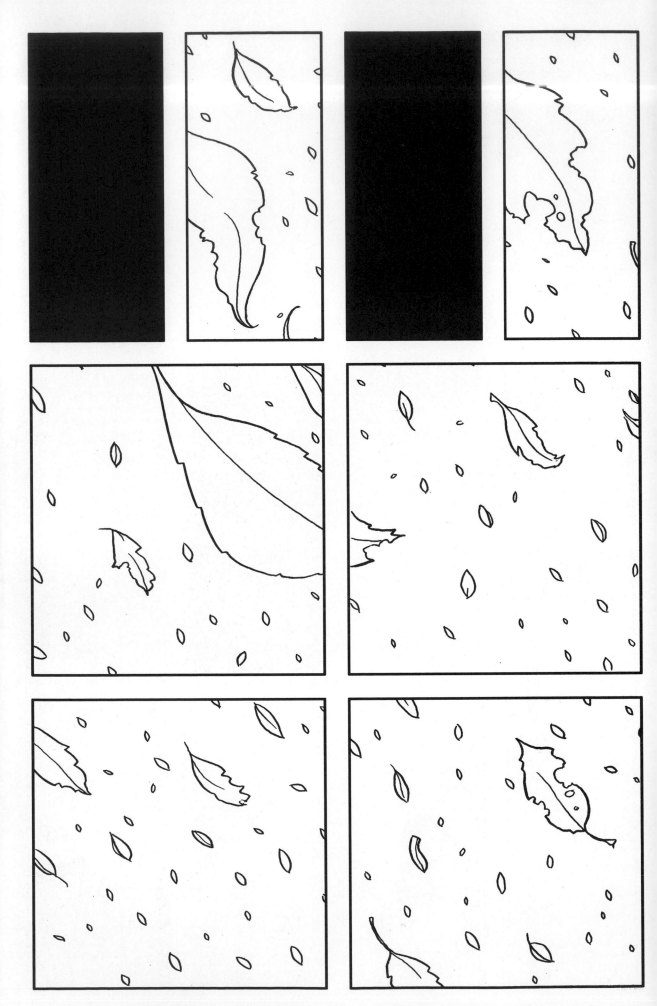

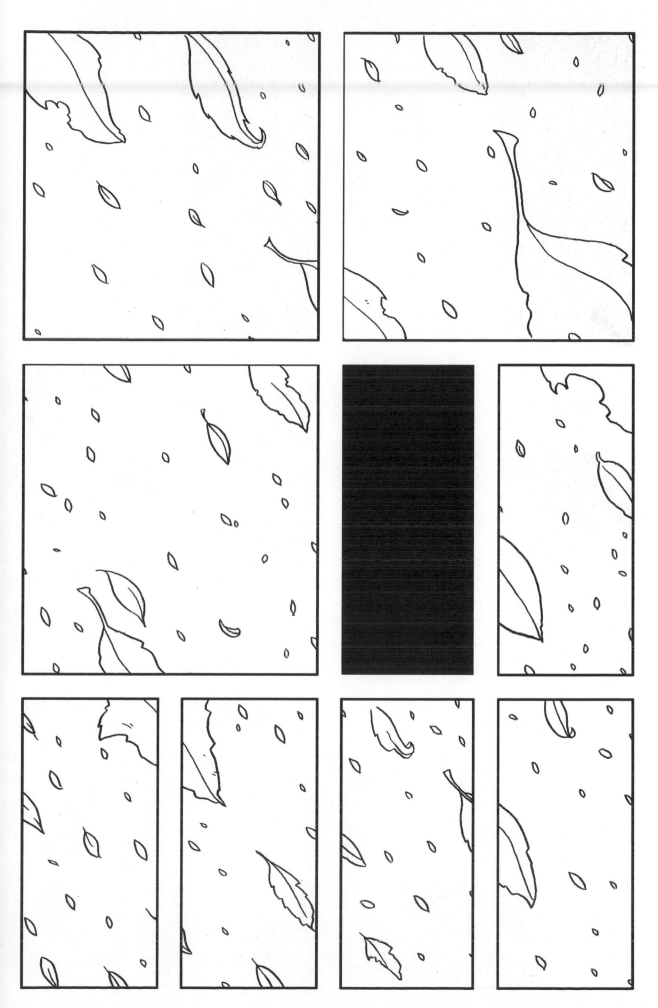

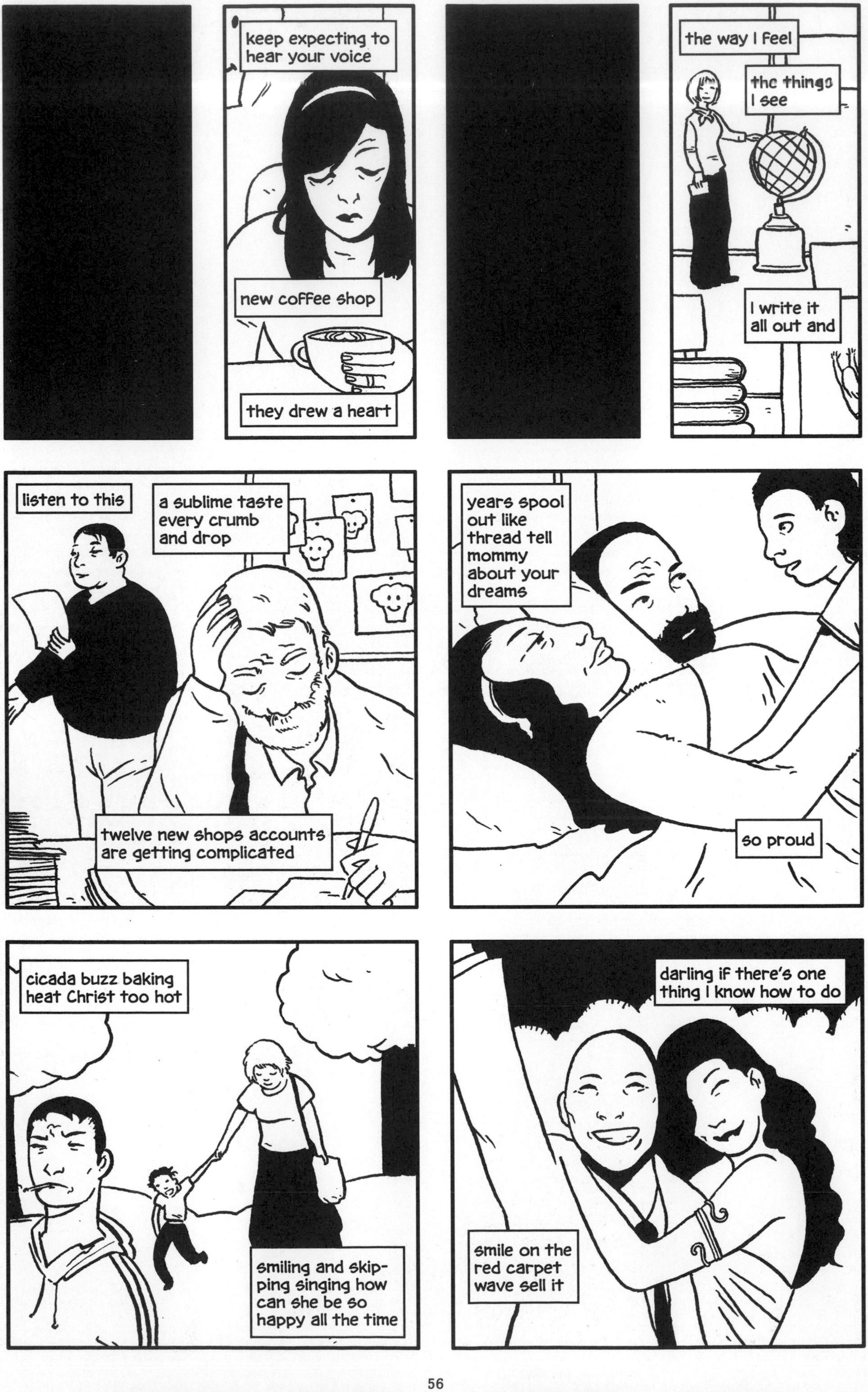

keep expecting to hear your voice
new coffee shop
they drew a heart
the way I feel
the things I see
I write it all out and
listen to this
a sublime taste every crumb and drop
twelve new shops accounts are getting complicated
years spool out like thread tell mommy about your dreams
so proud
cicada buzz baking heat Christ too hot
smiling and skip-ping singing how can she be so happy all the time
darling if there's one thing I know how to do
smile on the red carpet wave sell it

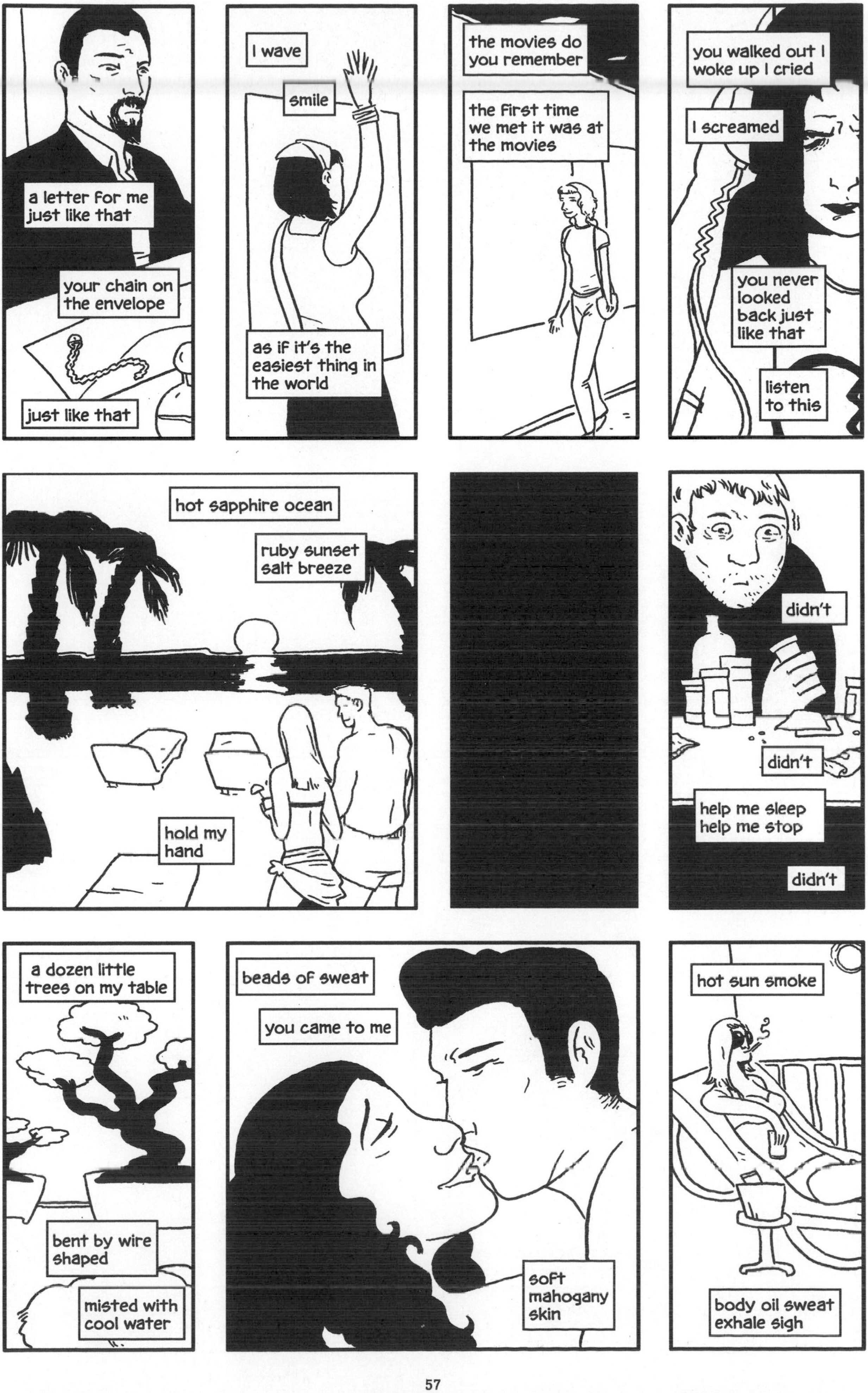
a letter for me just like that
your chain on the envelope
just like that
I wave
smile
as if it's the easiest thing in the world
the movies do you remember
the first time we met it was at the movies
you walked out I woke up I cried
I screamed
you never looked back just like that
listen to this
hot sapphire ocean
ruby sunset salt breeze
hold my hand
didn't
didn't
help me sleep help me stop
didn't
a dozen little trees on my table
bent by wire shaped
misted with cool water
beads of sweat
you came to me
soft mahogany skin
hot sun smoke
body oil sweat exhale sigh

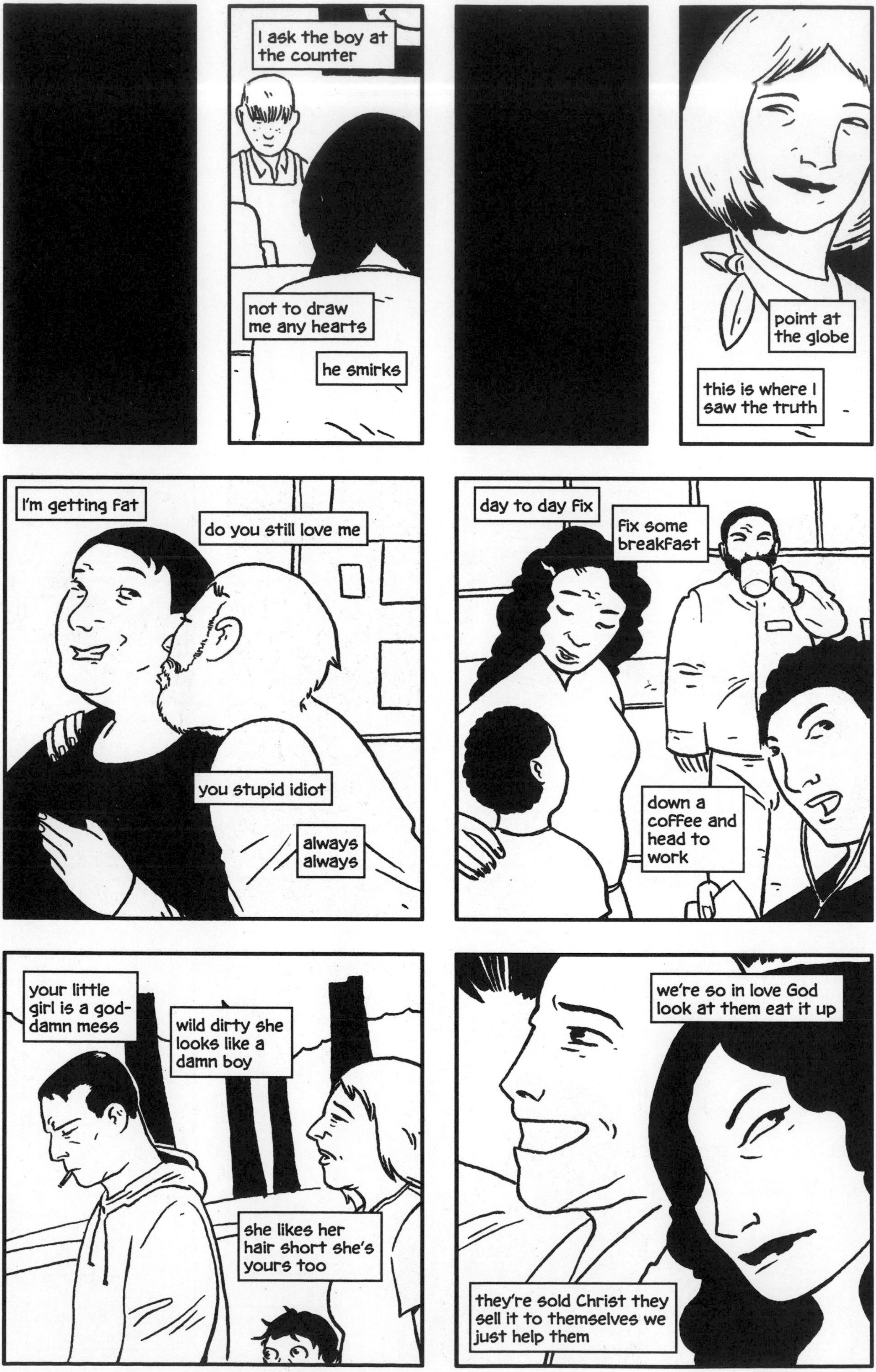
I ask the boy at the counter
not to draw me any hearts
he smirks
point at the globe
this is where I saw the truth
I'm getting fat
do you still love me
you stupid idiot
always always
day to day fix
fix some breakfast
down a coffee and head to work
your little girl is a god-damn mess
wild dirty she looks like a damn boy
she likes her hair short she's yours too
we're so in love God look at them eat it up
they're sold Christ they sell it to themselves we just help them

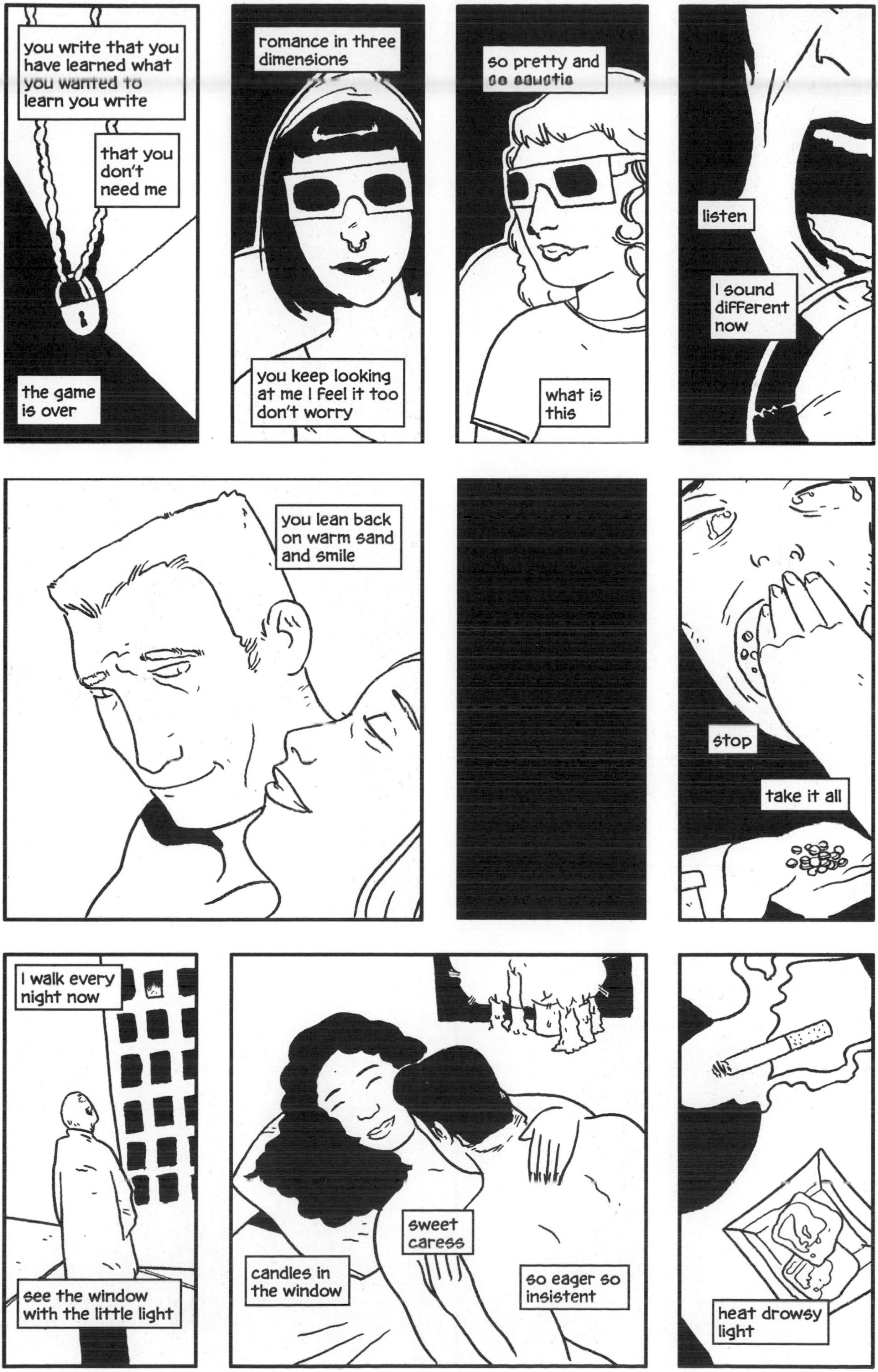
you write that you have learned what you wanted to learn you write
that you don't need me
the game is over
romance in three dimensions
you keep looking at me I feel it too don't worry
so pretty and so caustic
what is this
listen
I sound different now
you lean back on warm sand and smile
stop
take it all
I walk every night now
see the window with the little light
sweet caress
candles in the window
so eager so insistent
heat drowsy light

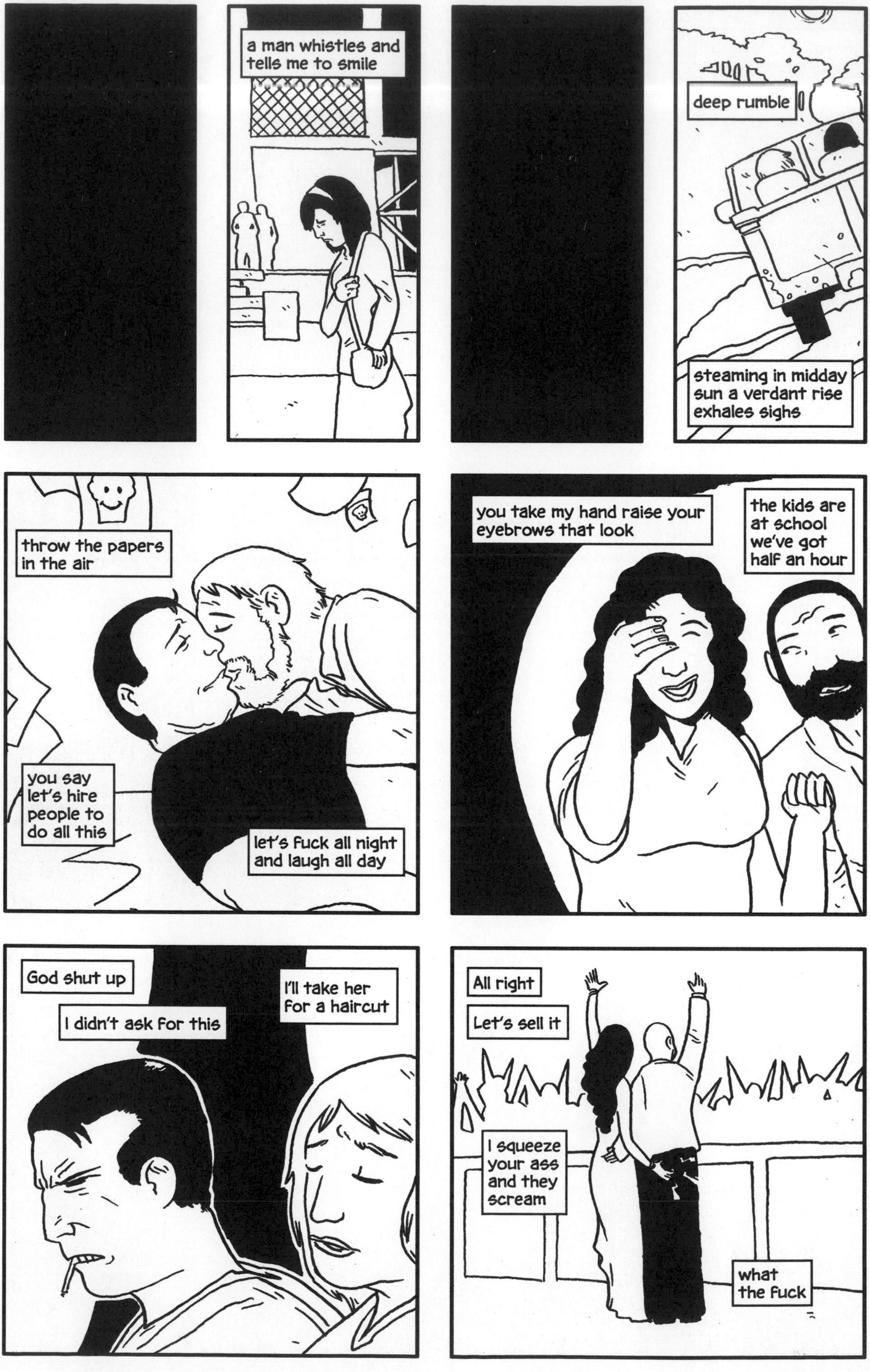
a man whistles and tells me to smile
deep rumble
steaming in midday sun a verdant rise exhales sighs
throw the papers in the air
you say let's hire people to do all this
let's fuck all night and laugh all day
you take my hand raise your eyebrows that look
the kids are at school we've got half an hour
God shut up
I didn't ask for this
I'll take her for a haircut
All right
Let's sell it
I squeeze your ass and they scream
what the fuck

you don't need me

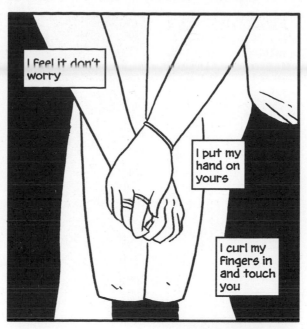

I feel it don't worry

I put my hand on yours

I curl my fingers in and touch you

rip the head-phones out and scream

we fly

Floating

the light wavers up there

I breathe down here

candles gutter burning down to the wick gasp

go deep

all right

sweat cooling smoke curling

then what

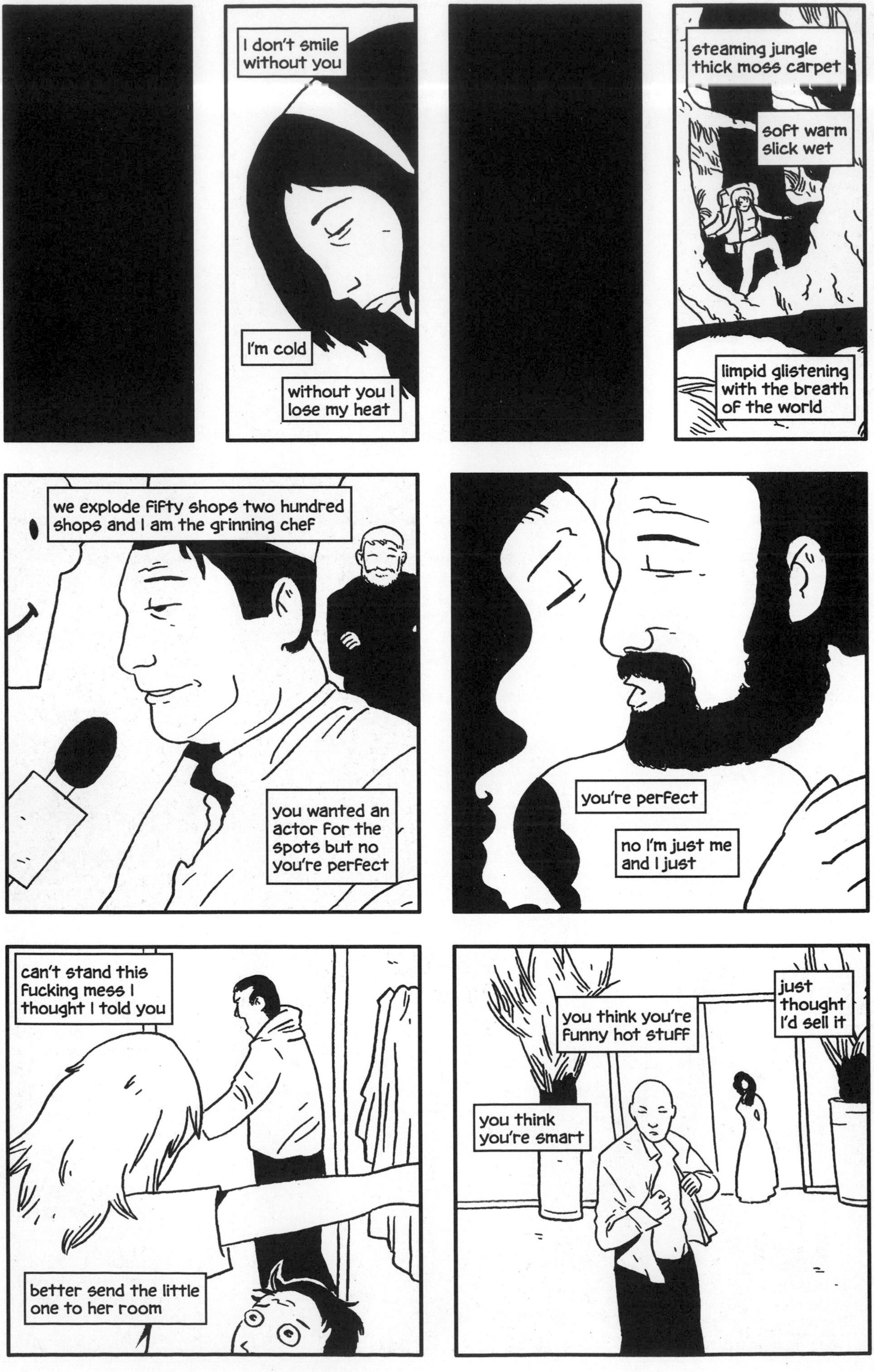
I don't smile
without you
I'm cold
without you I
lose my heat
steaming jungle
thick moss carpet
soft warm
slick wet
limpid glistening
with the breath
of the world
we explode fifty shops two hundred
shops and I am the grinning chef
you wanted an
actor for the
spots but no
you're perfect
you're perfect
no I'm just me
and I just
can't stand this
fucking mess I
thought I told you
better send the little
one to her room
you think you're
funny hot stuff
just
thought
I'd sell it
you think
you're smart

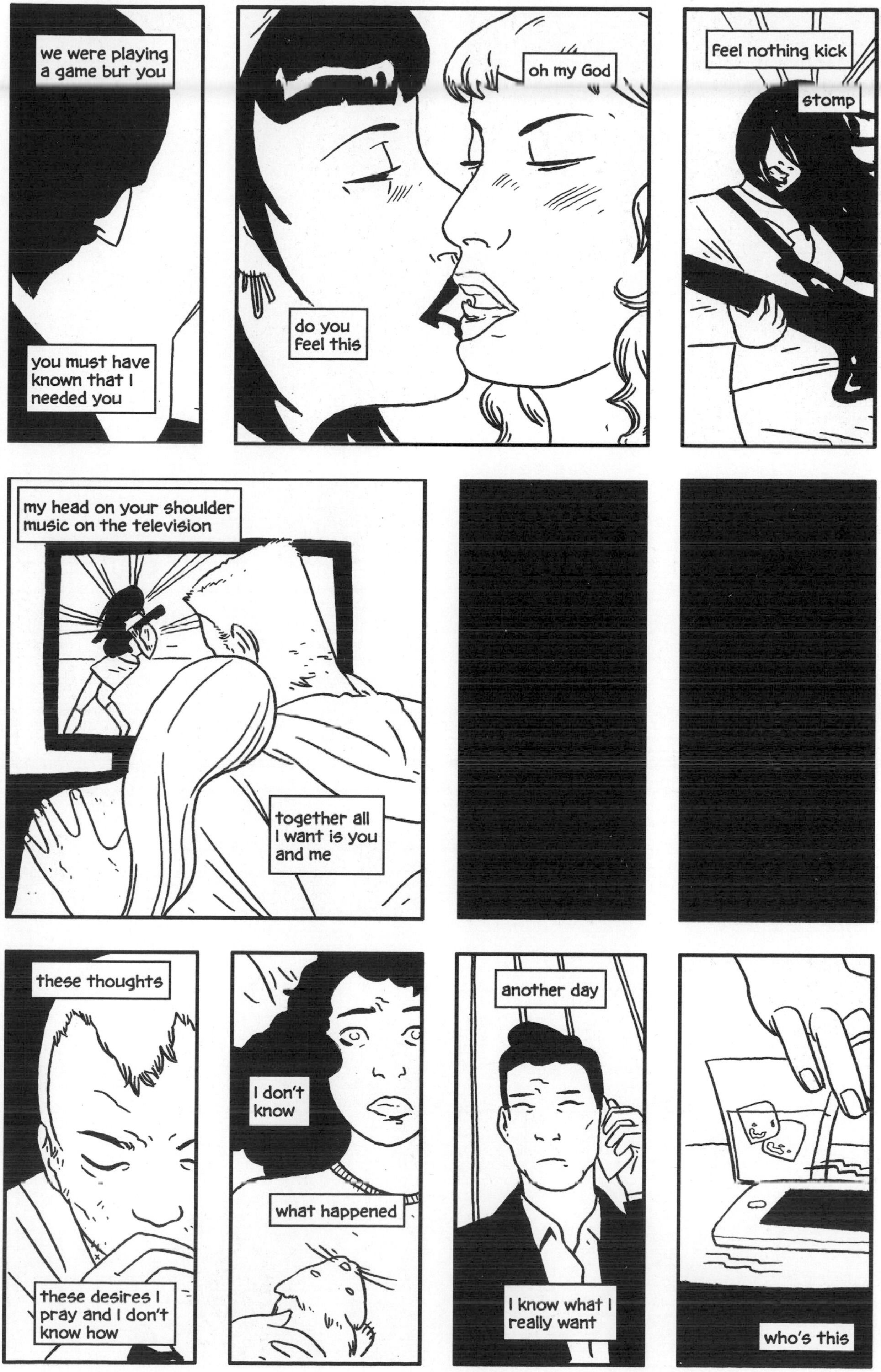
we were playing a game but you
you must have known that I needed you
oh my God
do you feel this
feel nothing kick
stomp
my head on your shoulder music on the television
together all I want is you and me
these thoughts
these desires I pray and I don't know how
I don't know
what happened
another day
I know what I really want
who's this

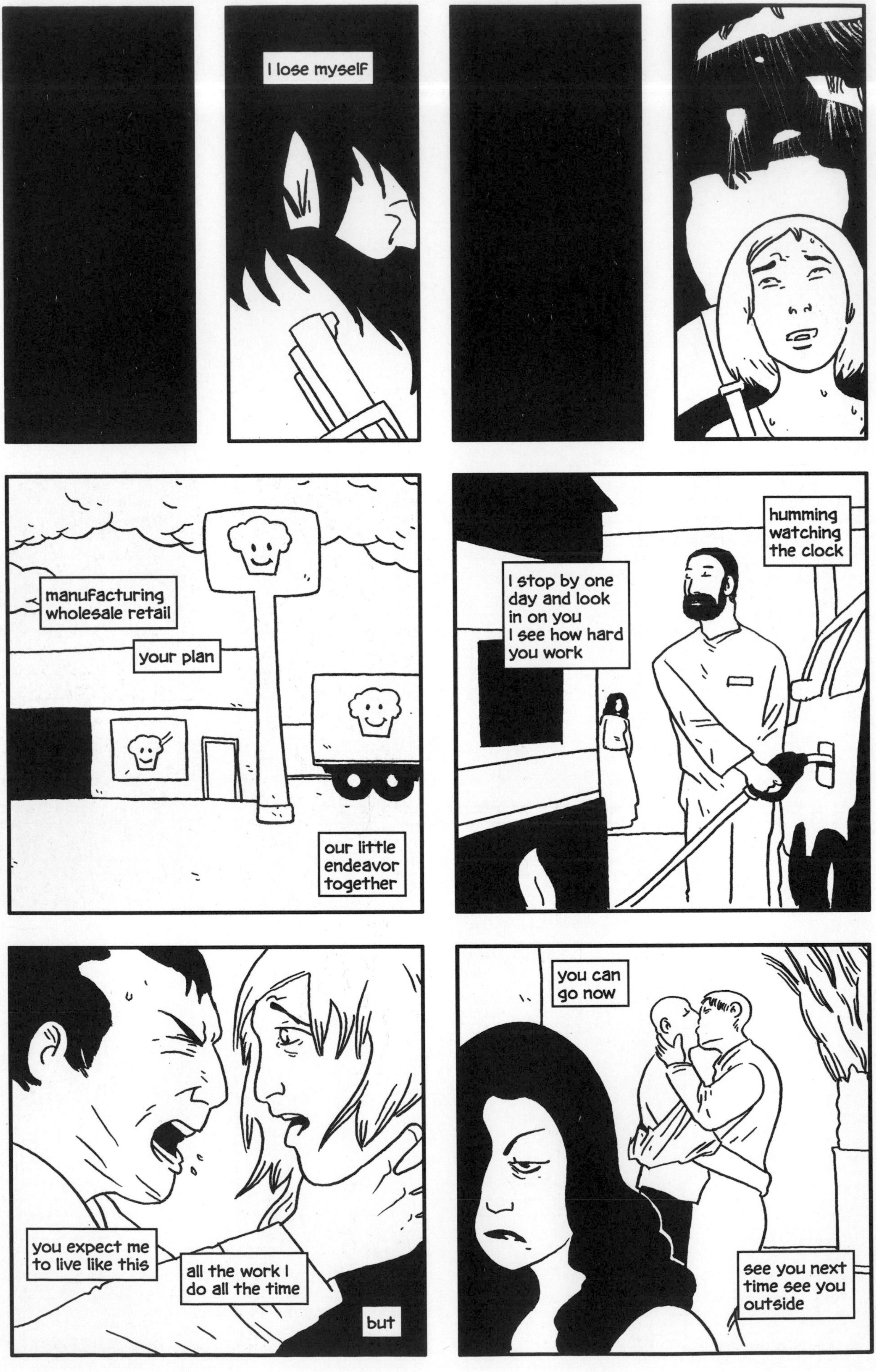
I lose myself
manufacturing wholesale retail
your plan
our little endeavor together
I stop by one day and look in on you I see how hard you work
humming watching the clock
you expect me to live like this
all the work I do all the time
but
you can go now
see you next time see you outside

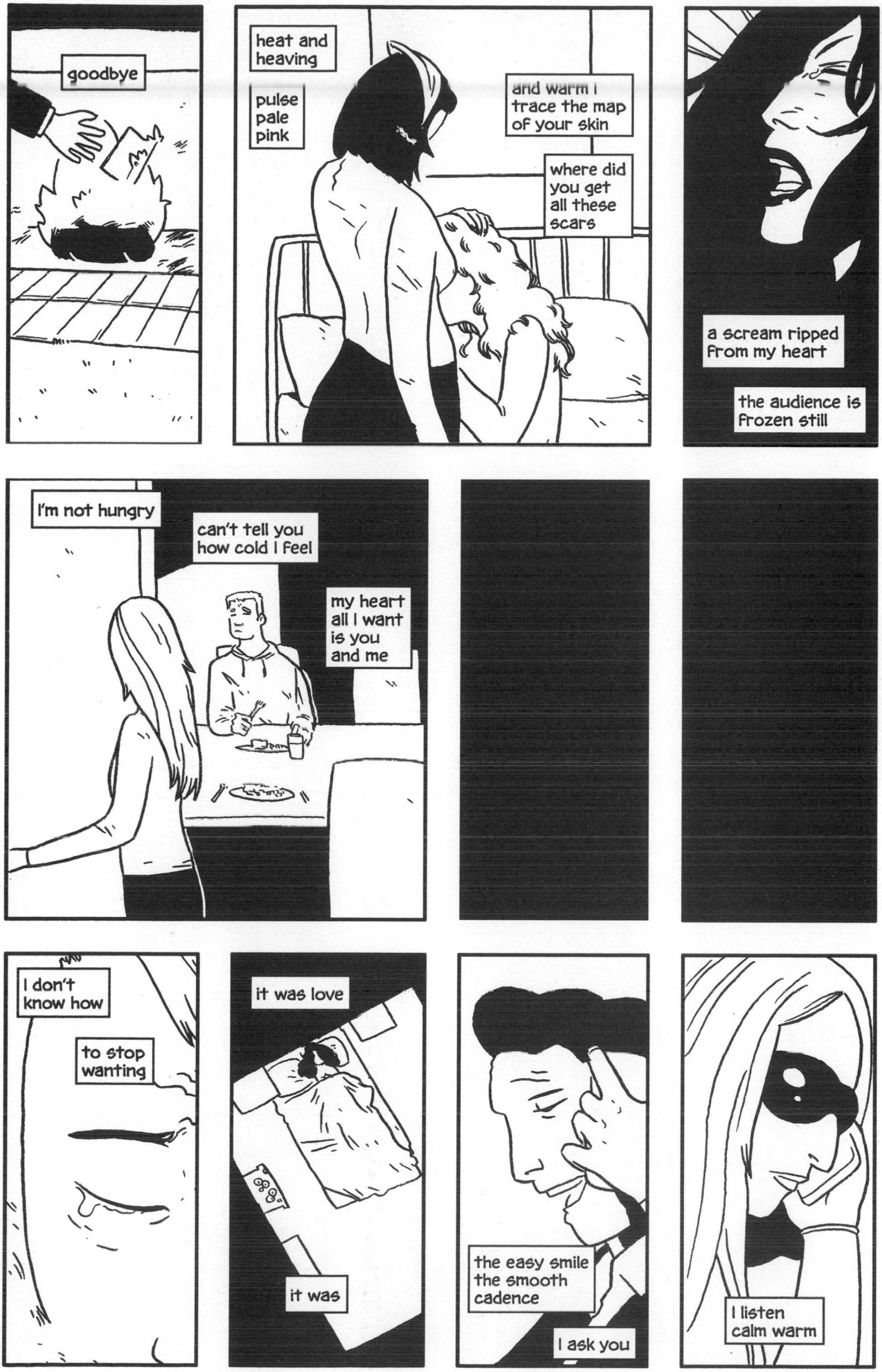
goodbye
heat and heaving
pulse pale pink
and warm I trace the map of your skin
where did you get all these scars
a scream ripped from my heart
the audience is frozen still
I'm not hungry
can't tell you how cold I feel
my heart all I want is you and me
I don't know how
to stop wanting
it was love
it was
the easy smile the smooth cadence
I ask you
I listen calm warm

hey baby hey
beautiful hey
smile for me hey

speechless

hot sun
high hedge

not a
word

sigh

days together

walk in the
door tired
but alive

exhale

turn I
know

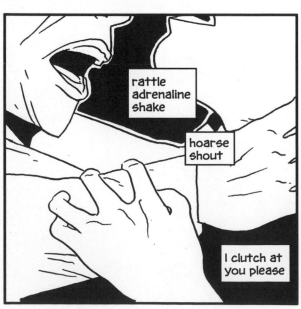

rattle
adrenaline
shake

hoarse
shout

I clutch at
you please

gazing at
our stills our
promos

funny love
steamy love

brave love
dying love

popular love
lucrative love

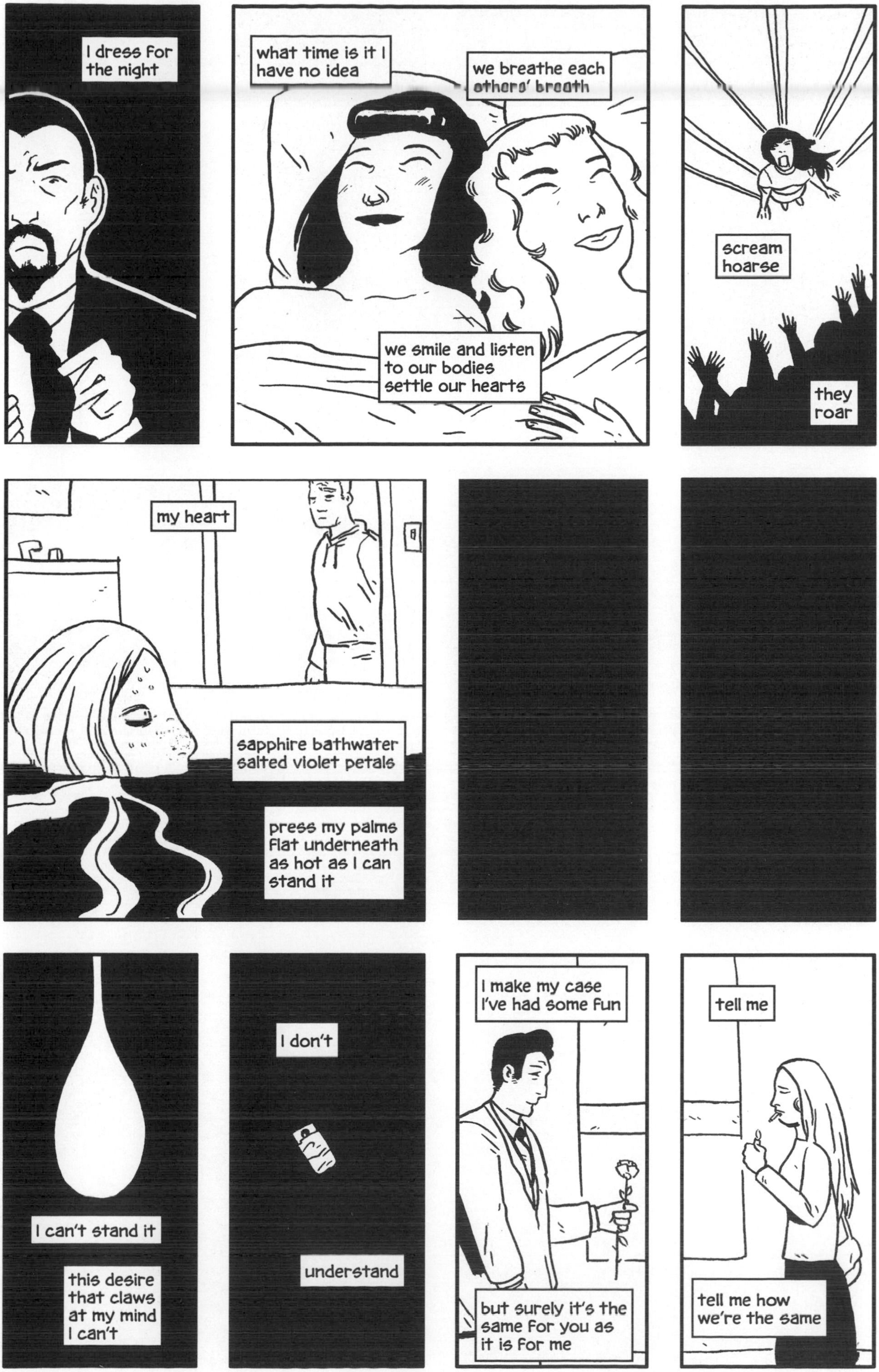
I dress for the night
what time is it I have no idea
we breathe each others' breath
we smile and listen to our bodies settle our hearts
scream hoarse
they roar
my heart
sapphire bathwater salted violet petals
press my palms flat underneath as hot as I can stand it
I can't stand it
this desire that claws at my mind I can't
I don't
understand
I make my case I've had some fun
but surely it's the same for you as it is for me
tell me
tell me how we're the same

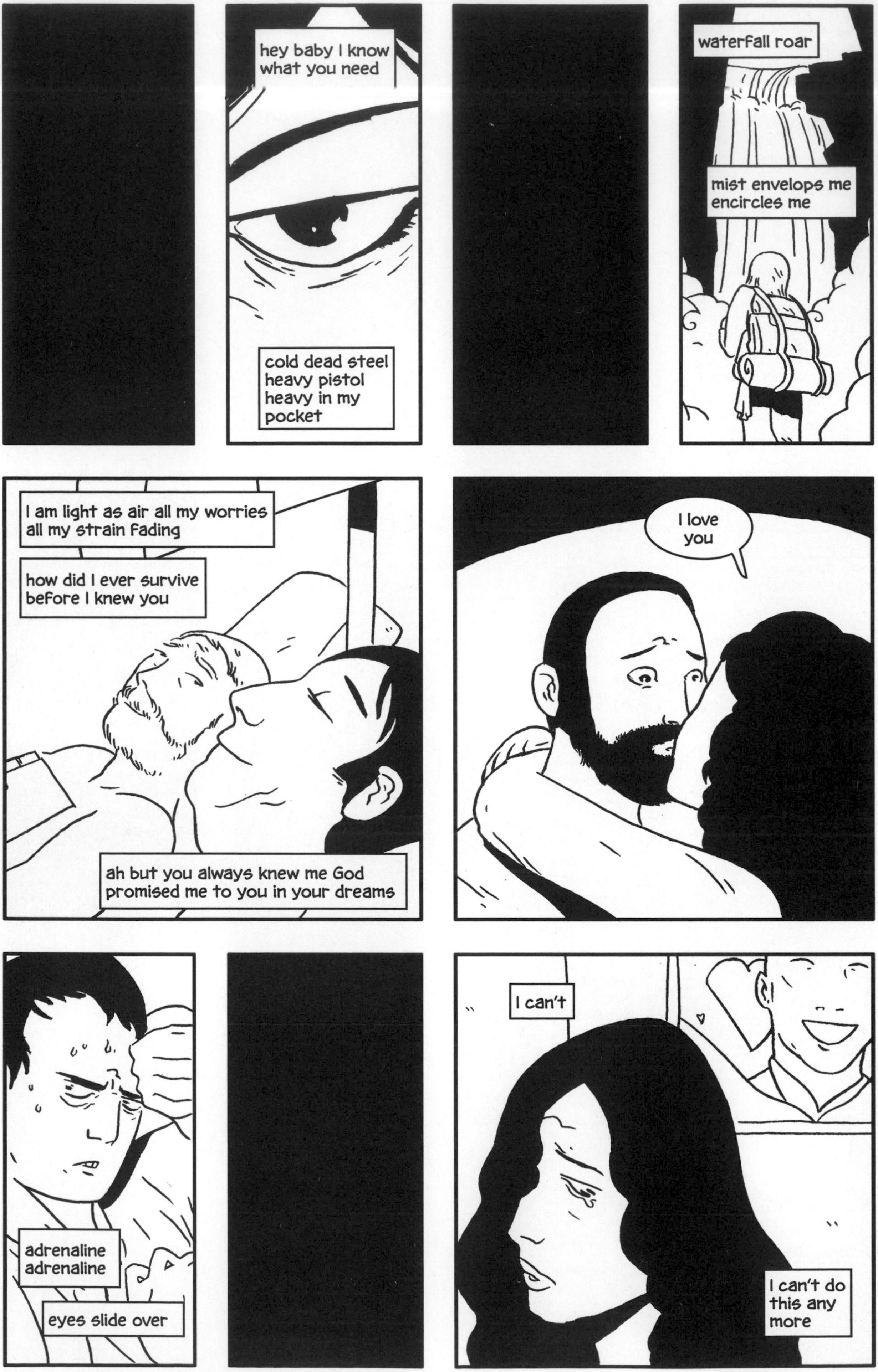
hey baby I know what you need
cold dead steel heavy pistol heavy in my pocket
waterfall roar
mist envelops me encircles me
I am light as air all my worries all my strain fading
how did I ever survive before I knew you
ah but you always knew me God promised me to you in your dreams
I love you
adrenaline adrenaline
eyes slide over
I can't
I can't do this any more

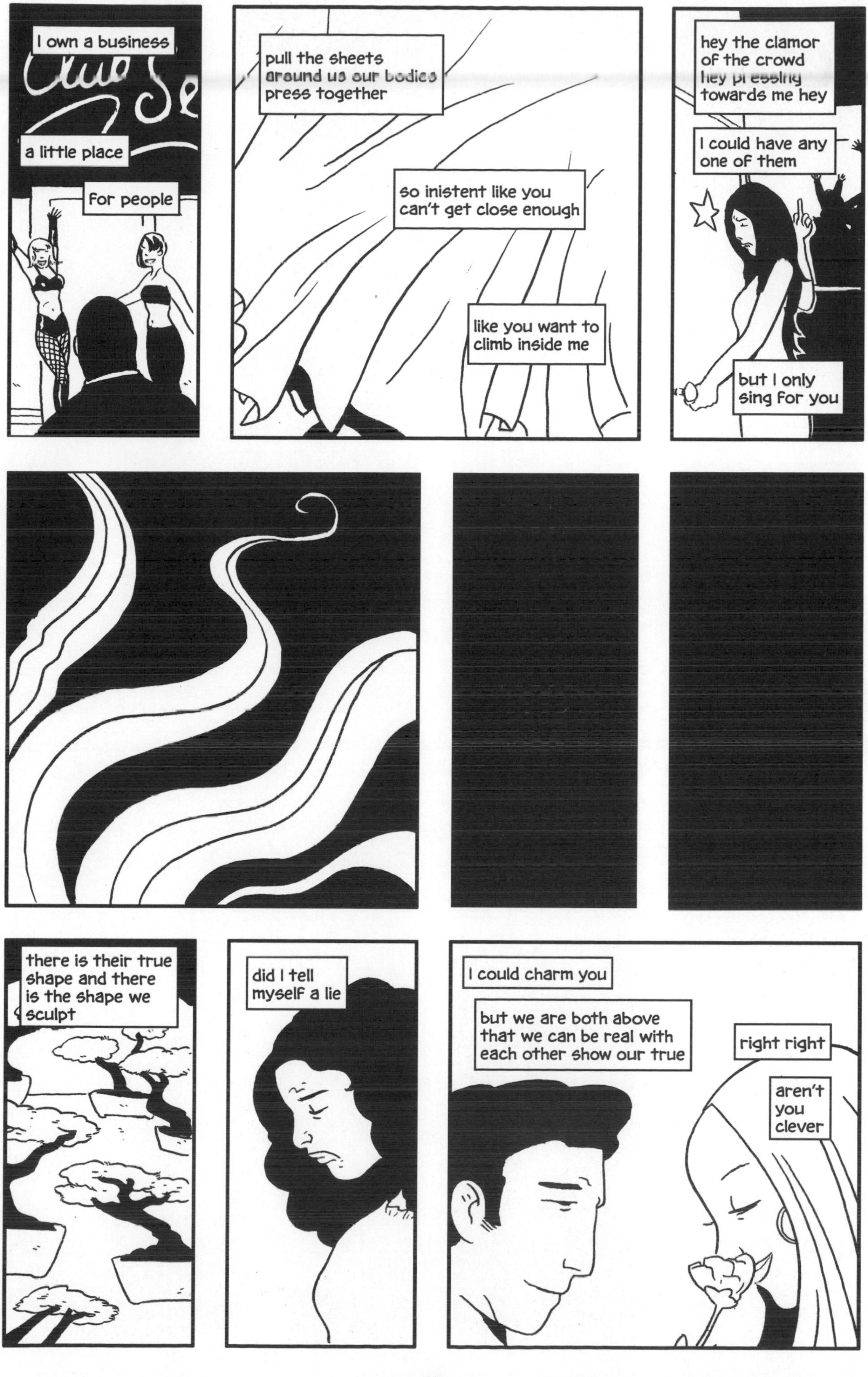
I own a business
a little place
for people
pull the sheets around us our bodies press together
so inistent like you can't get close enough
like you want to climb inside me
hey the clamor of the crowd hey pressing towards me hey
I could have any one of them
but I only sing for you
there is their true shape and there is the shape we sculpt
did I tell myself a lie
I could charm you
but we are both above that we can be real with each other show our true
right right
aren't you clever

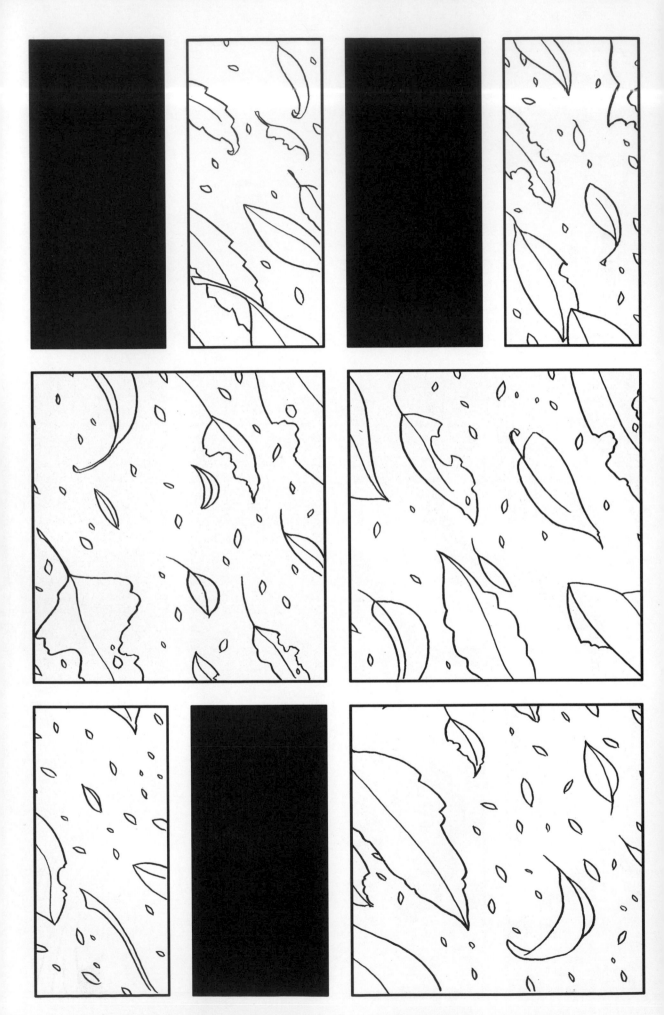

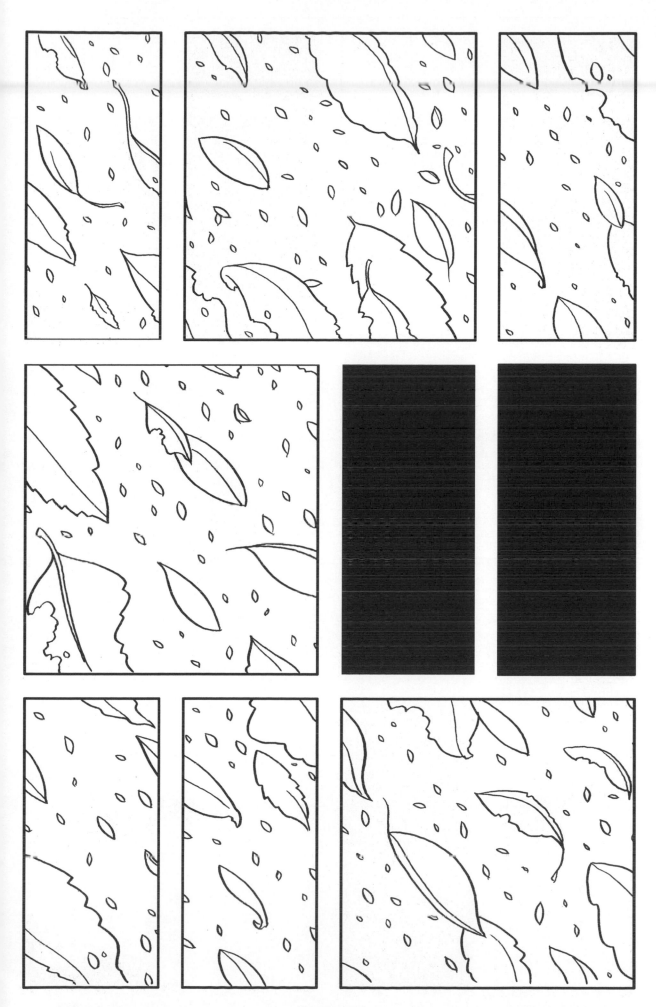

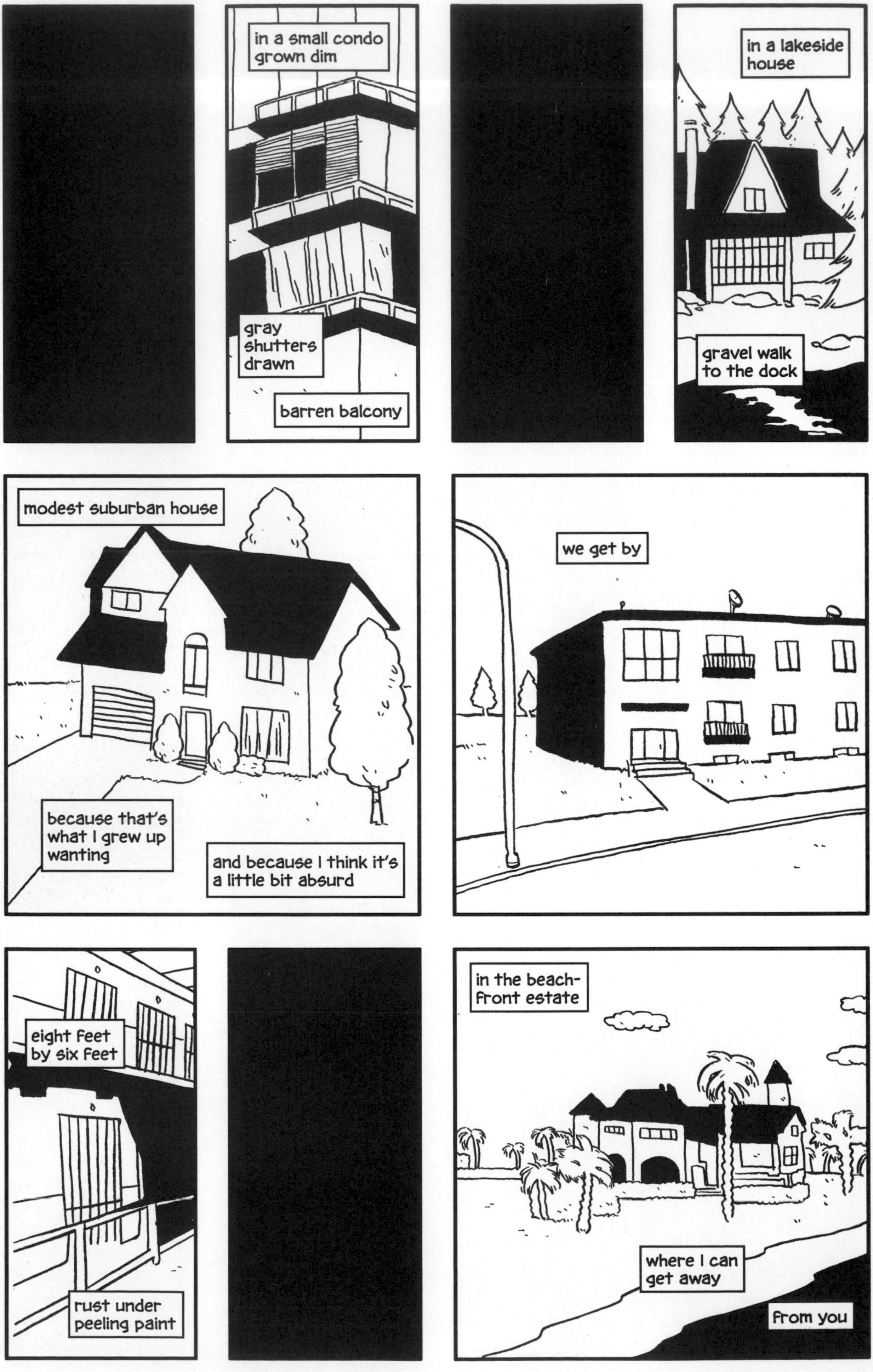
in a small condo grown dim
gray shutters drawn
barren balcony
in a lakeside house
gravel walk to the dock
modest suburban house
because that's what I grew up wanting
and because I think it's a little bit absurd
we get by
eight feet by six feet
rust under peeling paint
in the beach-front estate
where I can get away
from you

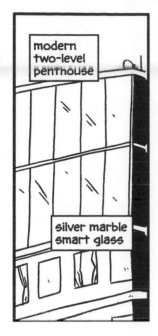

modern two-level penthouse

silver marble smart glass

the brown-stone with its two trees out front

branches inter-mingled we gave them names

corner view

piled with boxes dishes in the trash

the small house

you inherited from your mother small lawn

cluttered apartment

I never intended to stay so long

in my little nook

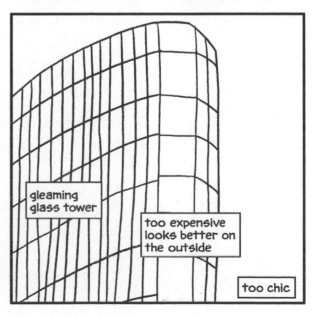

gleaming glass tower

too expensive looks better on the outside

too chic

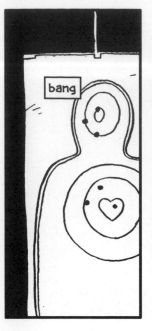

bang

propellor whine radio static hiss

sapphire skies clouds below

product launch

branded profile household name

smile

years fly

everything changes everything sags

everything but this one thing

hate

hate this

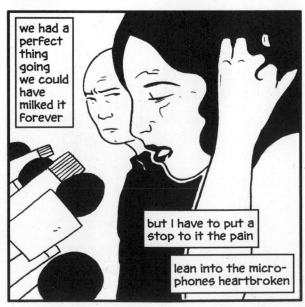

we had a perfect thing going we could have milked it forever

but I have to put a stop to it the pain

lean into the micro-phones heartbroken

I preside in the dim haze

redolent of sex and incense

they bow to me

legs touch under the table

you still make me blush

garbage

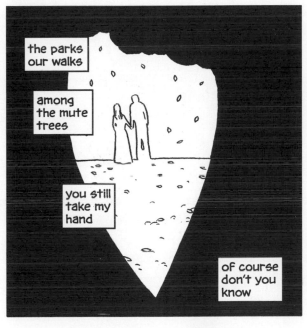

the parks our walks

among the mute trees

you still take my hand

of course don't you know

years and I study

I study myself

learn quiet

in my isolation

sure I'll bite you're the clever one

you're the one that almost got away

75

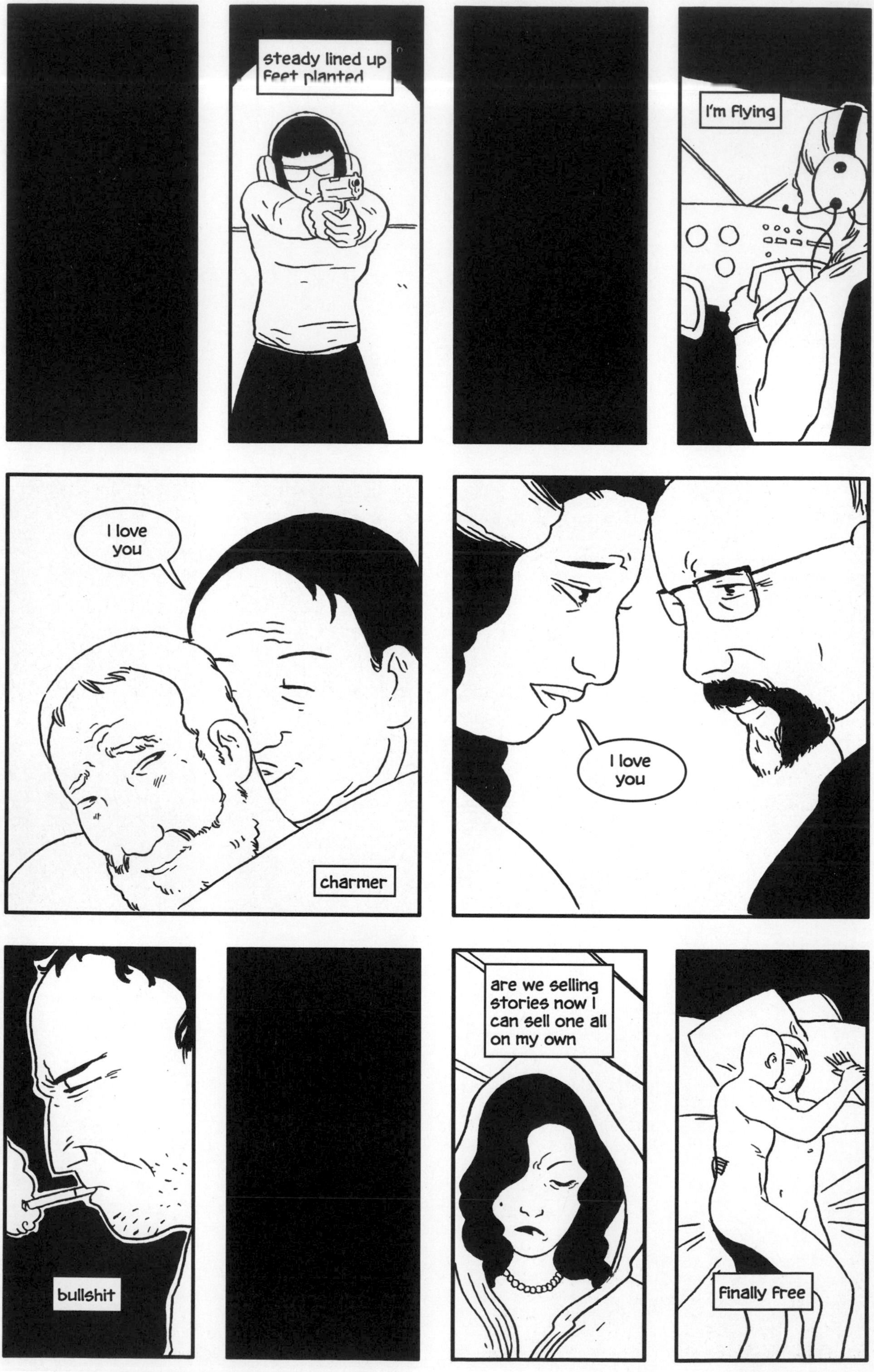
steady lined up
feet planted
I'm flying
I love you
charmer
I love you
bullshit
are we selling stories now I can sell one all on my own
finally free

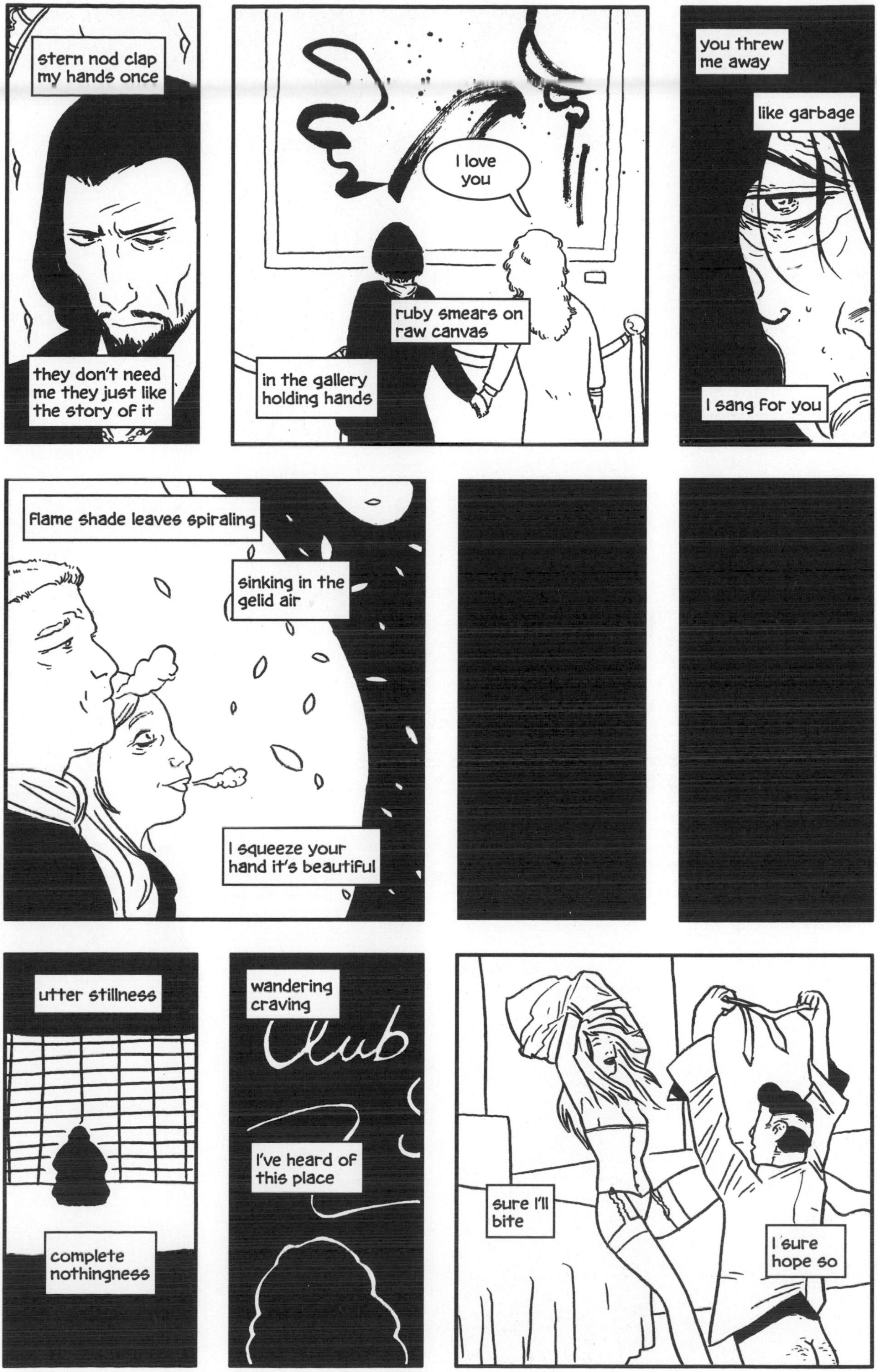

stern nod clap my hands once
they don't need me they just like the story of it
I love you
ruby smears on raw canvas
in the gallery holding hands
you threw me away
like garbage
I sang for you
flame shade leaves spiraling
sinking in the gelid air
I squeeze your hand it's beautiful
utter stillness
complete nothingness
wandering craving
Club
I've heard of this place
sure I'll bite
I sure hope so

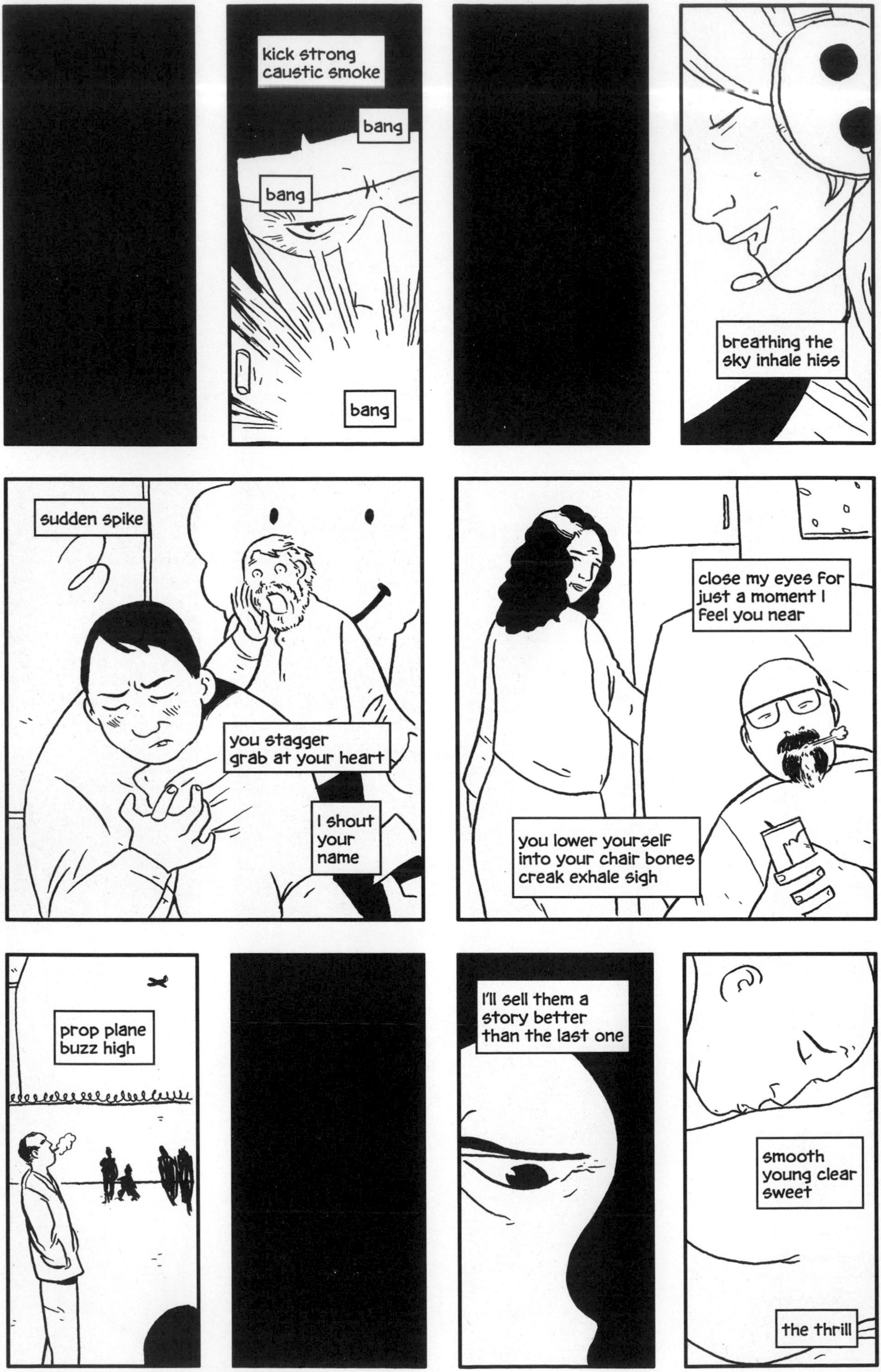
kick strong
caustic smoke
bang
bang
bang
breathing the
sky inhale hiss
sudden spike
you stagger
grab at your heart
I shout
your
name
close my eyes for
just a moment I
feel you near
you lower yourself
into your chair bones
creak exhale sigh
prop plane
buzz high
I'll sell them a
story better
than the last one
smooth
young clear
sweet
the thrill

I made this farce of myself

cast the role

she buys me a book of paintings and I don't know why I start to cry

I mean I lose it

I don't understand did I do something wrong

did I take something I shouldn't have did I give up too much

did I learn to forget

how sad I am

by taking these walks with you

the world is beautiful and you are beautiful

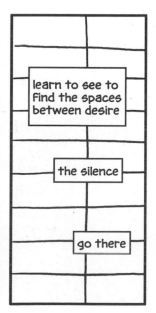

learn to see to find the spaces between desire

the silence

go there

writhing limbs mirrors multiply

I go in

my tongue in your ear your hand moves with my heartbeat

beautiful

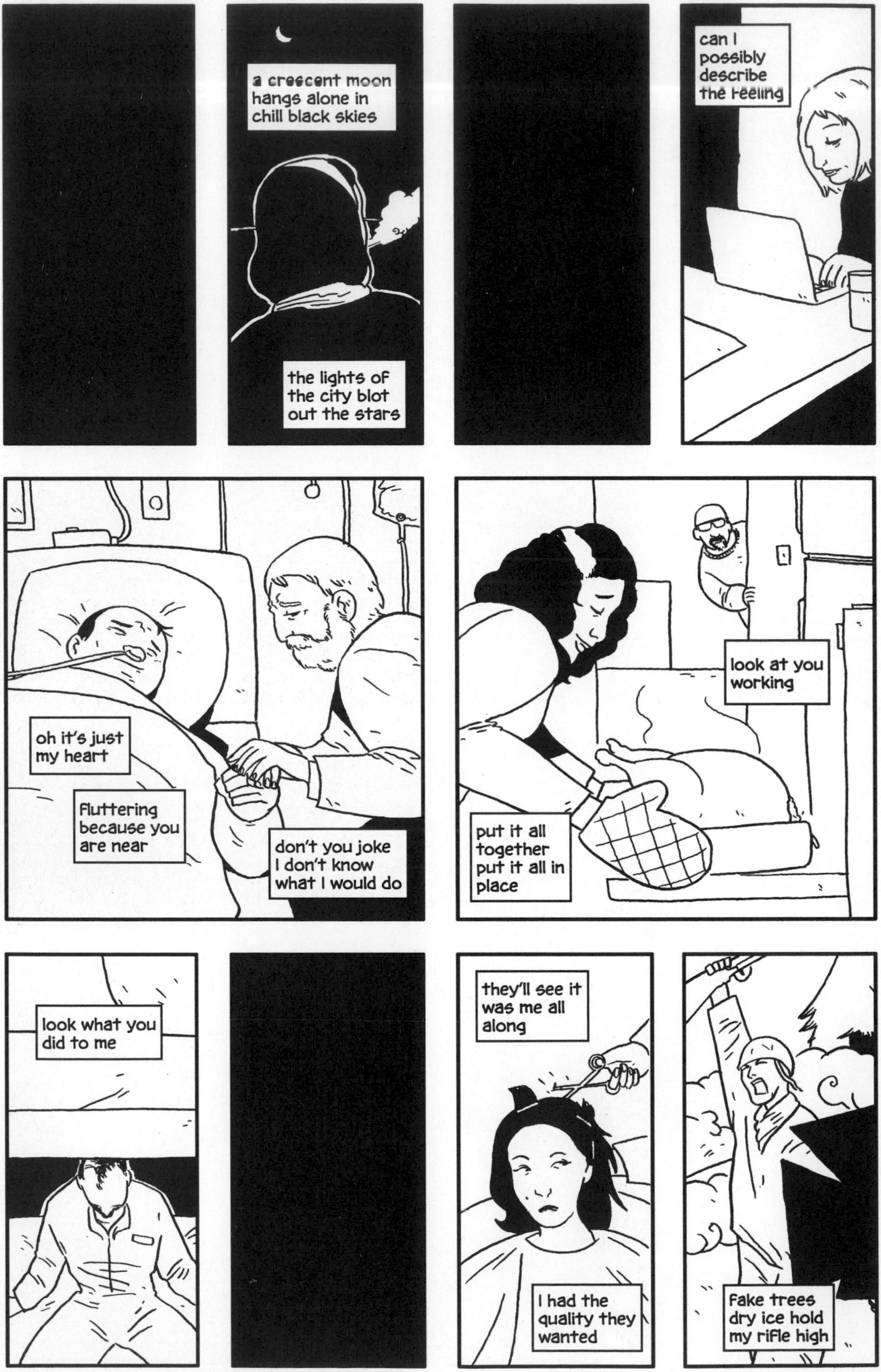

a crescent moon hangs alone in chill black skies
the lights of the city blot out the stars
can I possibly describe the feeling
oh it's just my heart
fluttering because you are near
don't you joke I don't know what I would do
look at you working
put it all together put it all in place
look what you did to me
they'll see it was me all along
I had the quality they wanted
fake trees dry ice hold my rifle high

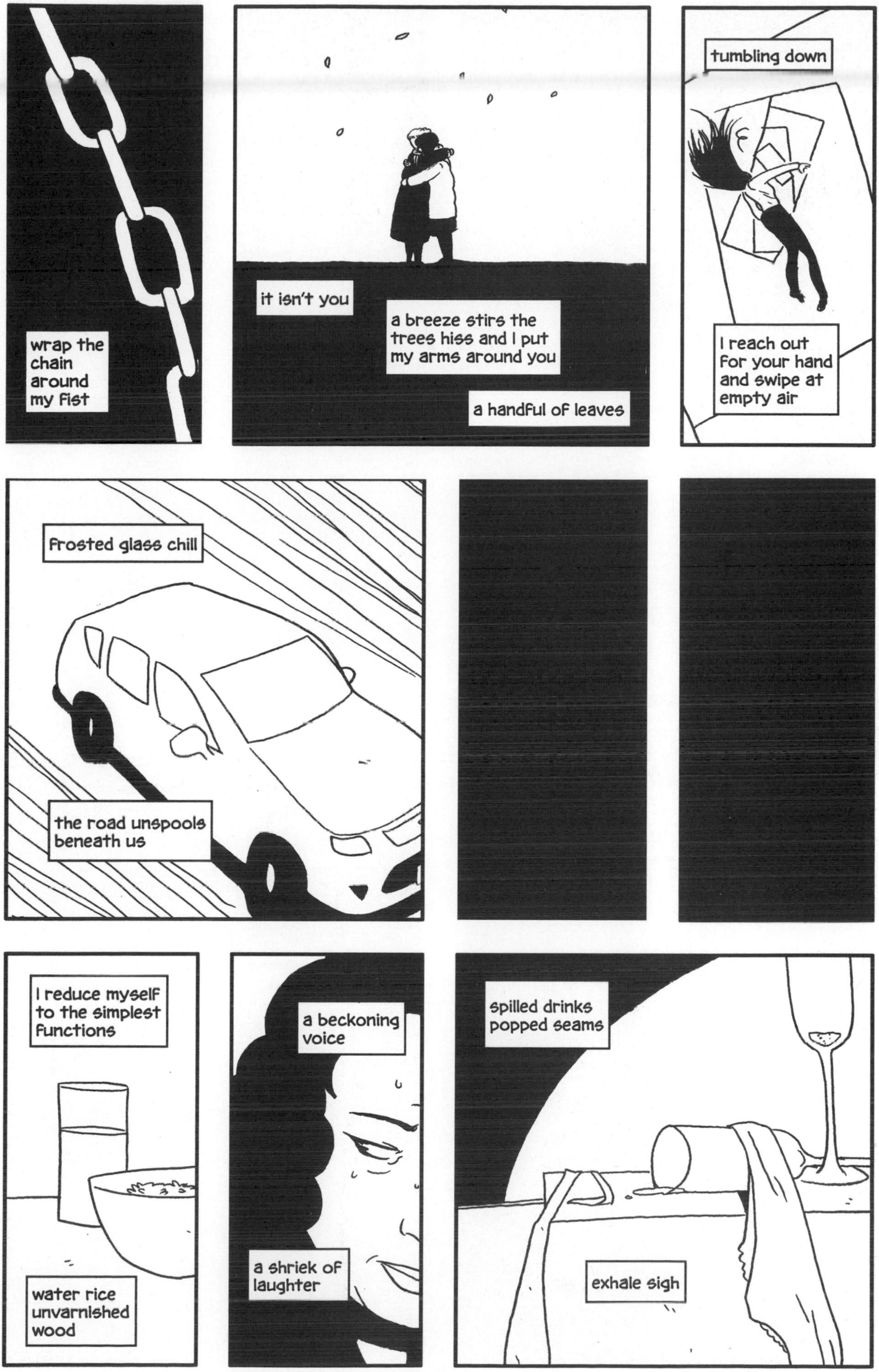
wrap the chain around my fist
it isn't you
a breeze stirs the trees hiss and I put my arms around you
a handful of leaves
tumbling down
I reach out for your hand and swipe at empty air
frosted glass chill
the road unspools beneath us
I reduce myself to the simplest functions
water rice unvarnished wood
a beckoning voice
a shriek of laughter
spilled drinks popped seams
exhale sigh

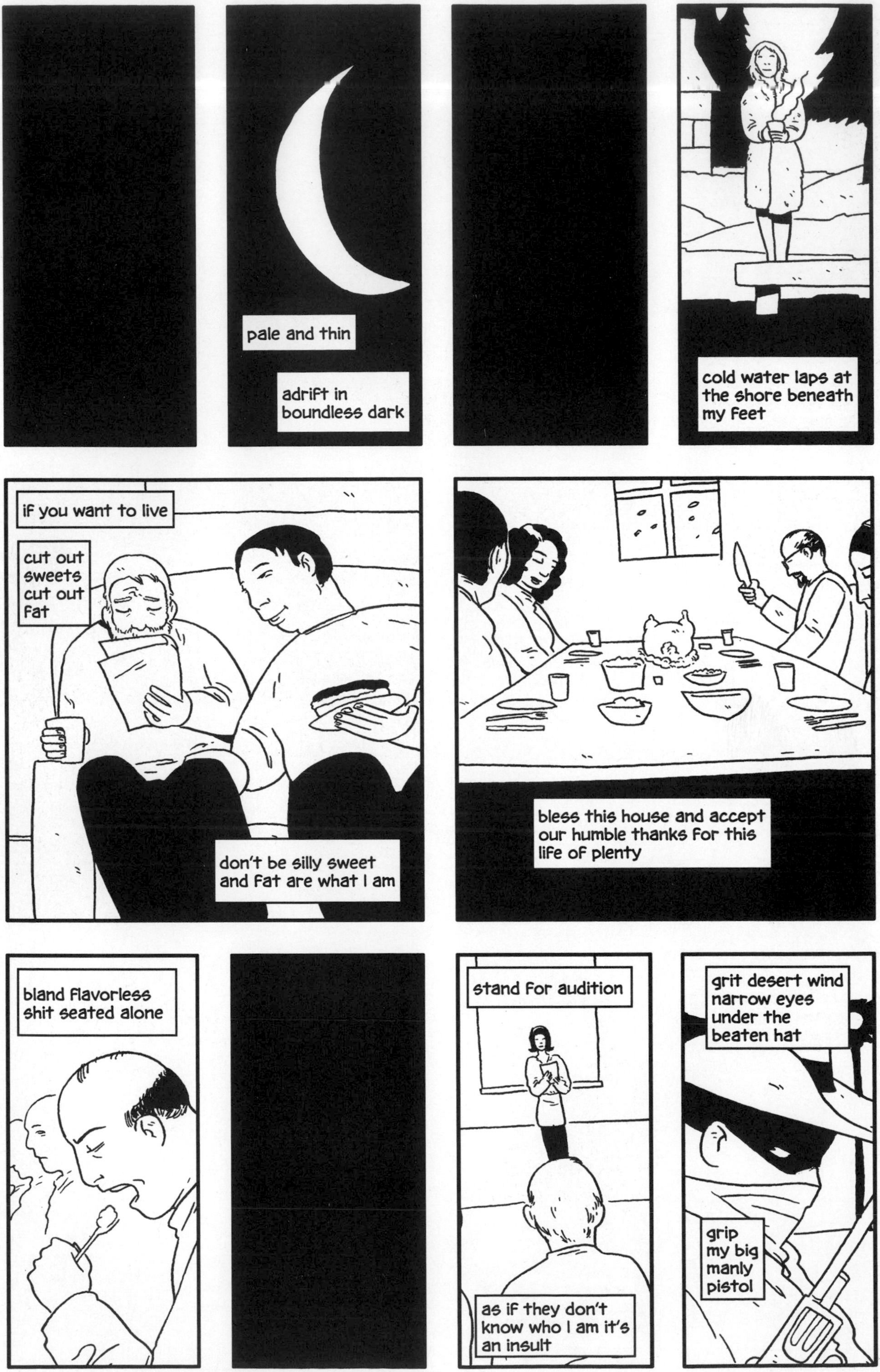

pale and thin
adrift in boundless dark
cold water laps at the shore beneath my feet
if you want to live
cut out sweets cut out fat
don't be silly sweet and fat are what I am
bless this house and accept our humble thanks for this life of plenty
bland flavorless shit seated alone
stand for audition
as if they don't know who I am it's an insult
grit desert wind narrow eyes under the beaten hat
grip my big manly pistol

young and smooth eager for my fiction

I grip her by the throat and frown

I love you

rolling forward already fading

this is how we live I love you I find ways to keep you alive with me

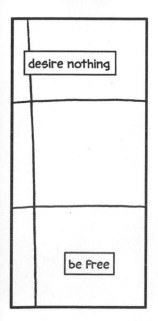

desire nothing

be free

be free

well how about that you were right it is better

with you

did you forget you really are the best

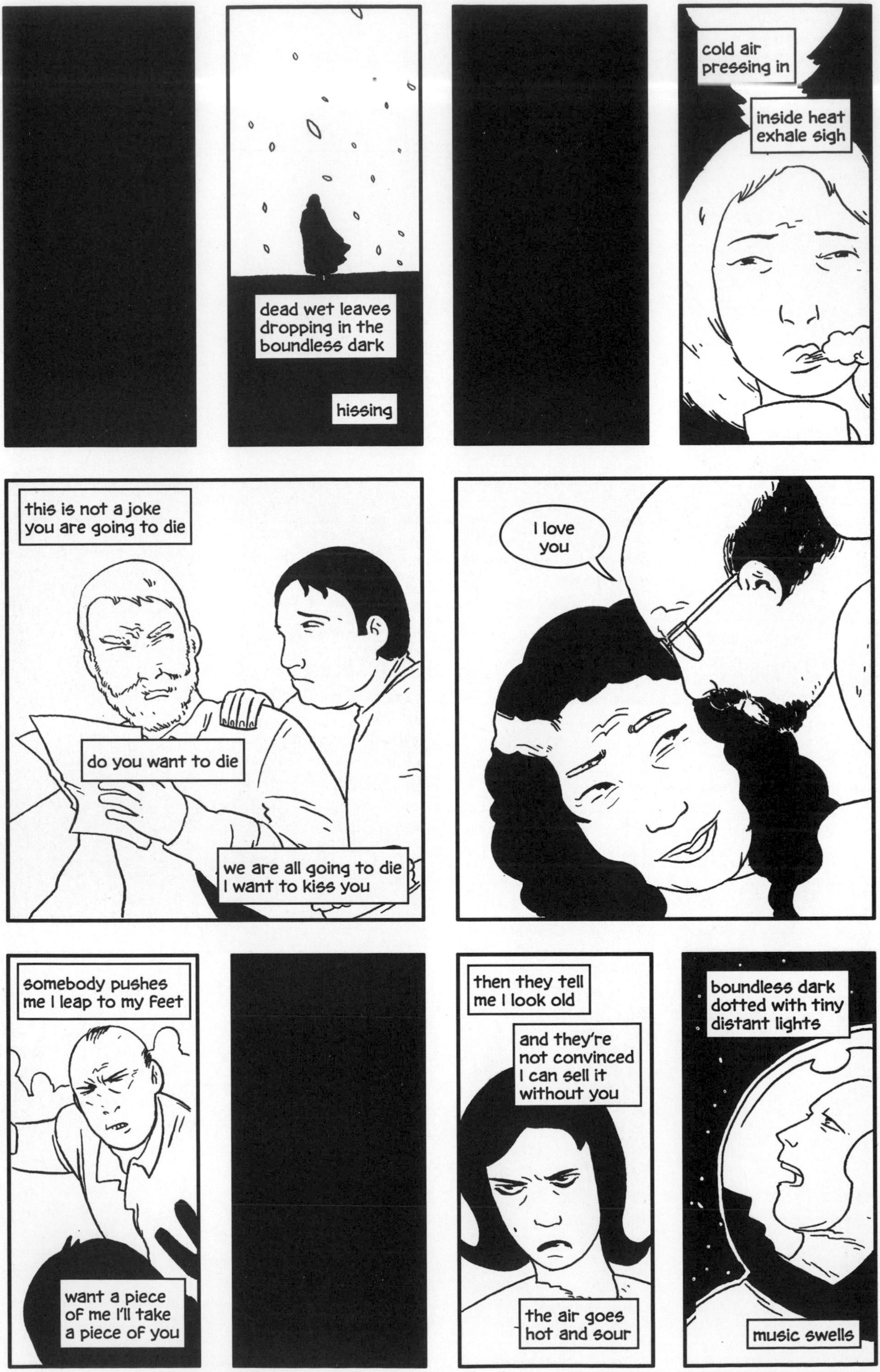
dead wet leaves dropping in the boundless dark
hissing
cold air pressing in
inside heat exhale sigh
this is not a joke you are going to die
do you want to die
we are all going to die I want to kiss you
I love you
somebody pushes me I leap to my feet
want a piece of me I'll take a piece of you
then they tell me I look old
and they're not convinced I can sell it without you
the air goes hot and sour
boundless dark dotted with tiny distant lights
music swells

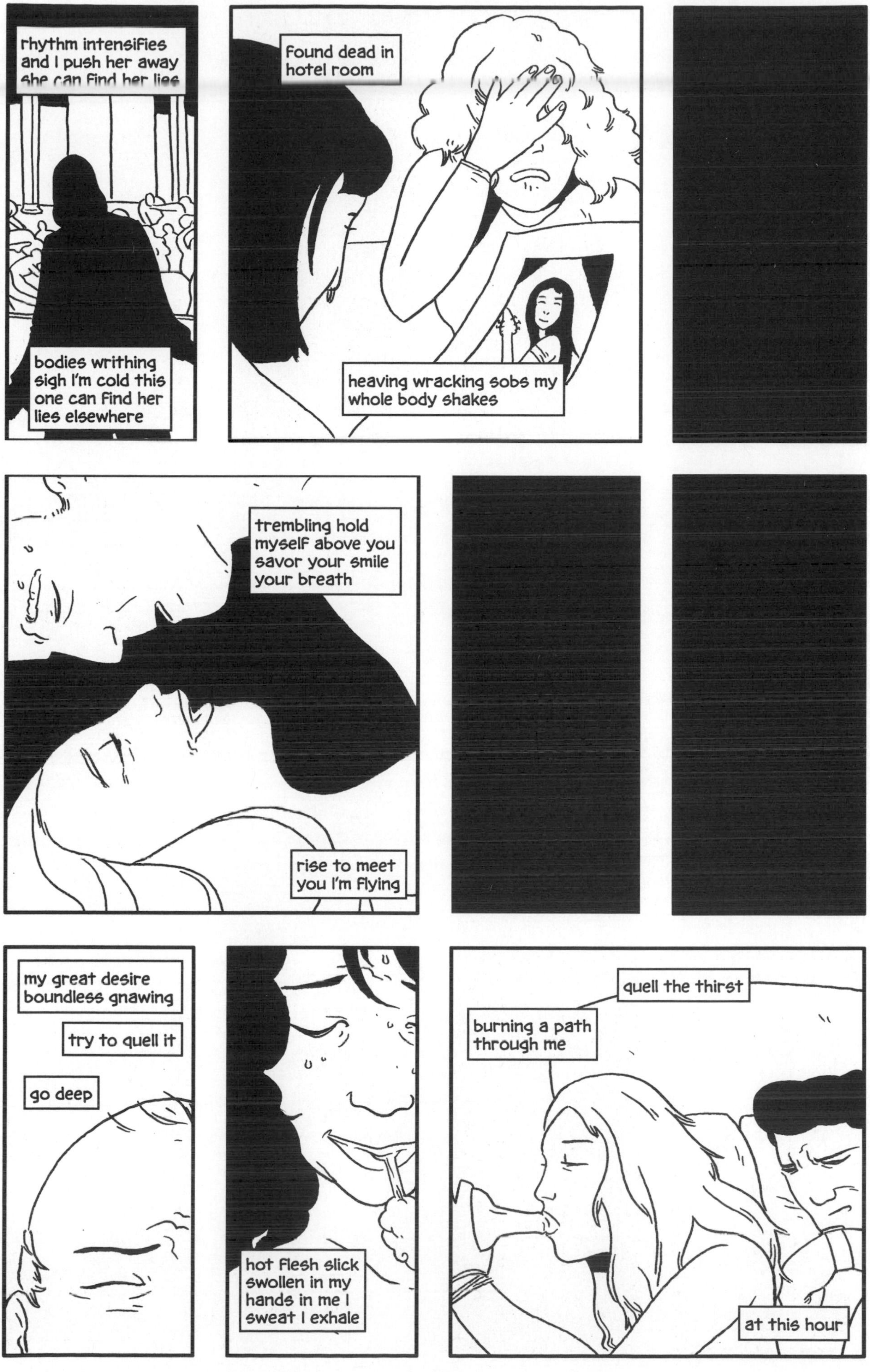
rhythm intensifies and I push her away she can find her lies
bodies writhing sigh I'm cold this one can find her lies elsewhere
found dead in hotel room
heaving wracking sobs my whole body shakes
trembling hold myself above you savor your smile your breath
rise to meet you I'm flying
my great desire boundless gnawing
try to quell it
go deep
hot flesh slick swollen in my hands in me I sweat I exhale
quell the thirst
burning a path through me
at this hour

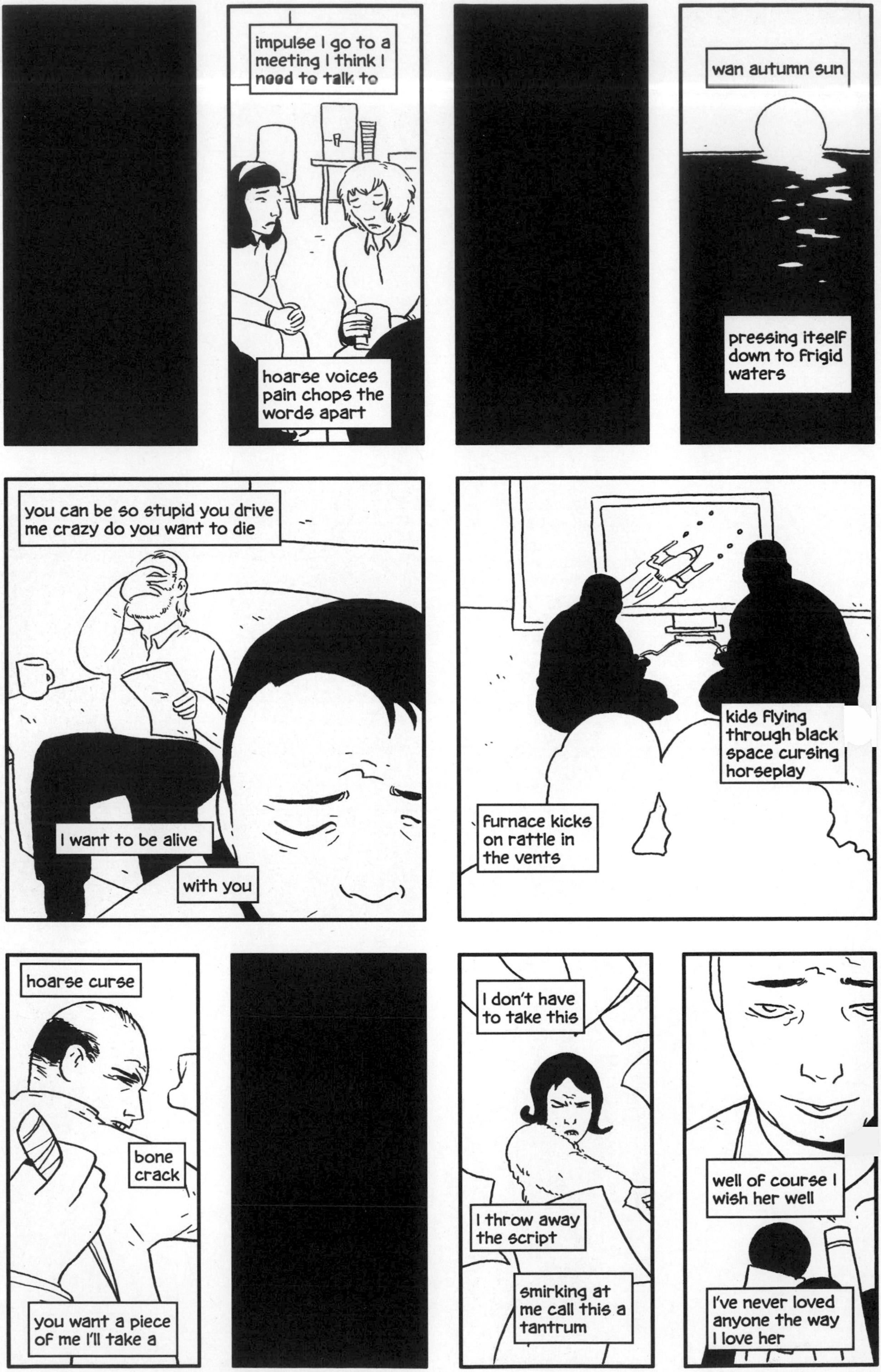
impulse I go to a meeting I think I need to talk to
hoarse voices pain chops the words apart
wan autumn sun
pressing itself down to frigid waters
you can be so stupid you drive me crazy do you want to die
I want to be alive
with you
kids flying through black space cursing horseplay
furnace kicks on rattle in the vents
hoarse curse
bone crack
you want a piece of me I'll take a
I don't have to take this
I throw away the script
smirking at me call this a tantrum
well of course I wish her well
I've never loved anyone the way I love her

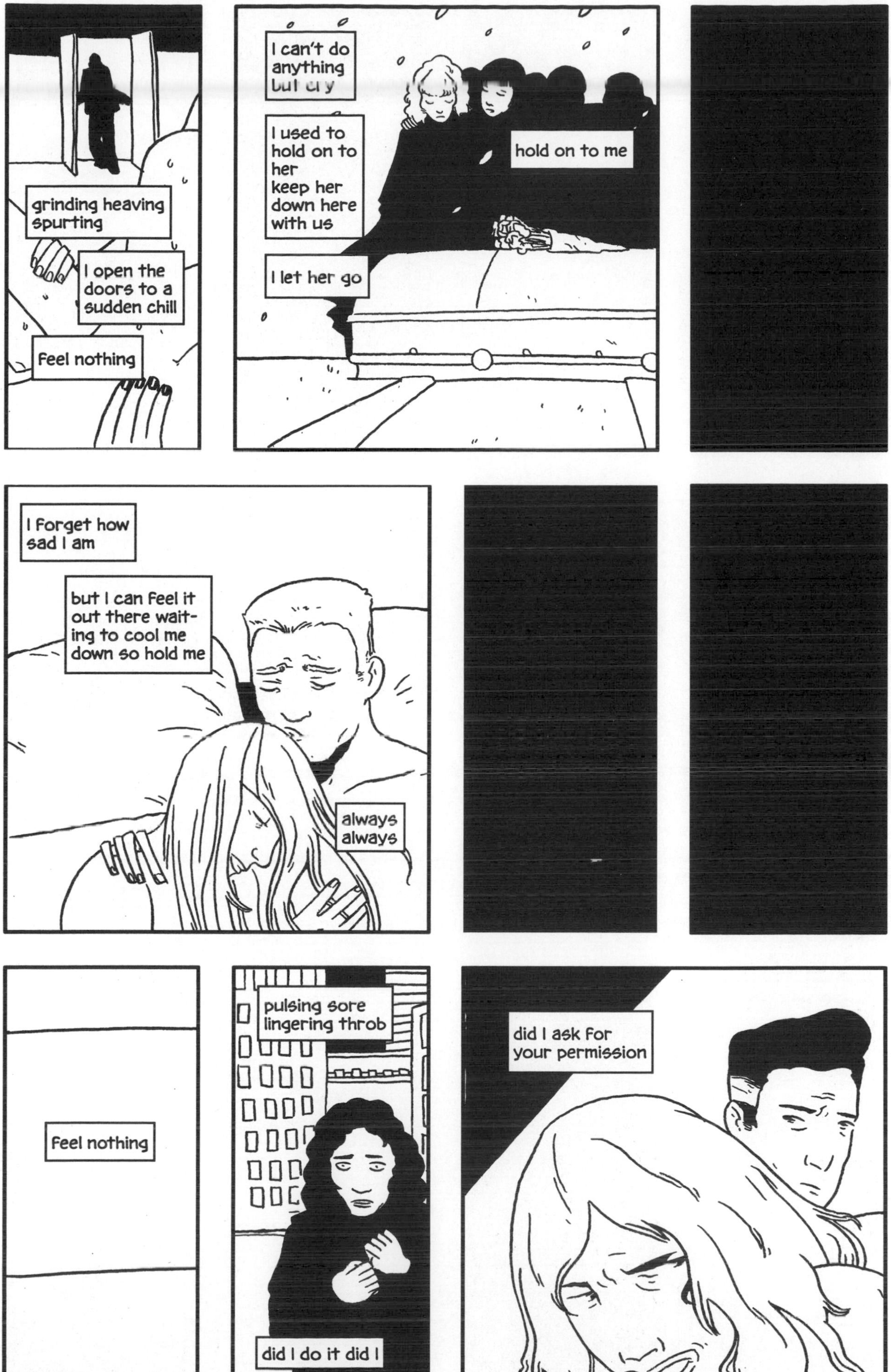
grinding heaving spurting
I open the doors to a sudden chill
feel nothing
I can't do anything but cry
I used to hold on to her keep her down here with us
I let her go
hold on to me
I forget how sad I am
but I can feel it out there wait-ing to cool me down so hold me
always always
feel nothing
pulsing sore lingering throb
did I do it did I
did I ask for your permission

I let it out

pain fear rage desire

pale golden light

subtle shift

to ruby to violet

I Follow you into your kitchen

when you are angry I cook

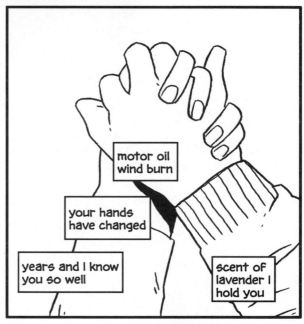
motor oil wind burn

your hands have changed

years and I know you so well

scent of lavender I hold you

you sons of bitches

you dirty shits

rage pain fear

you're going to love what comes next

step out into the still night

no sound but the wind

you can hold on to me

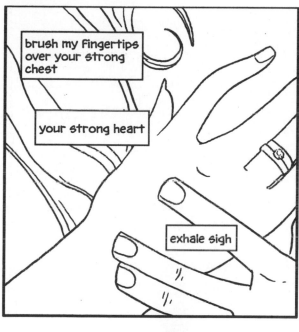

brush my fingertips over your strong chest

your strong heart

exhale sigh

let go

I did

and I loved it

inhale hiss

you signed up for this

you get me at night you get me in the morning too

sigh

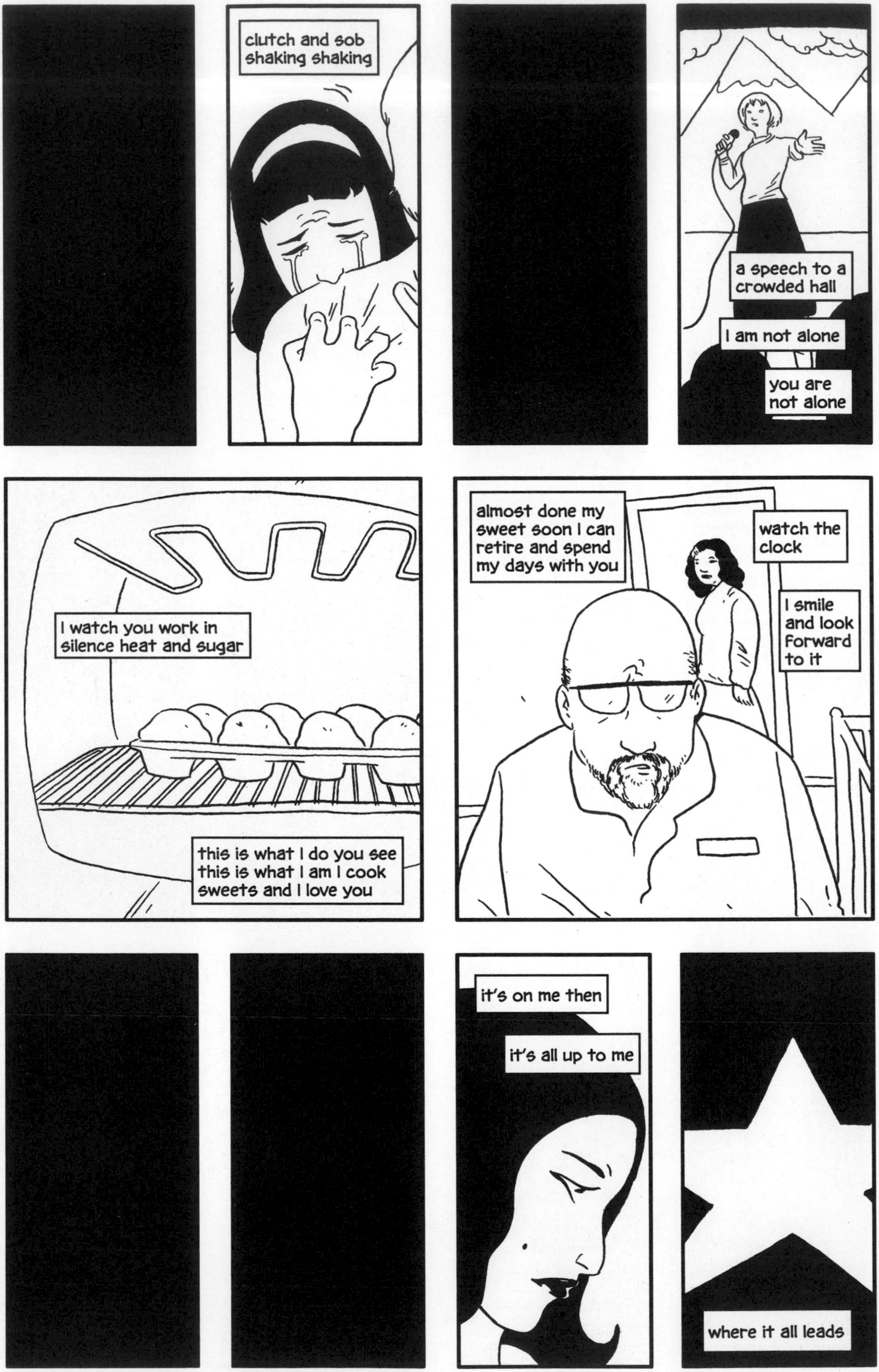
clutch and sob shaking shaking
a speech to a crowded hall
I am not alone
you are not alone
I watch you work in silence heat and sugar
this is what I do you see this is what I am I cook sweets and I love you
almost done my sweet soon I can retire and spend my days with you
watch the clock
I smile and look forward to it
it's on me then
it's all up to me
where it all leads

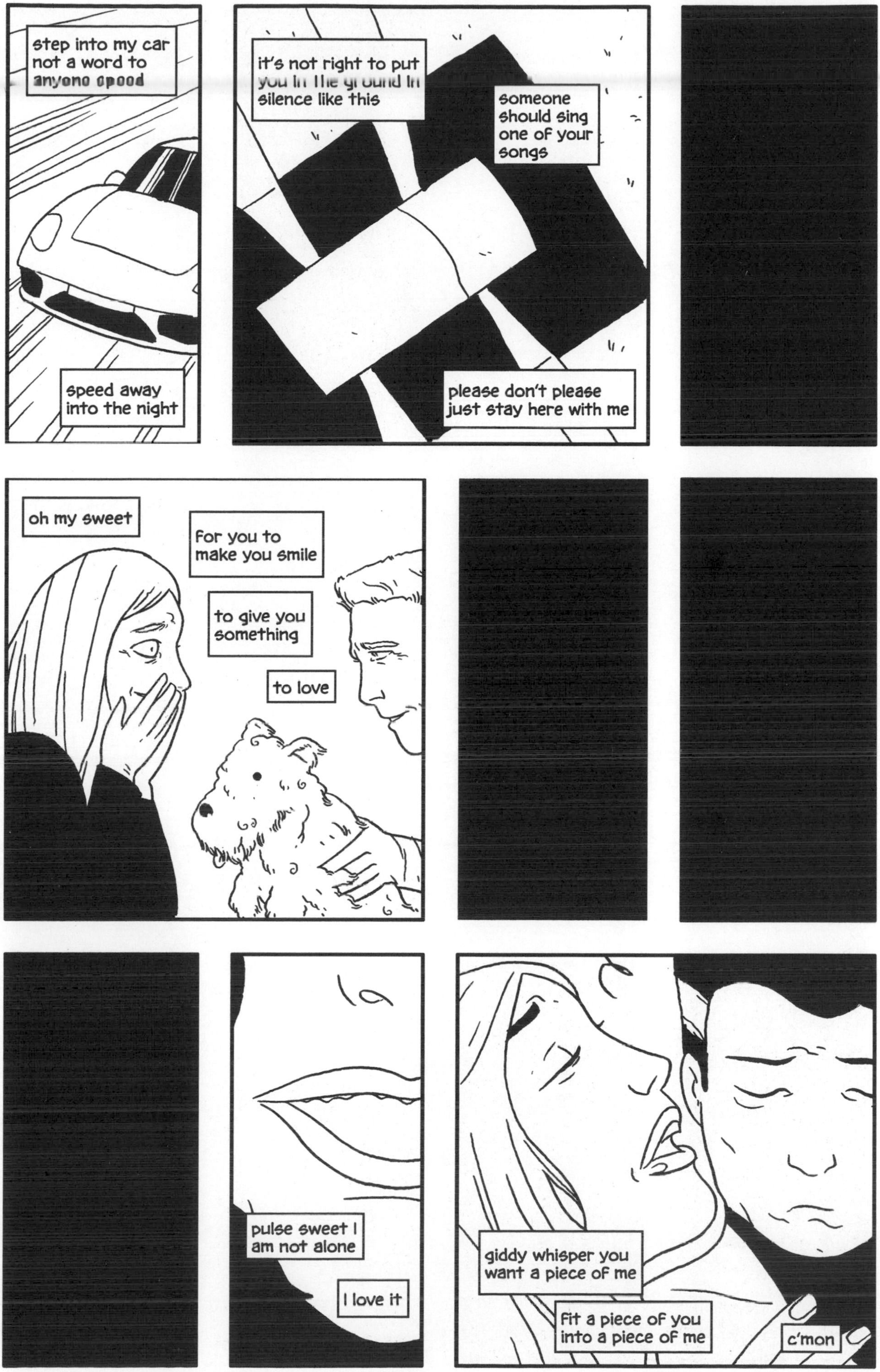
step into my car
not a word to
anyone speed
speed away
into the night
it's not right to put
you in the ground in
silence like this
someone
should sing
one of your
songs
please don't please
just stay here with me
oh my sweet
for you to
make you smile
to give you
something
to love
pulse sweet I
am not alone
I love it
giddy whisper you
want a piece of me
fit a piece of you
into a piece of me
c'mon

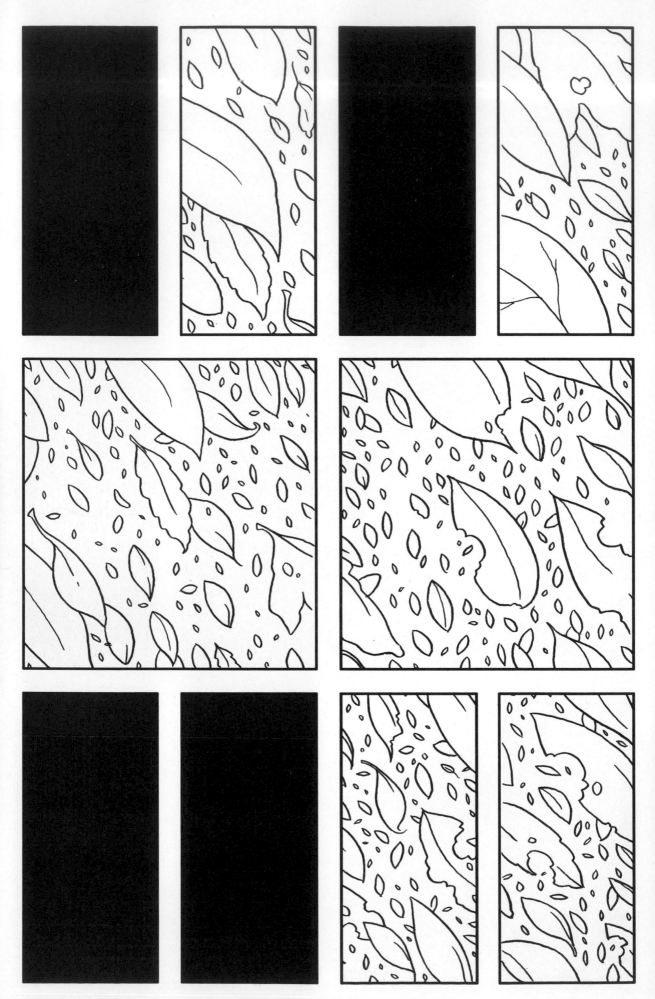

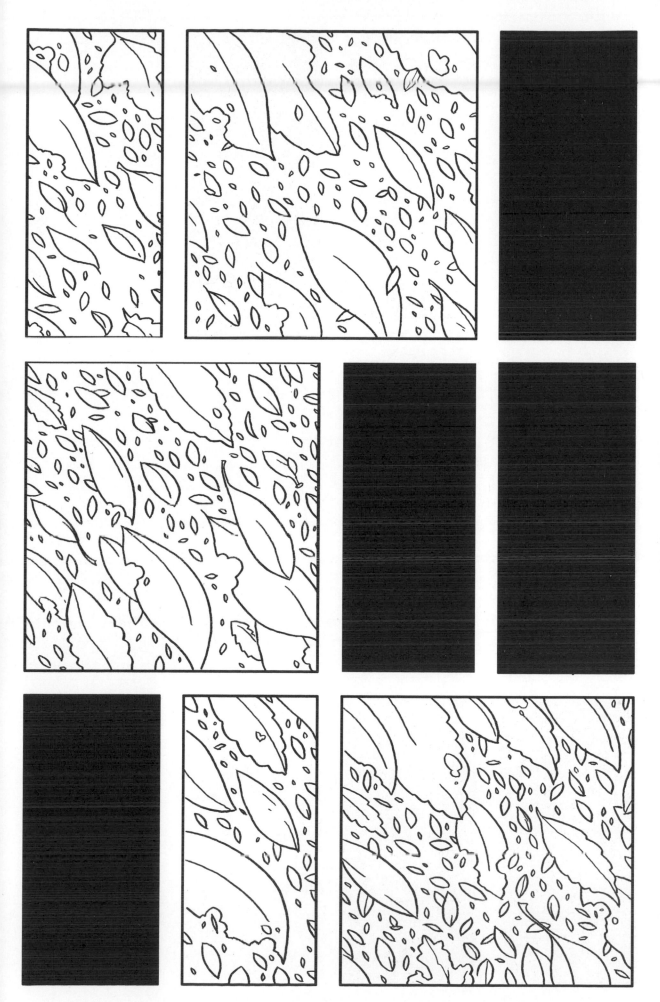

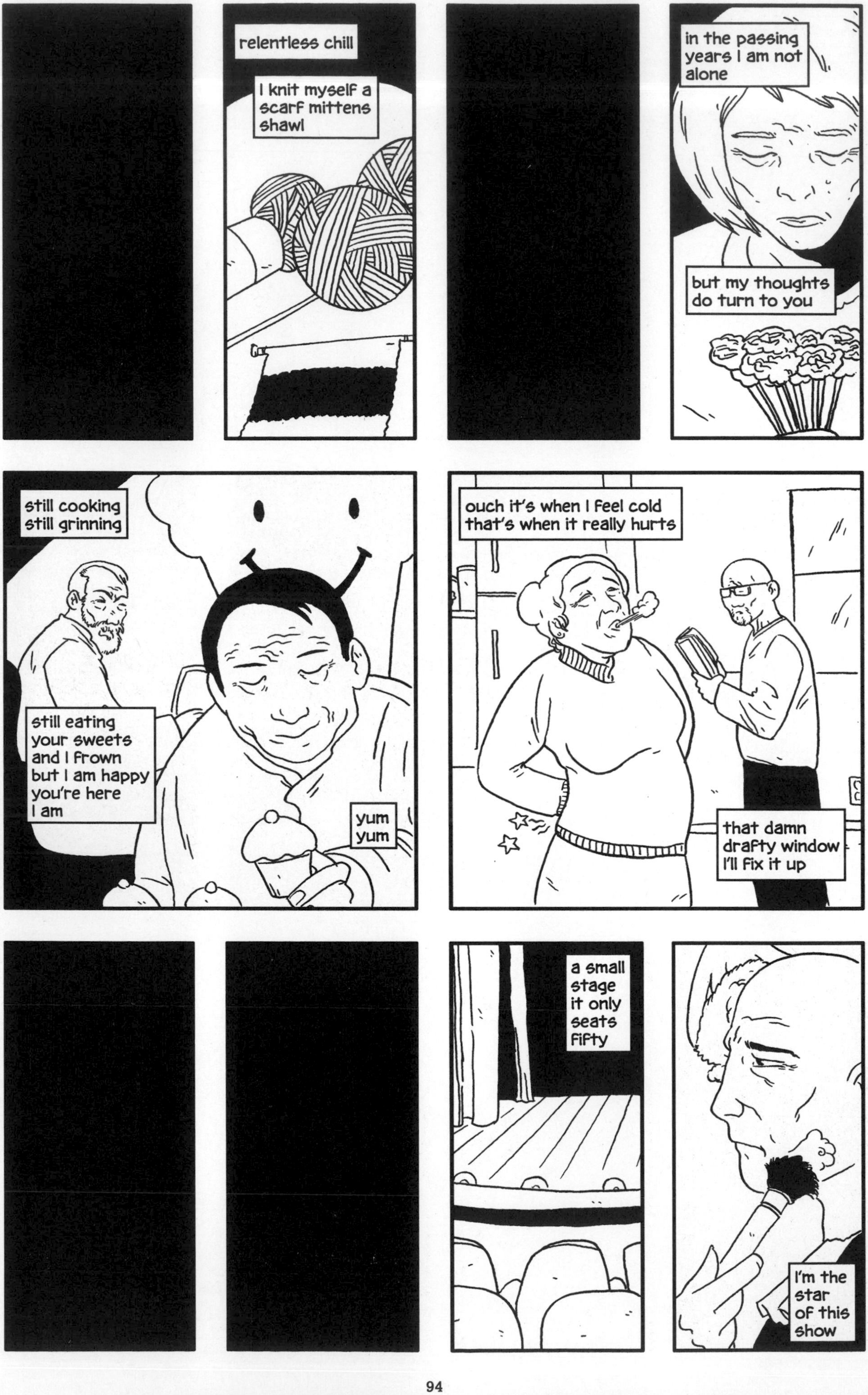
relentless chill
I knit myself a scarf mittens shawl
in the passing years I am not alone
but my thoughts do turn to you
still cooking still grinning
still eating your sweets and I frown but I am happy you're here I am
yum yum
ouch it's when I feel cold that's when it really hurts
that damn drafty window I'll fix it up
a small stage it only seats fifty
I'm the star of this show

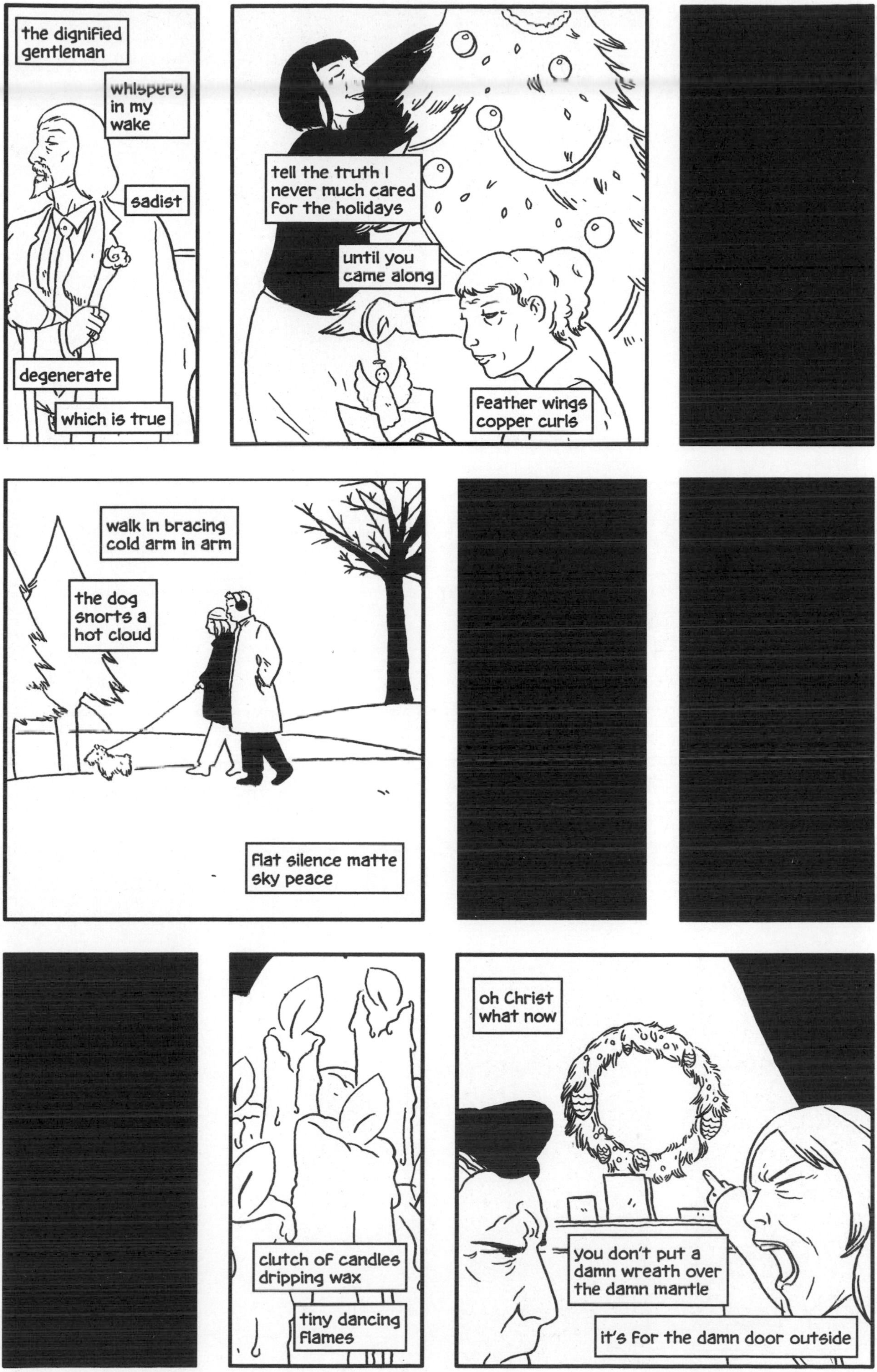
the dignified gentleman
whispers in my wake
sadist
degenerate
which is true
tell the truth I never much cared for the holidays
until you came along
feather wings copper curls
walk in bracing cold arm in arm
the dog snorts a hot cloud
flat silence matte sky peace
clutch of candles dripping wax
tiny dancing flames
oh Christ what now
you don't put a damn wreath over the damn mantle
it's for the damn door outside

For outside

violet blooms in hand

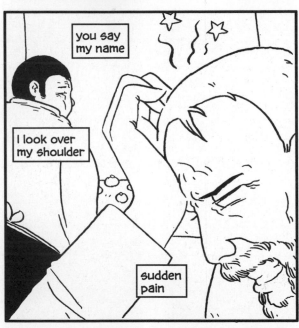
you say my name

I look over my shoulder

sudden pain

I'm starting to fall apart is all

I'll rub it for you I'll heat you up

and I show them

they are not alone I am not alone

diamond star

atop a trimmed tree

96

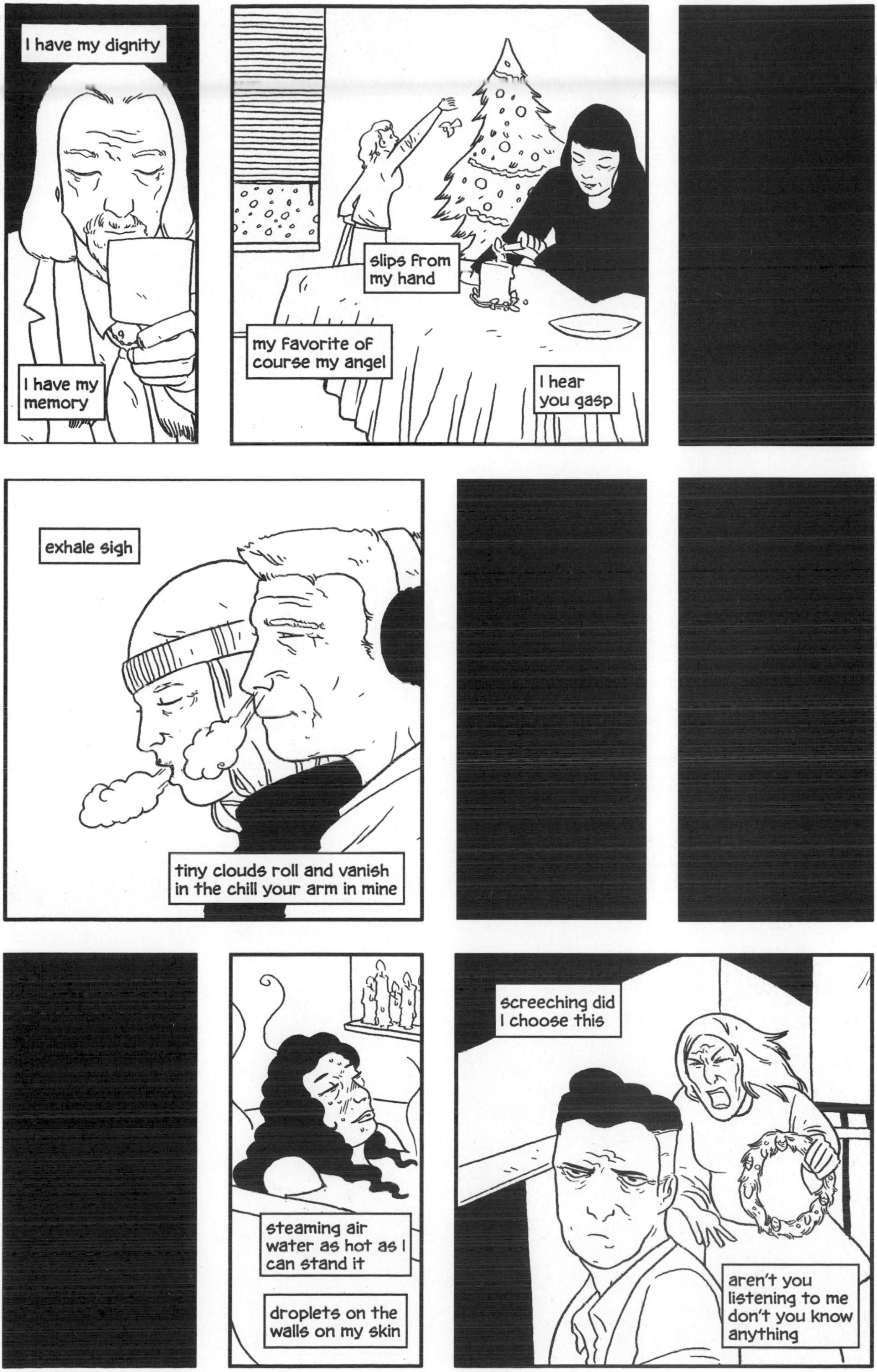
I have my dignity
I have my memory
my favorite of course my angel
slips from my hand
I hear you gasp
exhale sigh
tiny clouds roll and vanish in the chill your arm in mine
steaming air water as hot as I can stand it
droplets on the walls on my skin
screeching did I choose this
aren't you listening to me don't you know anything

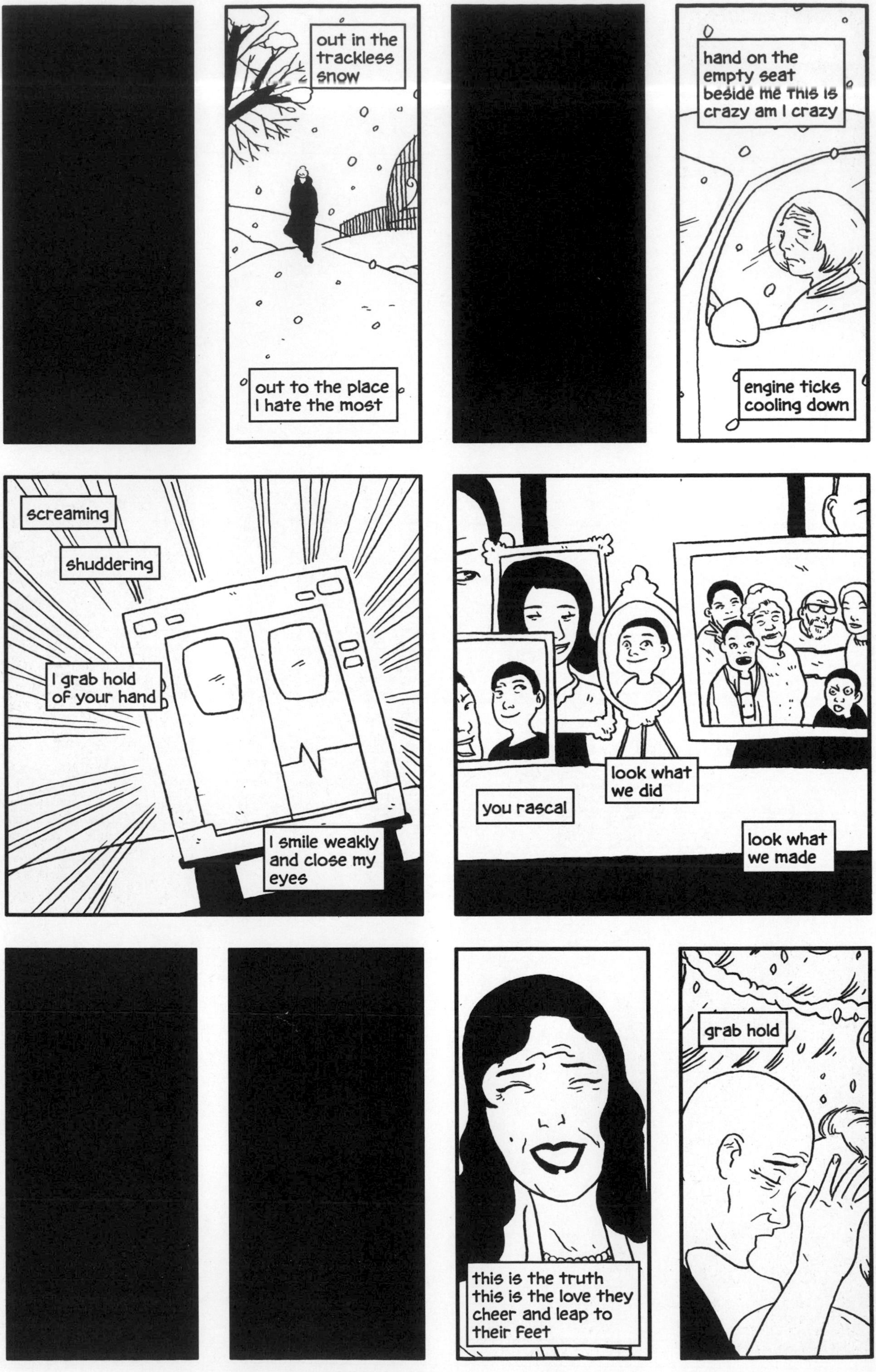
out in the trackless snow
out to the place I hate the most
hand on the empty seat beside me this is crazy am I crazy
engine ticks cooling down
screaming
shuddering
I grab hold of your hand
I smile weakly and close my eyes
you rascal
look what we did
look what we made
this is the truth this is the love they cheer and leap to their feet
grab hold

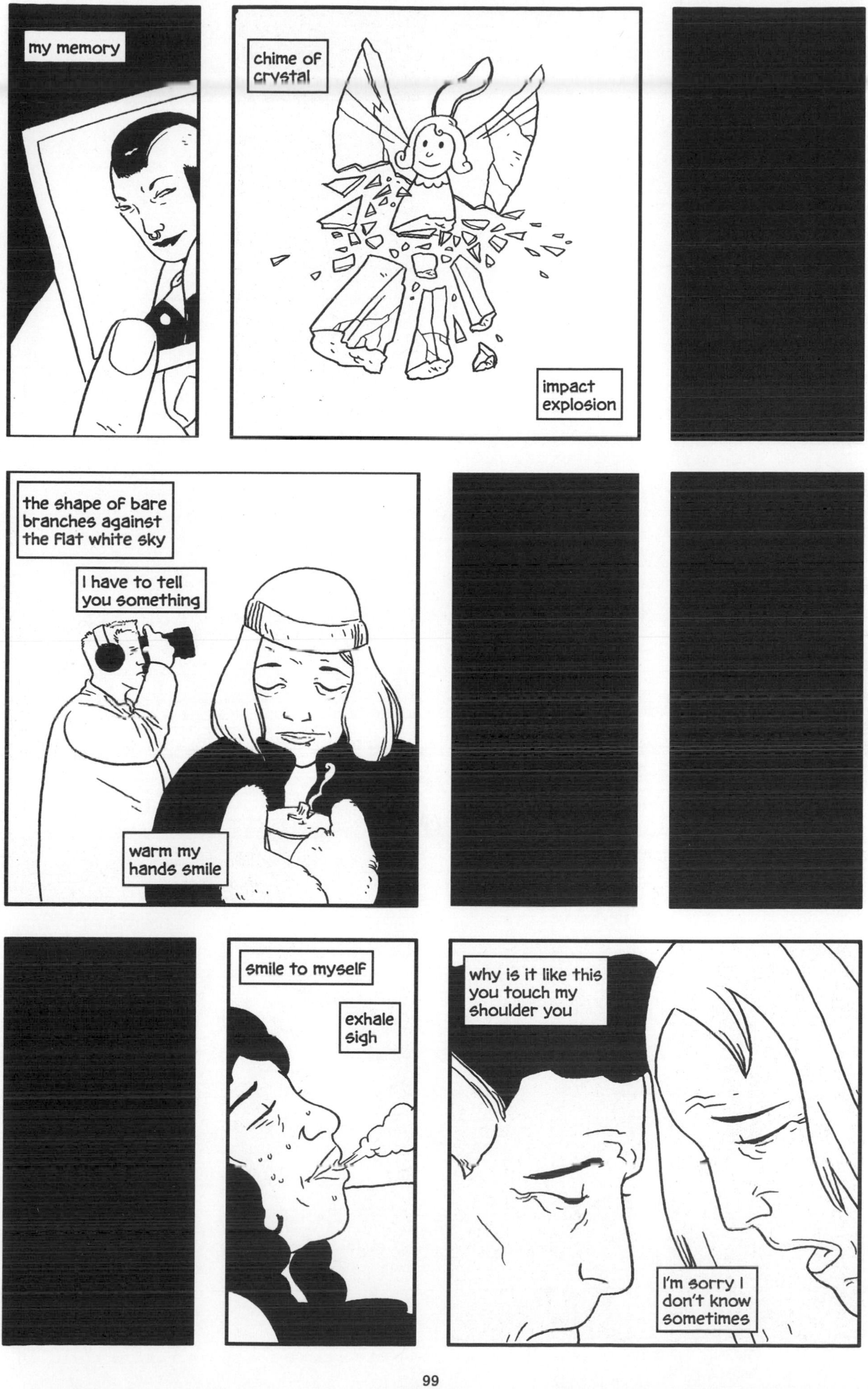

my memory

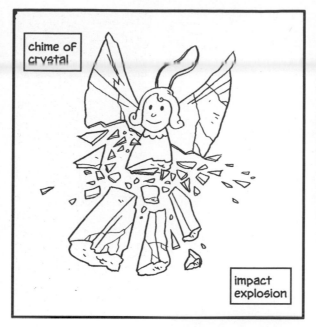

chime of crystal

impact explosion

the shape of bare branches against the flat white sky

I have to tell you something

warm my hands smile

smile to myself

exhale sigh

why is it like this you touch my shoulder you

I'm sorry I don't know sometimes

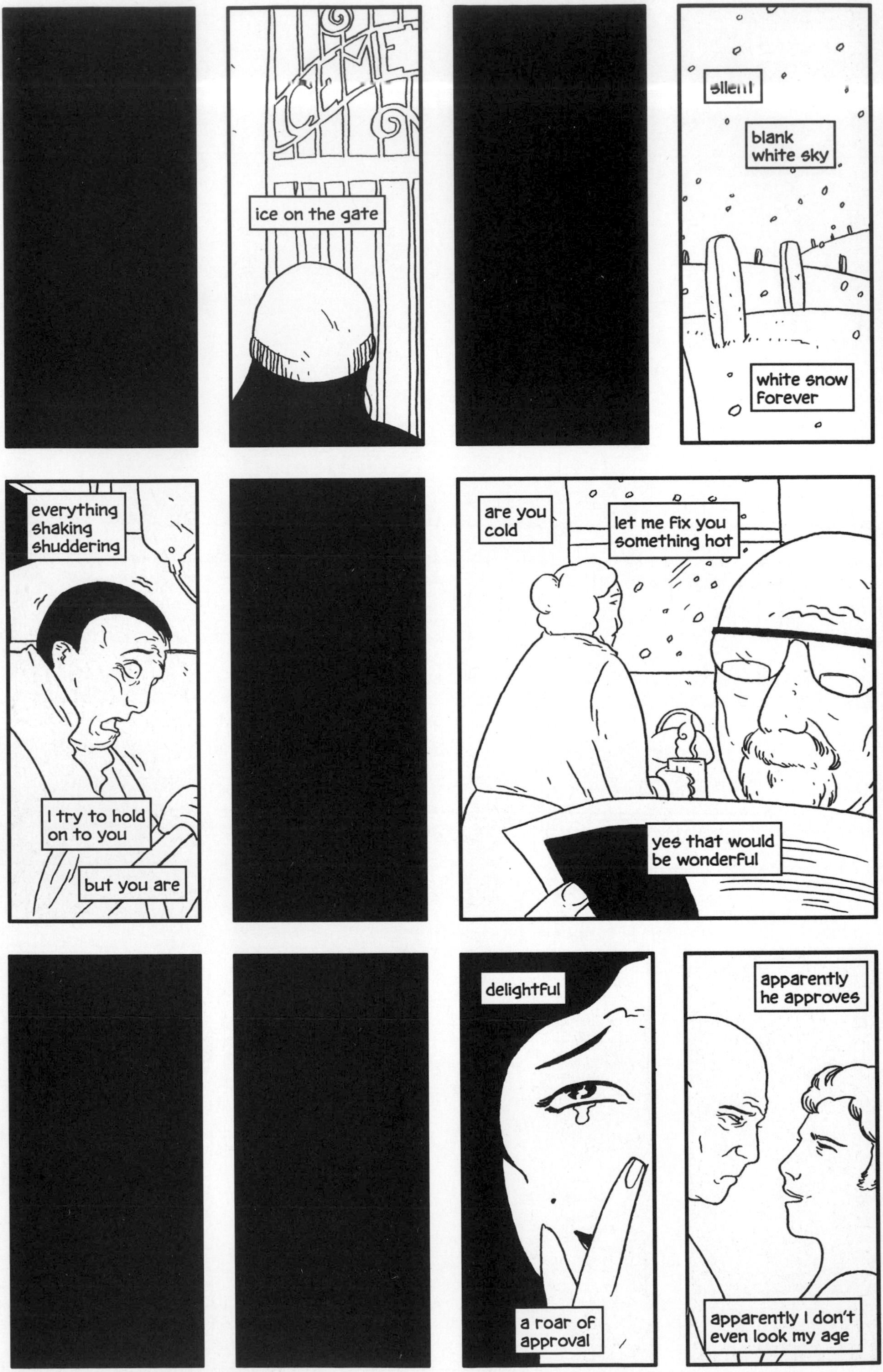

ice on the gate
silent
blank white sky
white snow forever
everything shaking shuddering
I try to hold on to you
but you are
are you cold
let me fix you something hot
yes that would be wonderful
delightful
a roar of approval
apparently he approves
apparently I don't even look my age

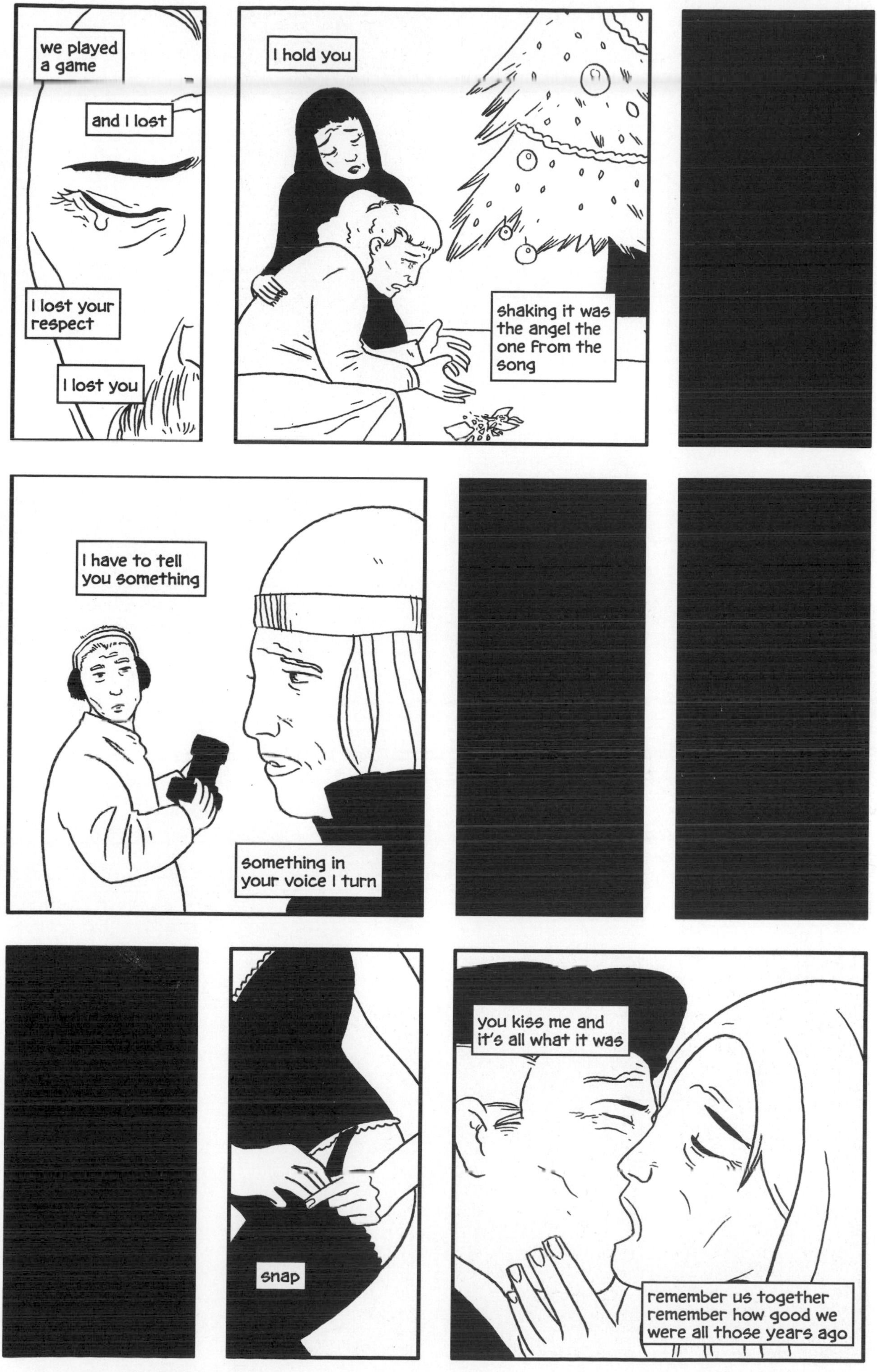
we played a game
and I lost
I lost your respect
I lost you
I hold you
shaking it was the angel the one from the song
I have to tell you something
something in your voice I turn
snap
you kiss me and it's all what it was
remember us together remember how good we were all those years ago

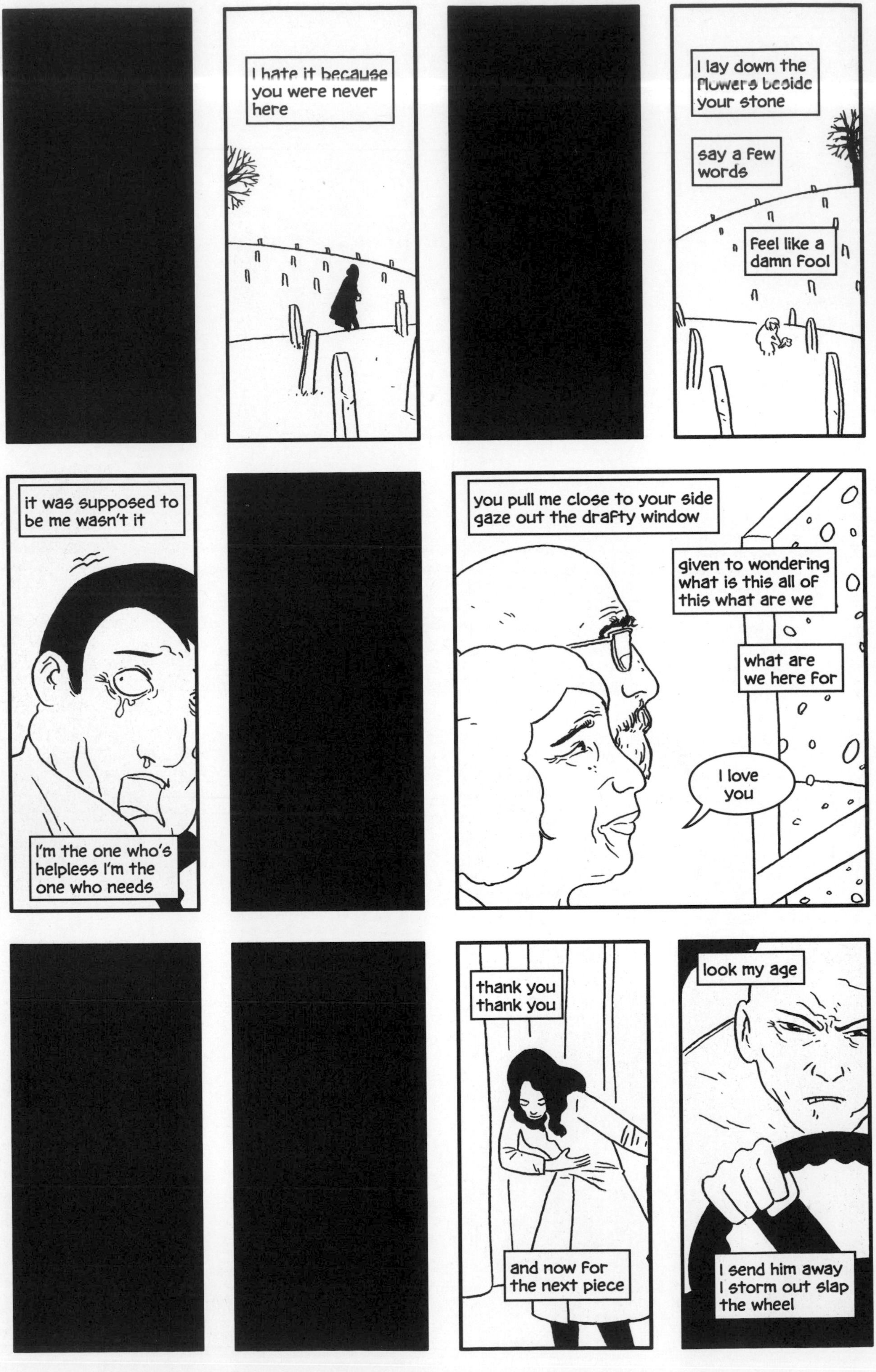
I hate it because you were never here
I lay down the flowers beside your stone
say a few words
feel like a damn fool
it was supposed to be me wasn't it
I'm the one who's helpless I'm the one who needs
you pull me close to your side gaze out the drafty window
given to wondering what is this all of this what are we
what are we here for
I love you
thank you thank you
and now for the next piece
look my age
I send him away I storm out slap the wheel

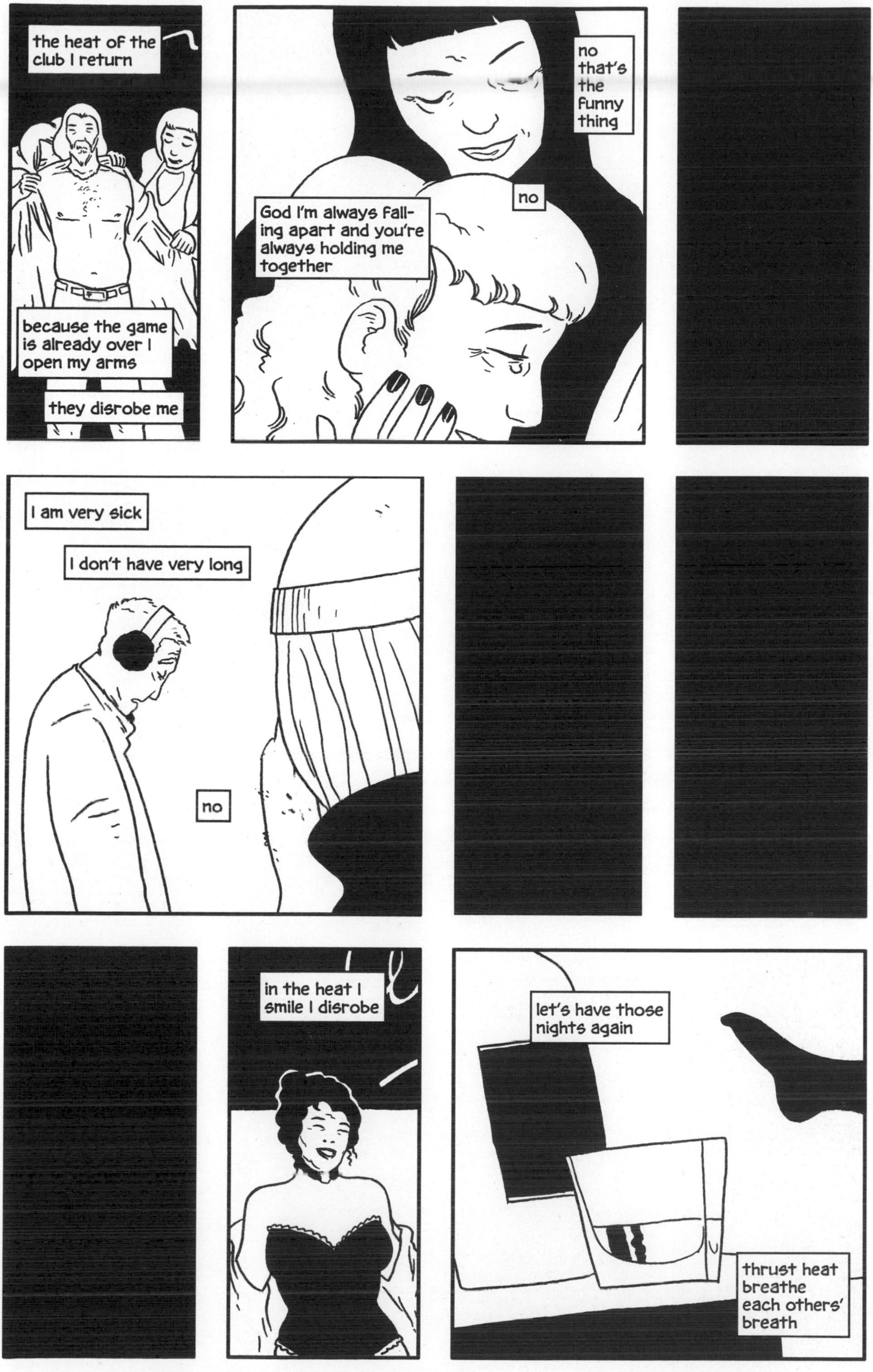
the heat of the club I return
because the game is already over I open my arms
they disrobe me
no that's the funny thing
no
God I'm always fall-ing apart and you're always holding me together
I am very sick
I don't have very long
no
in the heat I smile I disrobe
let's have those nights again
thrust heat breathe each others' breath

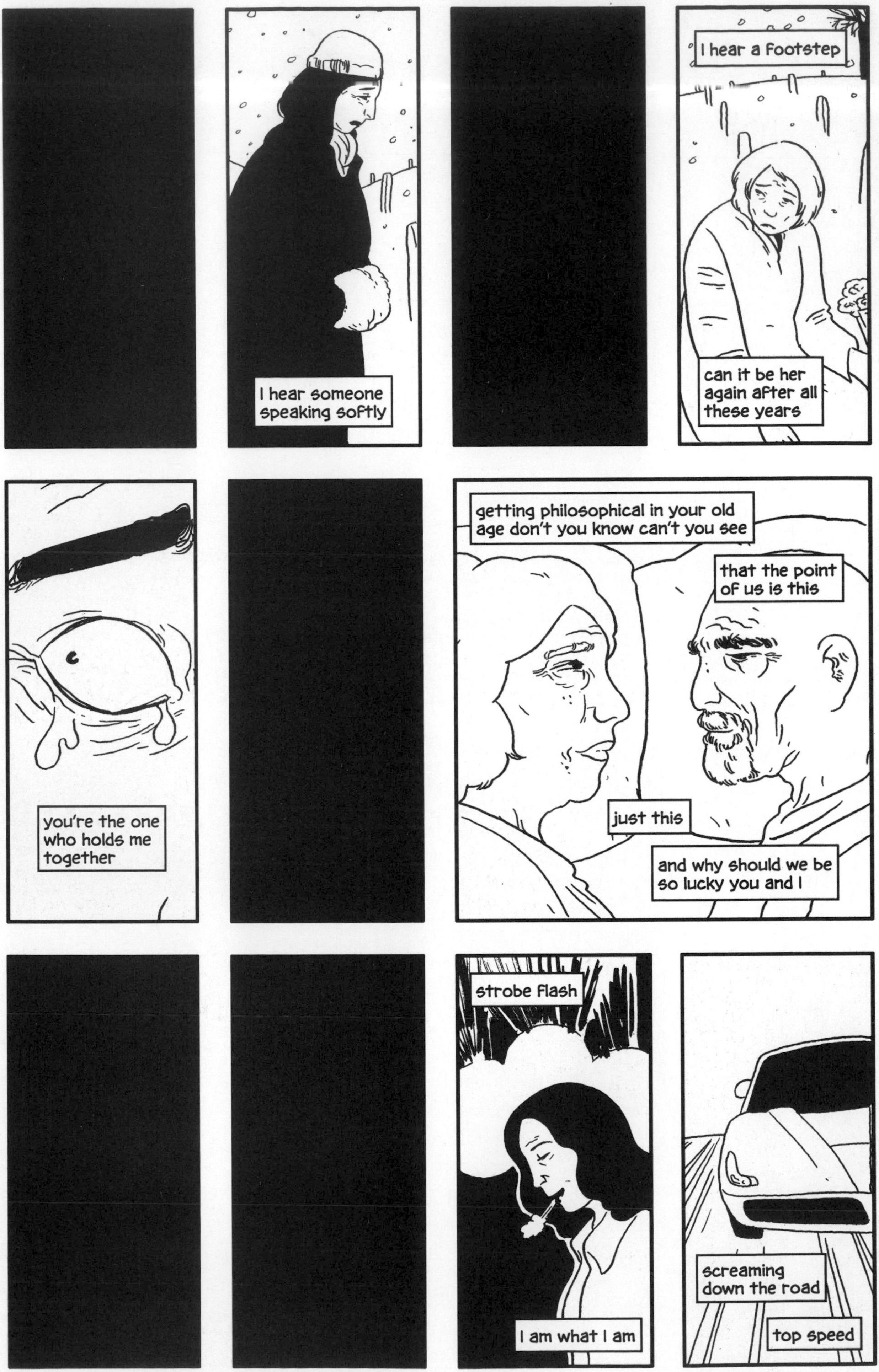
I hear someone
speaking softly
I hear a footstep
can it be her
again after all
these years
you're the one
who holds me
together
getting philosophical in your old
age don't you know can't you see
that the point
of us is this
just this
and why should we be
so lucky you and I
strobe flash
I am what I am
screaming
down the road
top speed

take me away

turn to kiss you scent of pine and cinnamon your ink black hair

taste of vanilla and my heart can still skip still flutter

you ask no questions you take my hand

the dog whines

we walk in the hissing snowfall

heat me kiss me

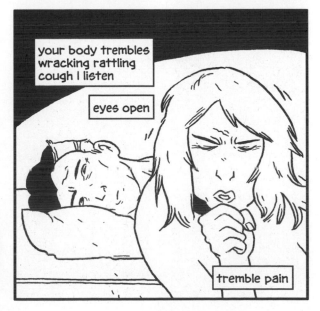

your body trembles wracking rattling cough I listen

eyes open

tremble pain

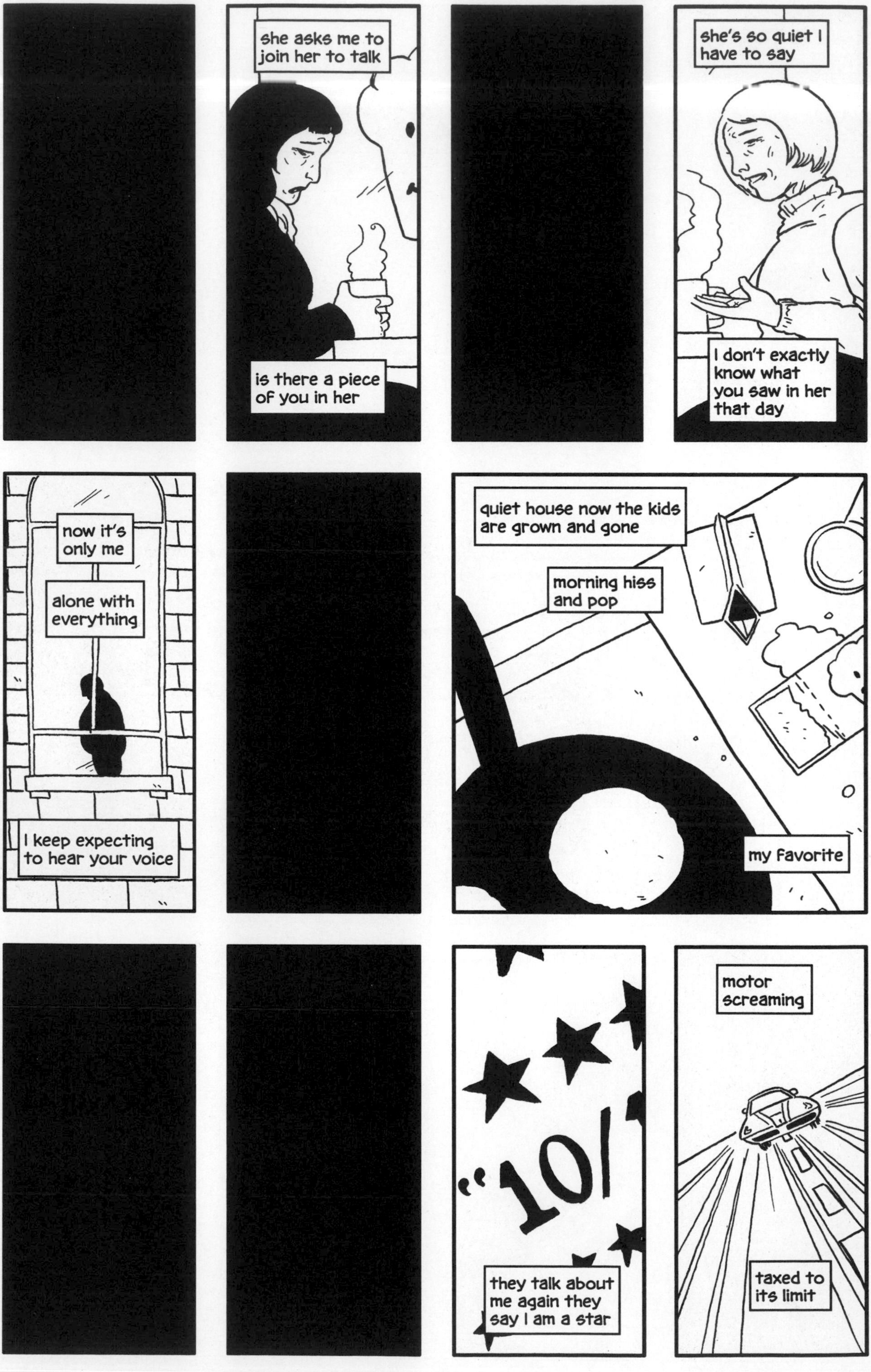
she asks me to join her to talk
is there a piece of you in her
she's so quiet I have to say
I don't exactly know what you saw in her that day
now it's only me
alone with everything
I keep expecting to hear your voice
quiet house now the kids are grown and gone
morning hiss and pop
my favorite
"10/
they talk about me again they say I am a star
motor screaming
taxed to its limit

Flesh heat slide slick beaded dew

I tremble

I go blank

steam curling into the air

whistling call shrill in the early light

you take the long shot treatment I beg you to

you hold my hand sit by me for hours

all over me around me inside me heat sigh sweat blush

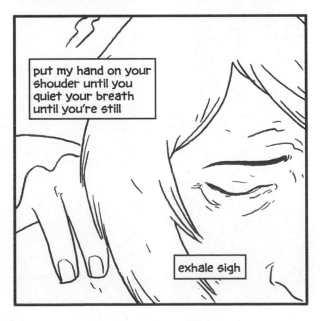

put my hand on your shouder until you quiet your breath until you're still

exhale sigh

it hurts I should just leave

just go

draw on sweet memories of you

I remember some- thing funny

all I have are memories

in this empty house

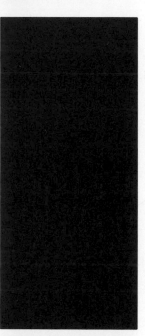

good morning kiss yes it is good

I didn't forget you know

yes are those pancakes

married forty years today my love

now this is an accomplishment

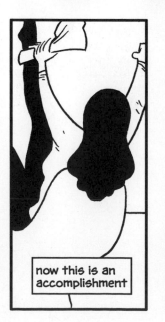

I let go

suddenly

 I wake suddenly in the small hours in the dark

was I dreaming

I press myself closer to you half awake how are you so warm

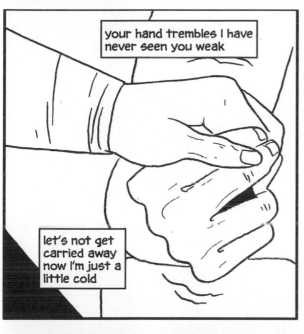 your hand trembles I have never seen you weak

let's not get carried away now I'm just a little cold

 somebody died

his heart right here
 don't worry I'm here

you're all right

shaking

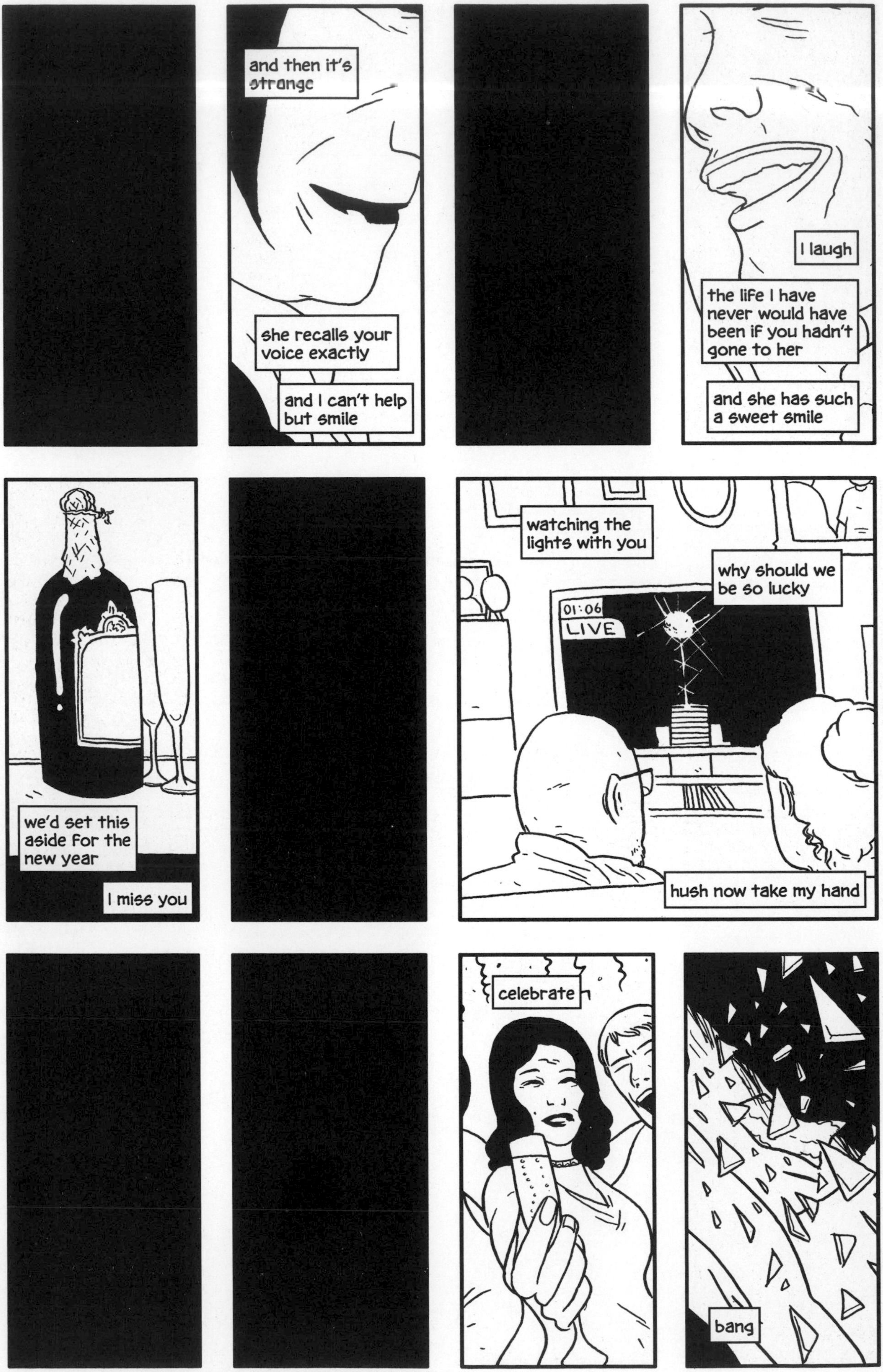
and then it's strange
she recalls your voice exactly
and I can't help but smile
I laugh
the life I have never would have been if you hadn't gone to her
and she has such a sweet smile
we'd set this aside for the new year
I miss you
watching the lights with you
why should we be so lucky
01:06
LIVE
hush now take my hand
celebrate
bang

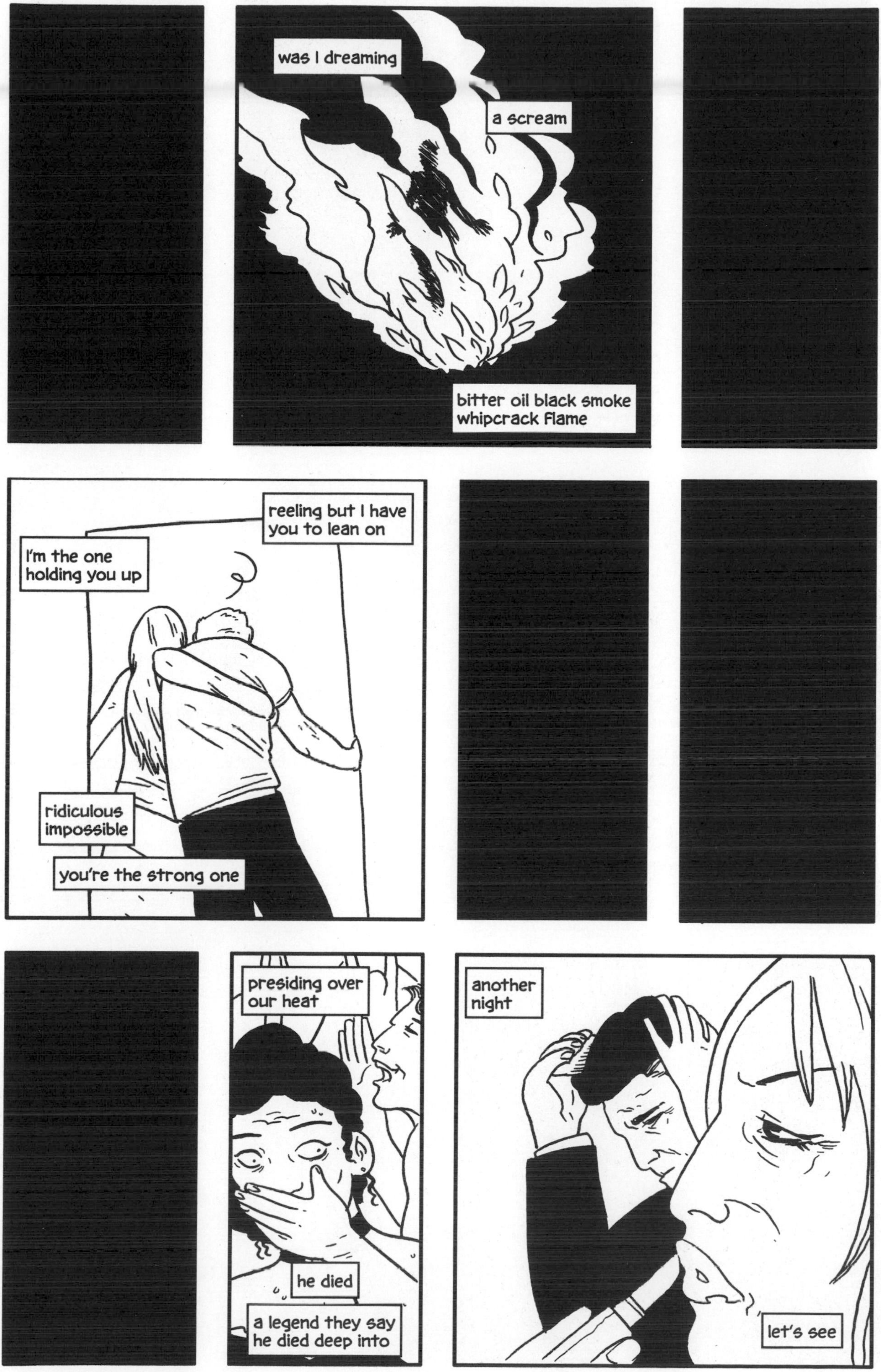
was I dreaming
a scream
bitter oil black smoke whipcrack flame
reeling but I have you to lean on
I'm the one holding you up
ridiculous impossible
you're the strong one
presiding over our heat
he died
a legend they say he died deep into
another night
let's see

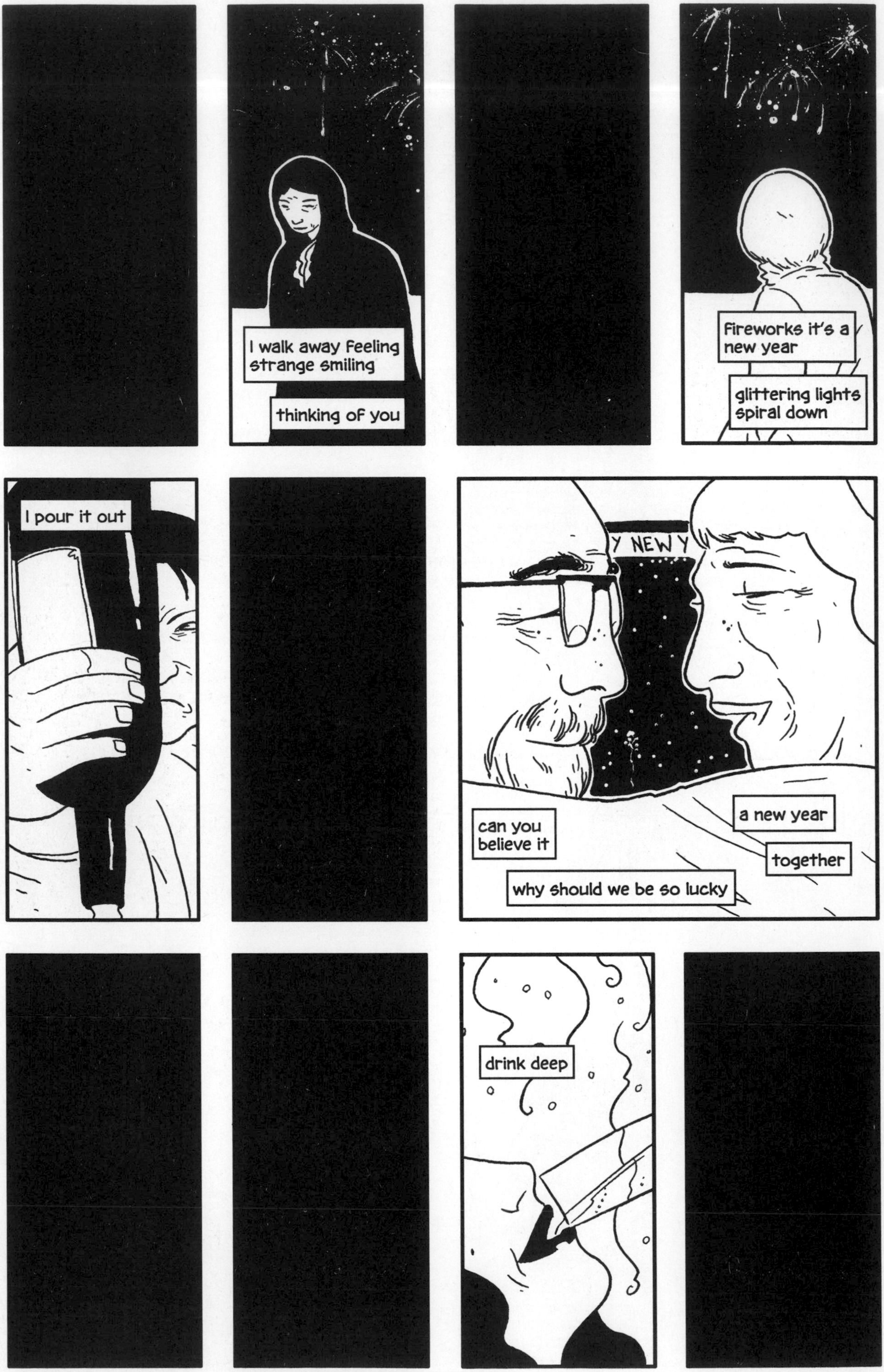
I walk away feeling strange smiling
thinking of you
fireworks it's a new year
glittering lights spiral down
I pour it out
Y NEW Y
can you believe it
a new year
together
why should we be so lucky
drink deep

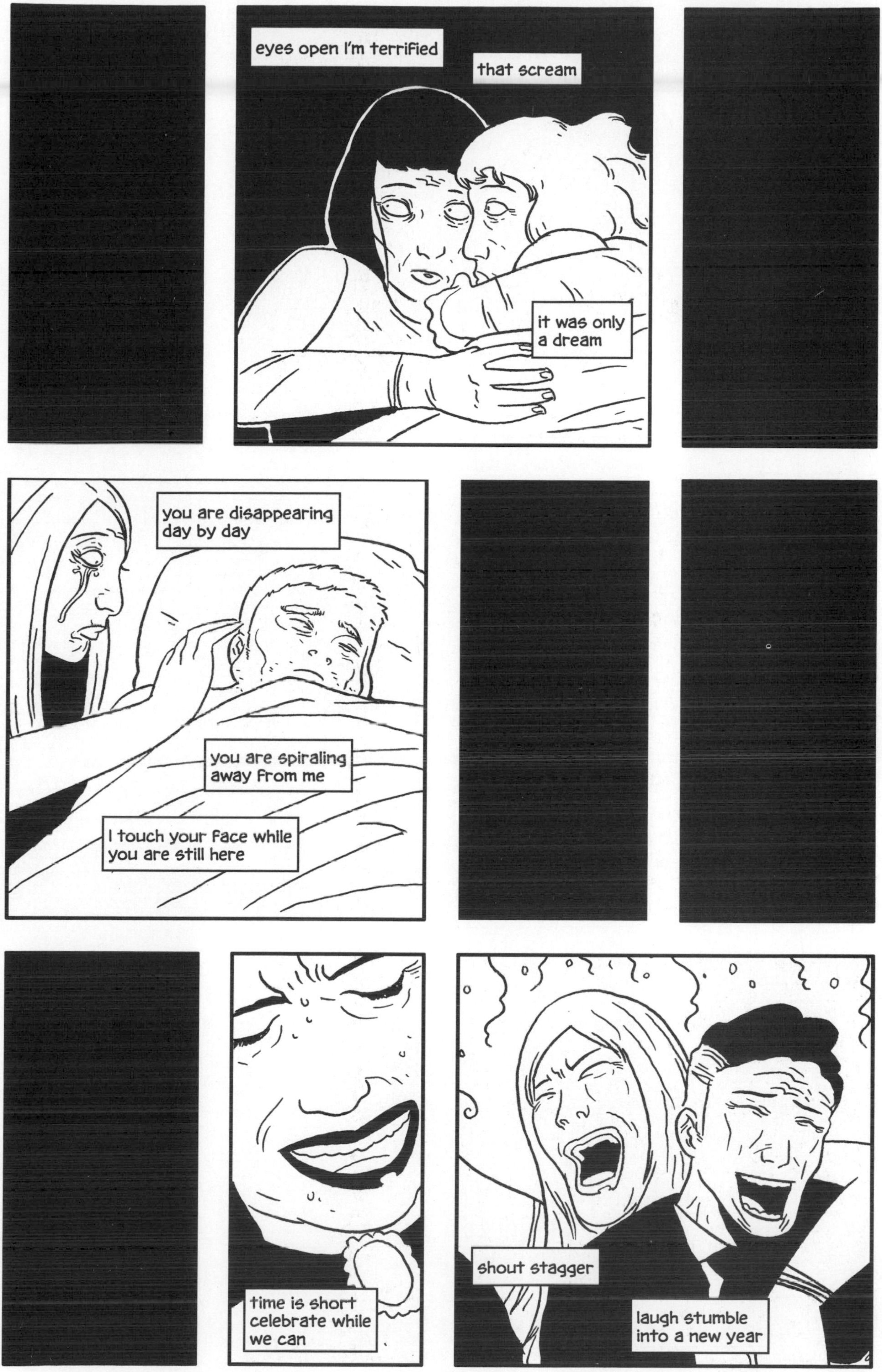
eyes open I'm terrified
that scream
it was only a dream
you are disappearing day by day
you are spiraling away from me
I touch your face while you are still here
time is short celebrate while we can
shout stagger
laugh stumble into a new year

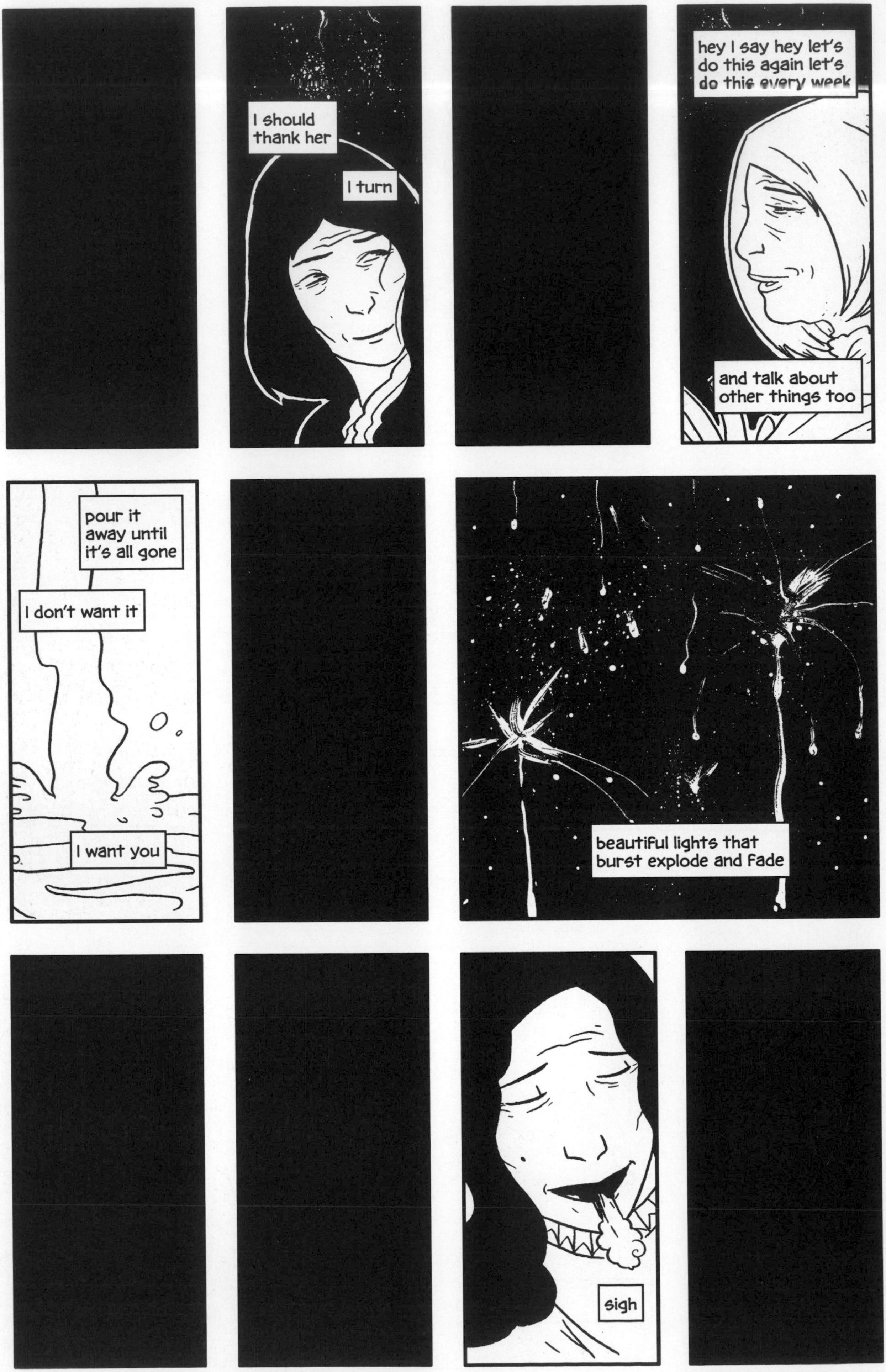
I should thank her
I turn
hey I say hey let's do this again let's do this every week
and talk about other things too
pour it away until it's all gone
I don't want it
I want you
beautiful lights that burst explode and fade
sigh

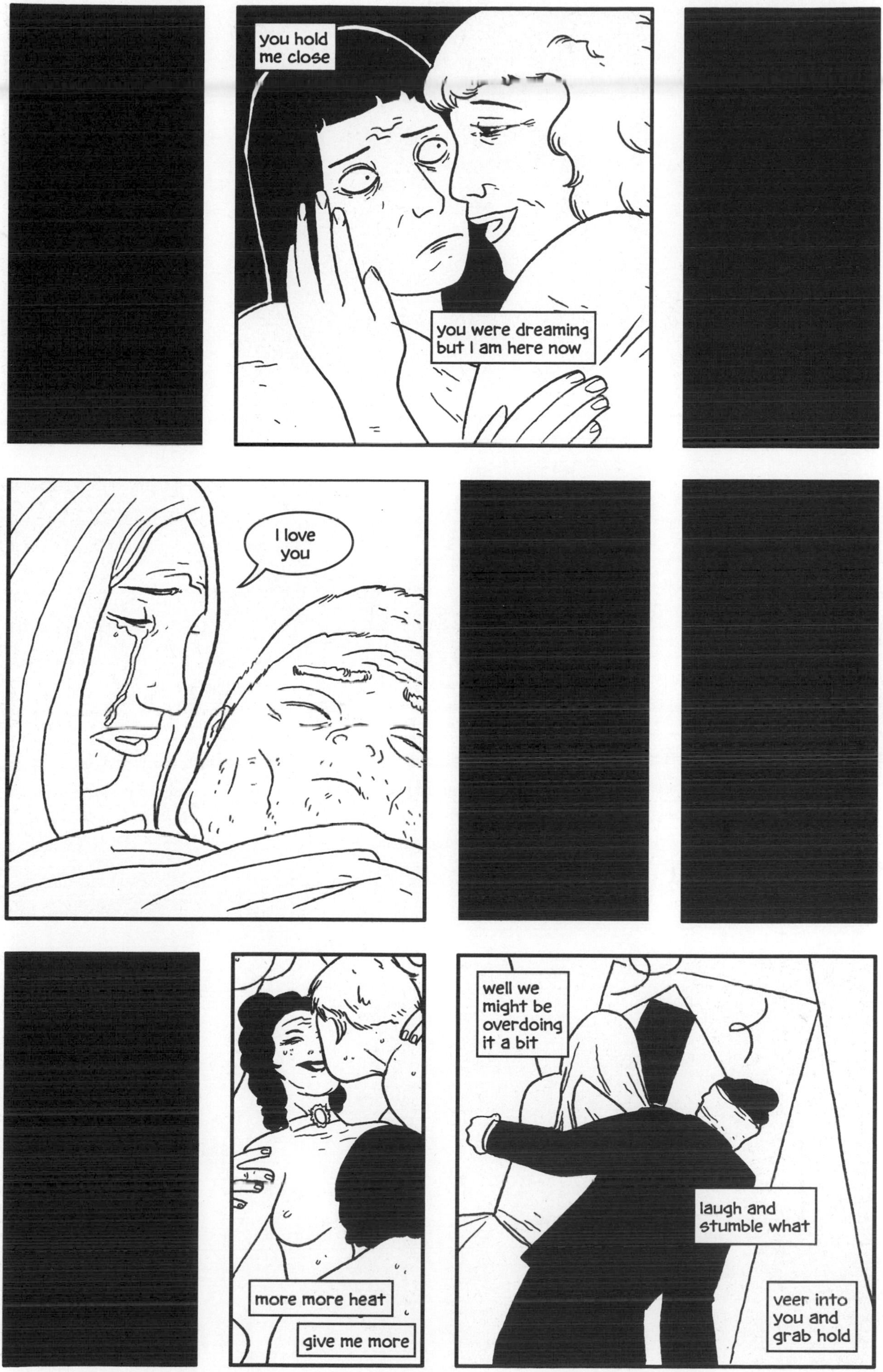
you hold me close
you were dreaming but I am here now
I love you
more more heat
give me more
well we might be overdoing it a bit
laugh and stumble what
veer into you and grab hold

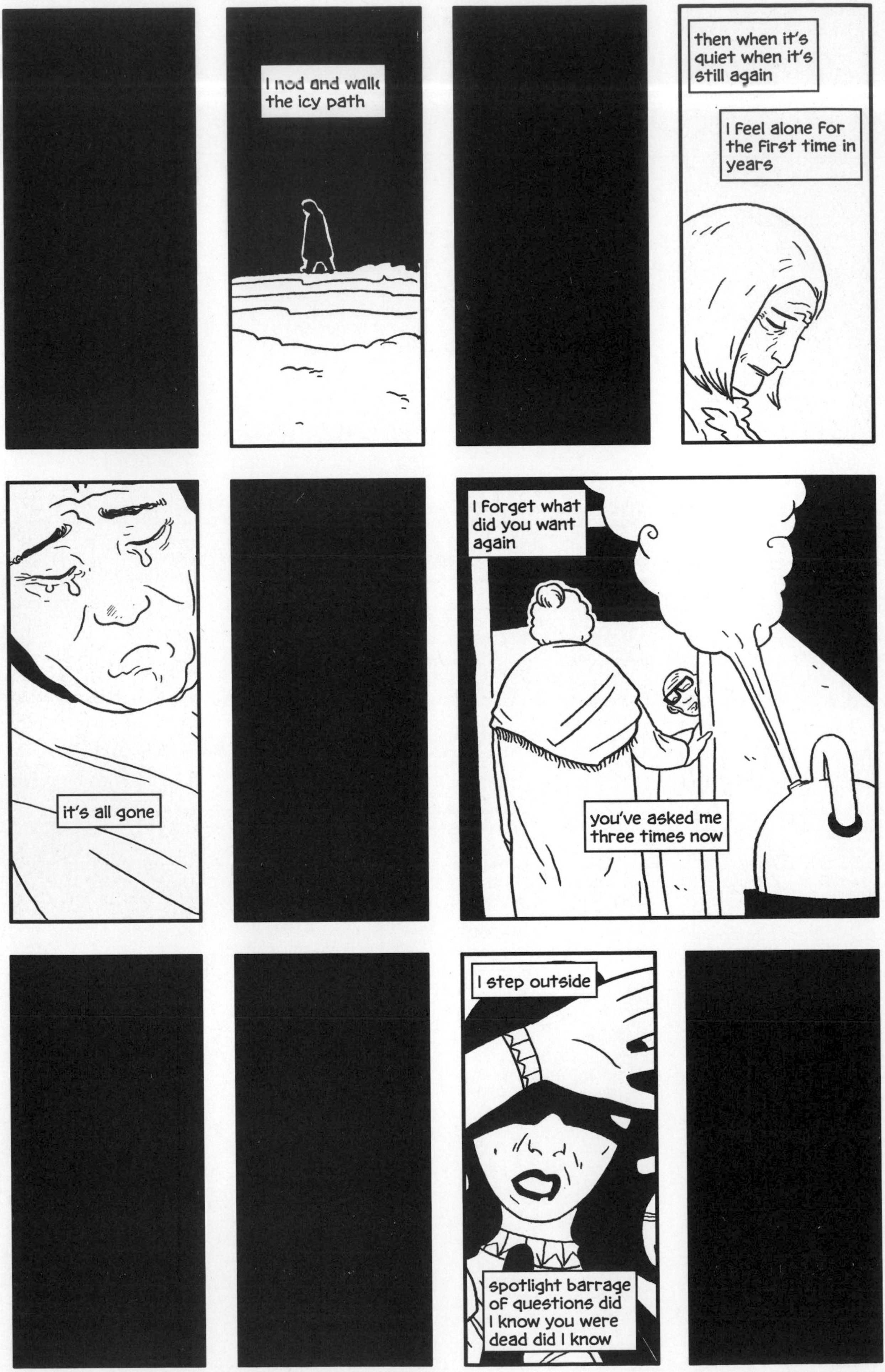
I nod and walk
the icy path
then when it's quiet when it's still again
I feel alone for the first time in years
it's all gone
I forget what did you want again
you've asked me three times now
I step outside
spotlight barrage of questions did I know you were dead did I know

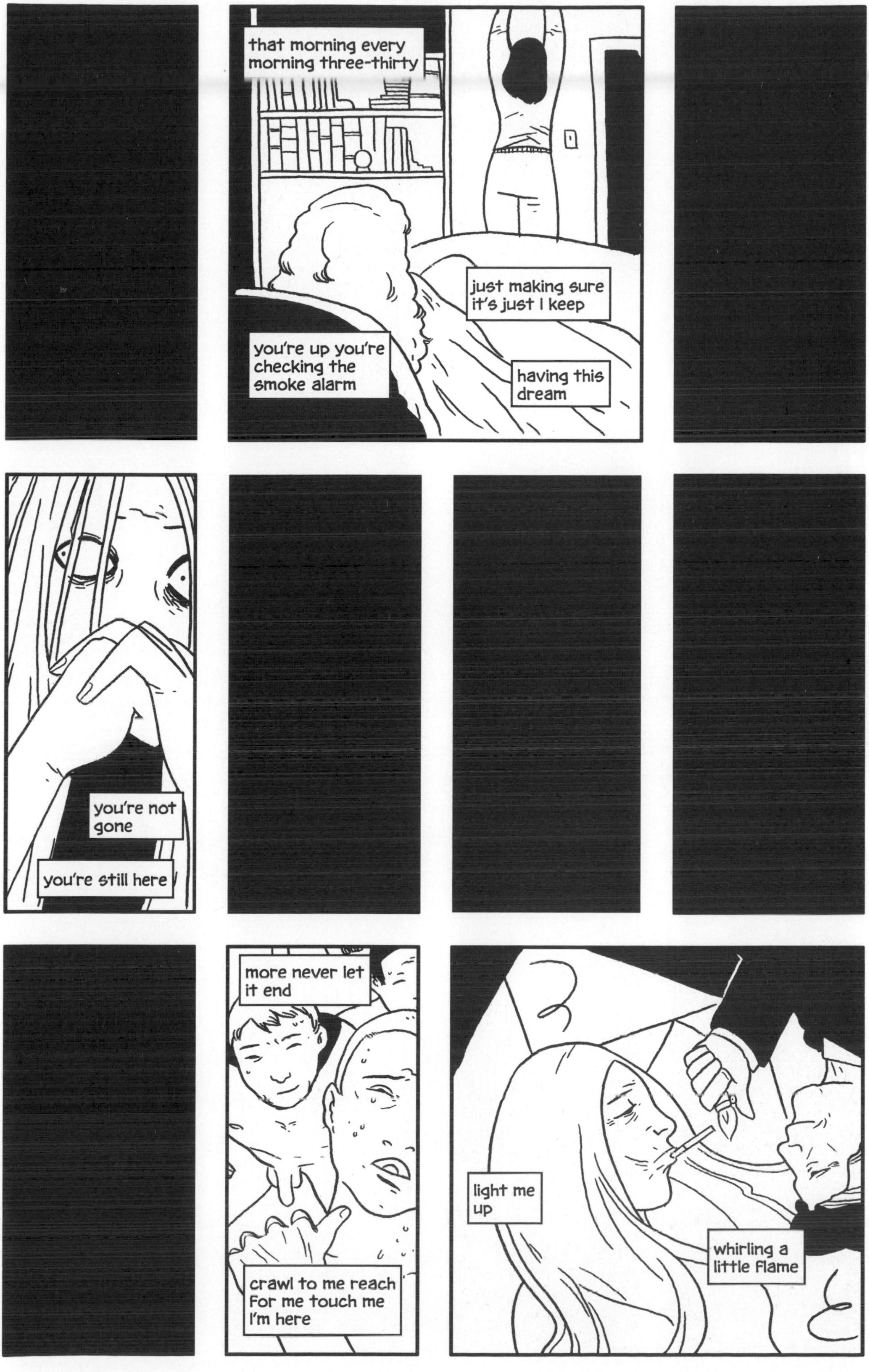
that morning every morning three-thirty
you're up you're checking the smoke alarm
just making sure it's just I keep
having this dream
you're not gone
you're still here
more never let it end
crawl to me reach for me touch me I'm here
light me up
whirling a little flame

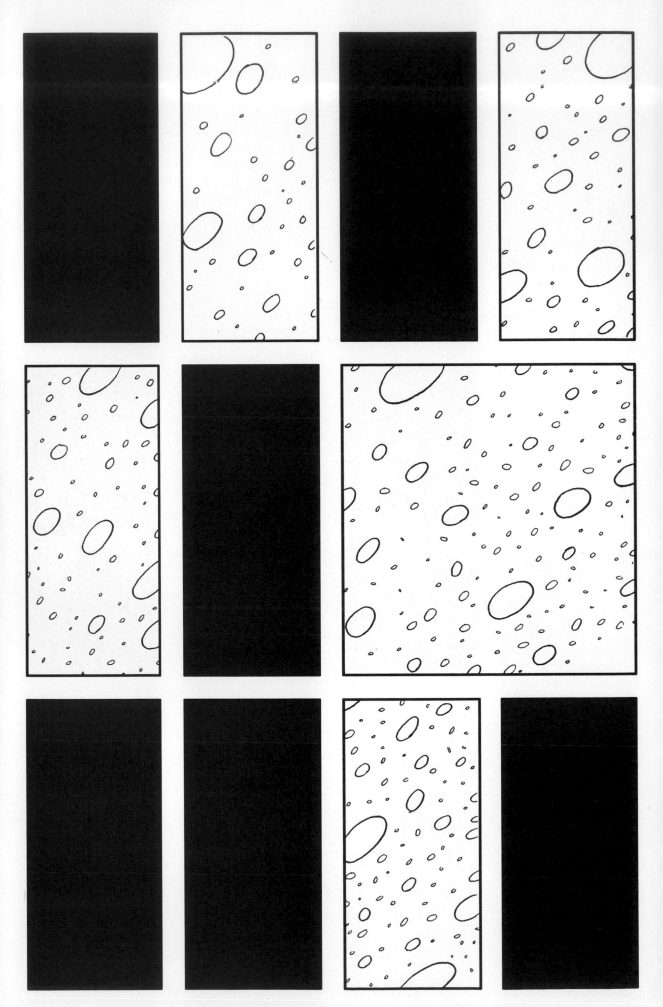

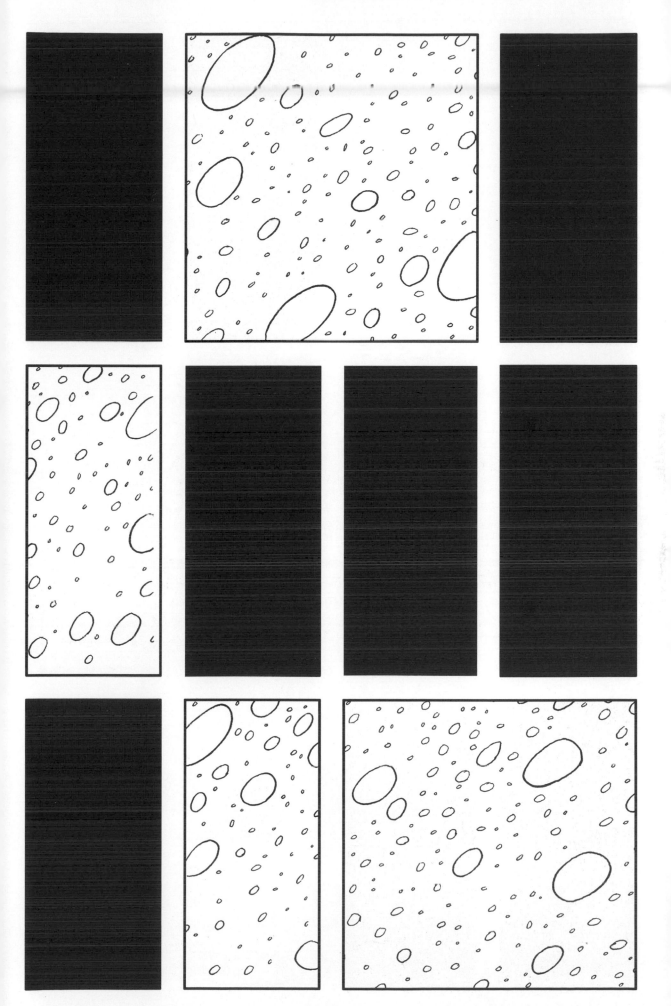

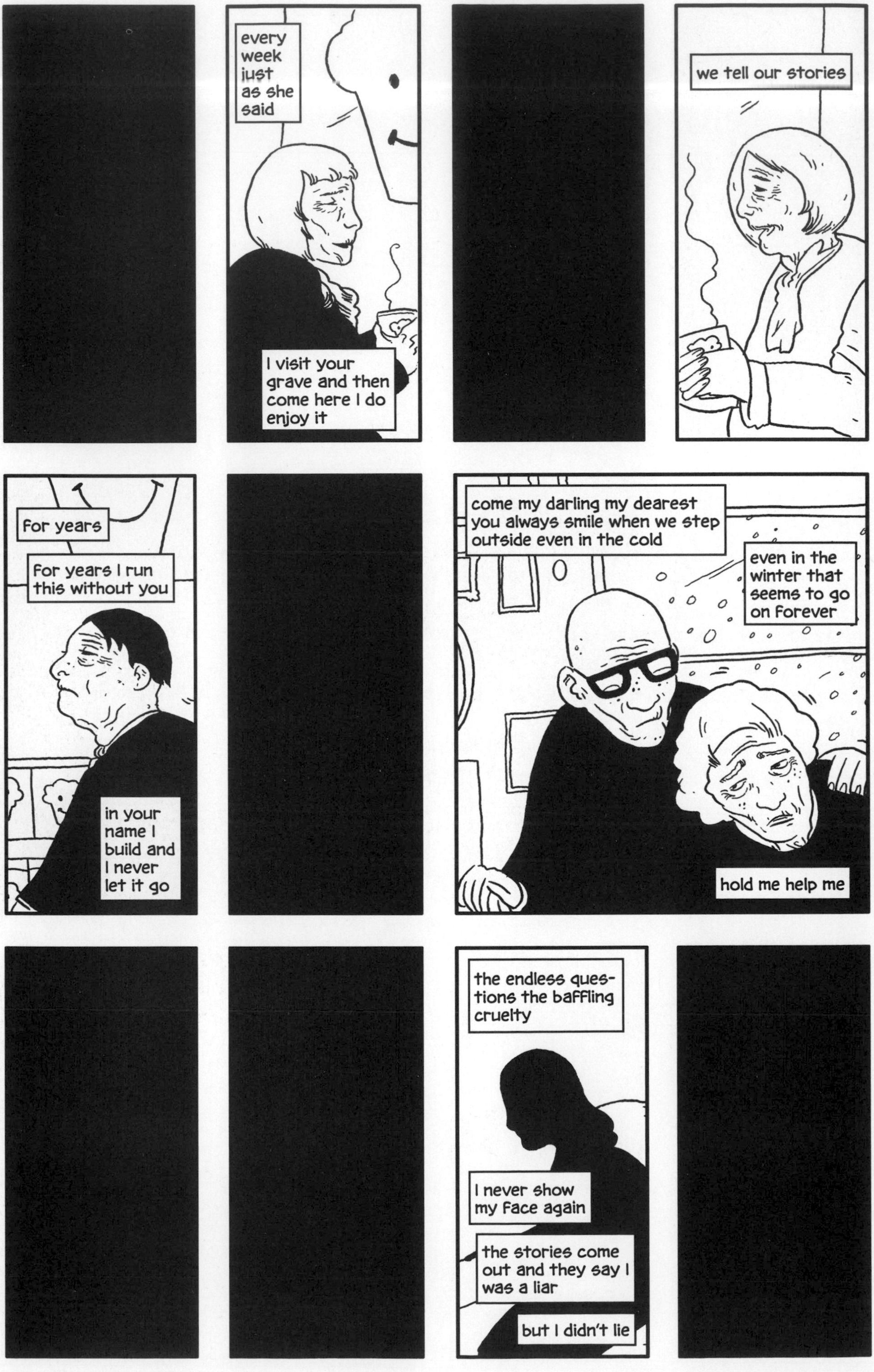
every week just as she said
I visit your grave and then come here I do enjoy it
we tell our stories
for years
for years I run this without you
in your name I build and I never let it go
come my darling my dearest you always smile when we step outside even in the cold
even in the winter that seems to go on forever
hold me help me
the endless ques-tions the baffling cruelty
I never show my face again
the stories come out and they say I was a liar
but I didn't lie

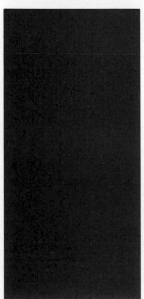

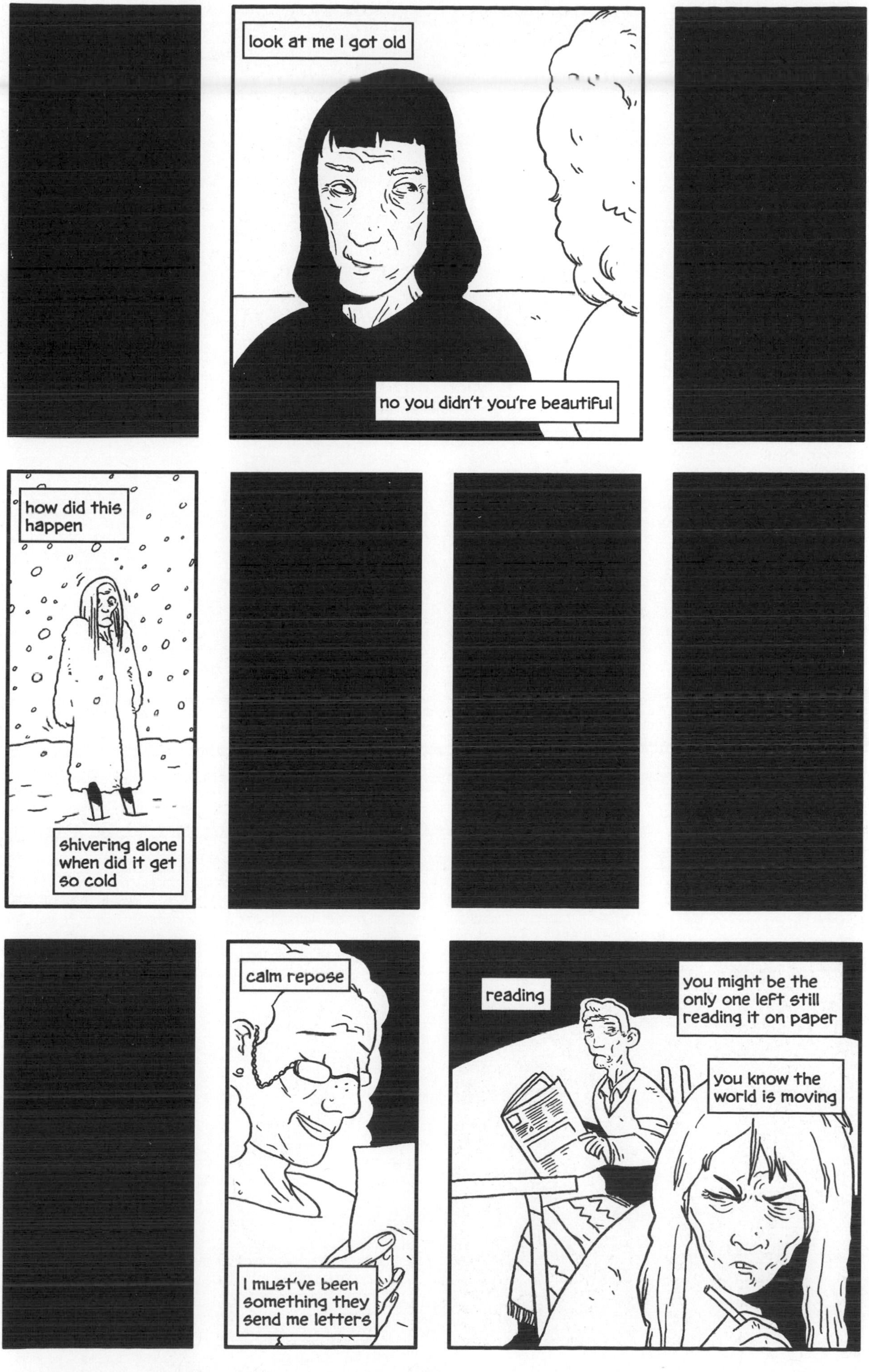
look at me I got old
no you didn't you're beautiful
how did this happen
shivering alone when did it get so cold
calm repose
I must've been something they send me letters
reading
you might be the only one left still reading it on paper
you know the world is moving

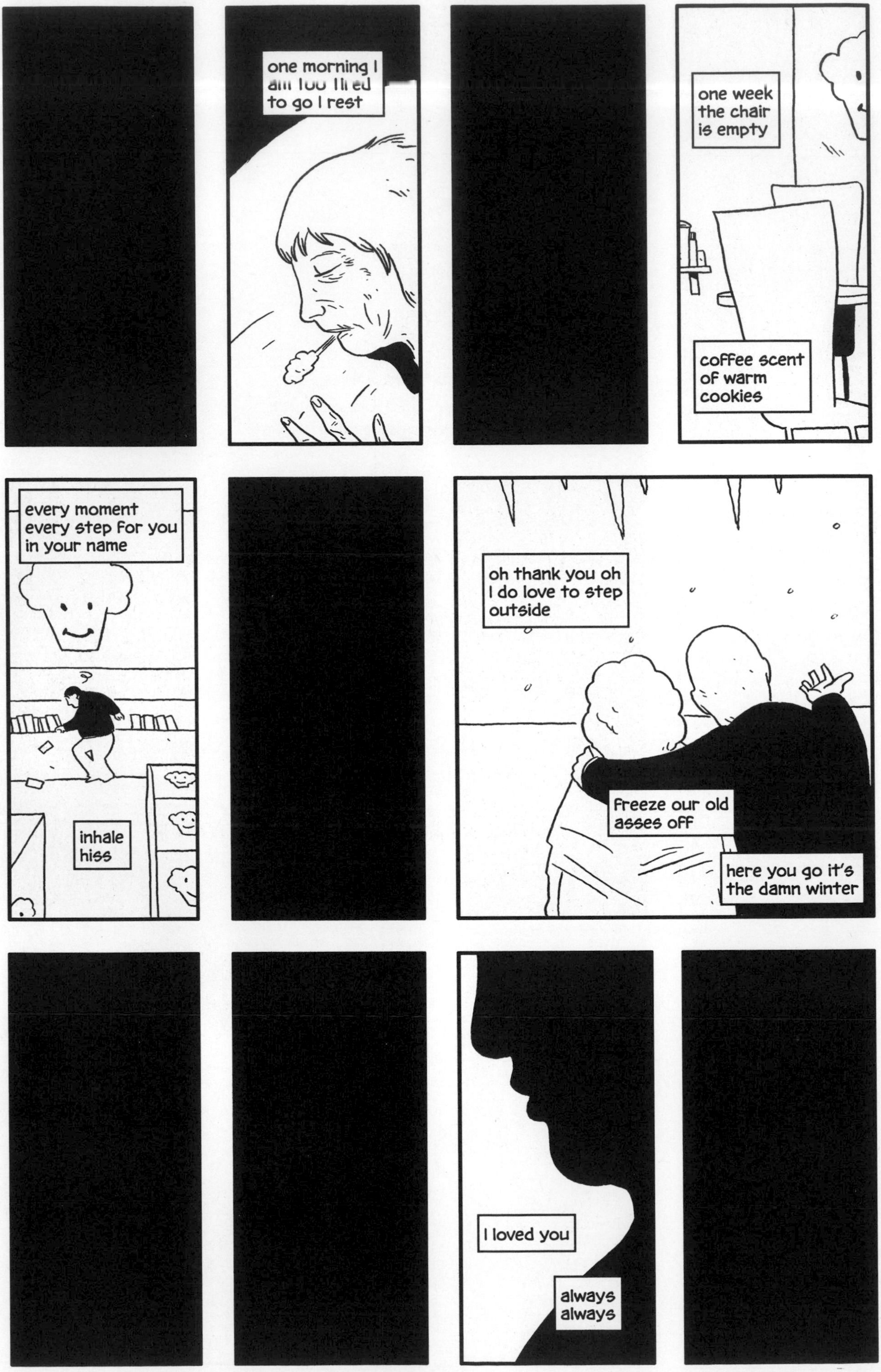
one morning I am too tired to go I rest
one week the chair is empty
coffee scent of warm cookies
every moment every step for you in your name
inhale hiss
oh thank you oh I do love to step outside
freeze our old asses off
here you go it's the damn winter
I loved you
always always

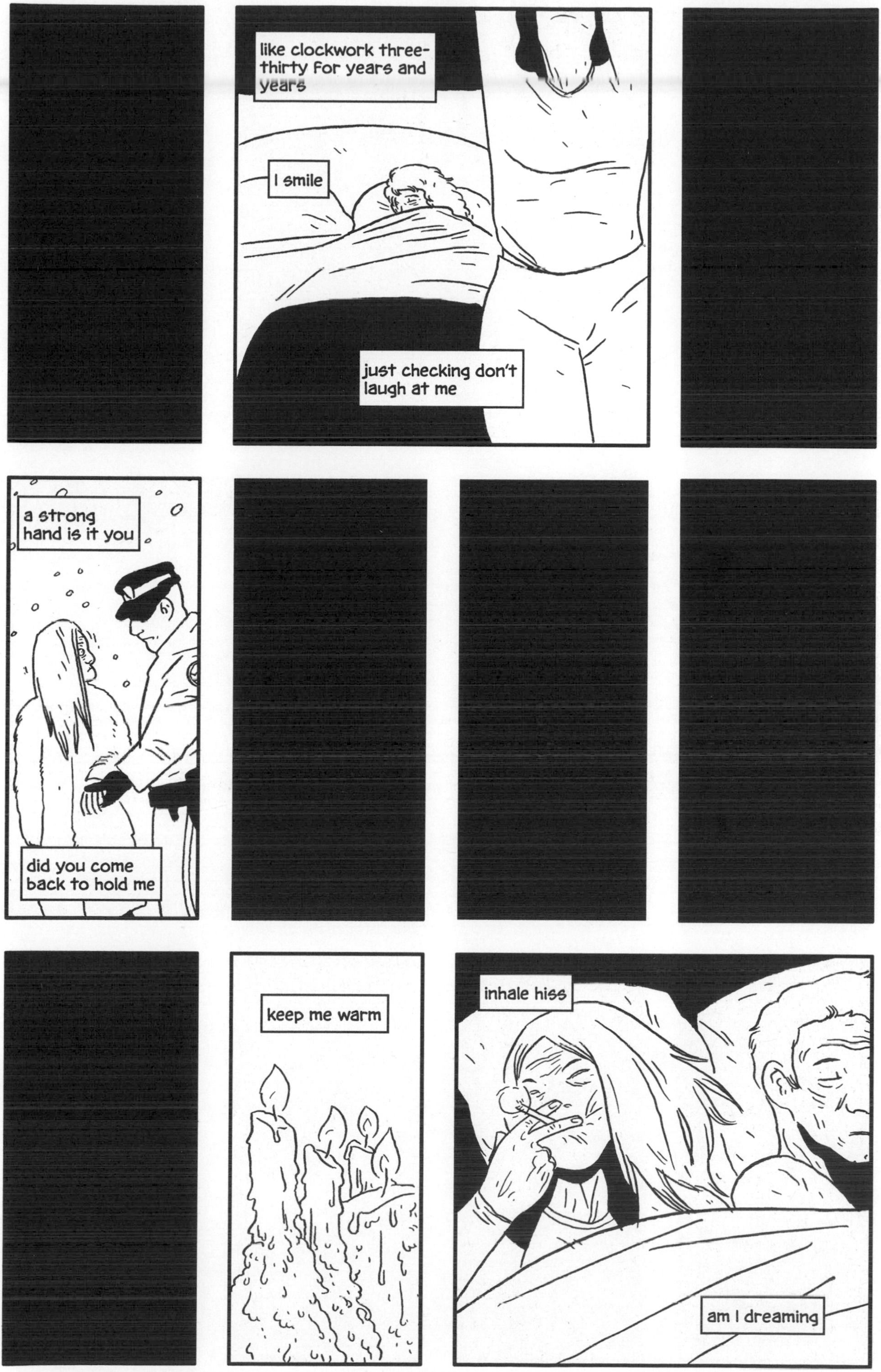
like clockwork three-thirty for years and years
I smile
just checking don't laugh at me
a strong hand is it you
did you come back to hold me
keep me warm
inhale hiss
am I dreaming

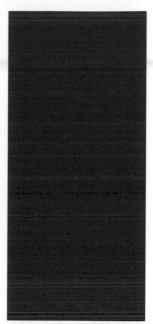

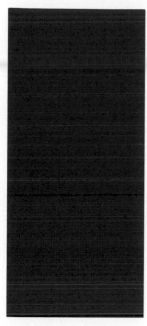

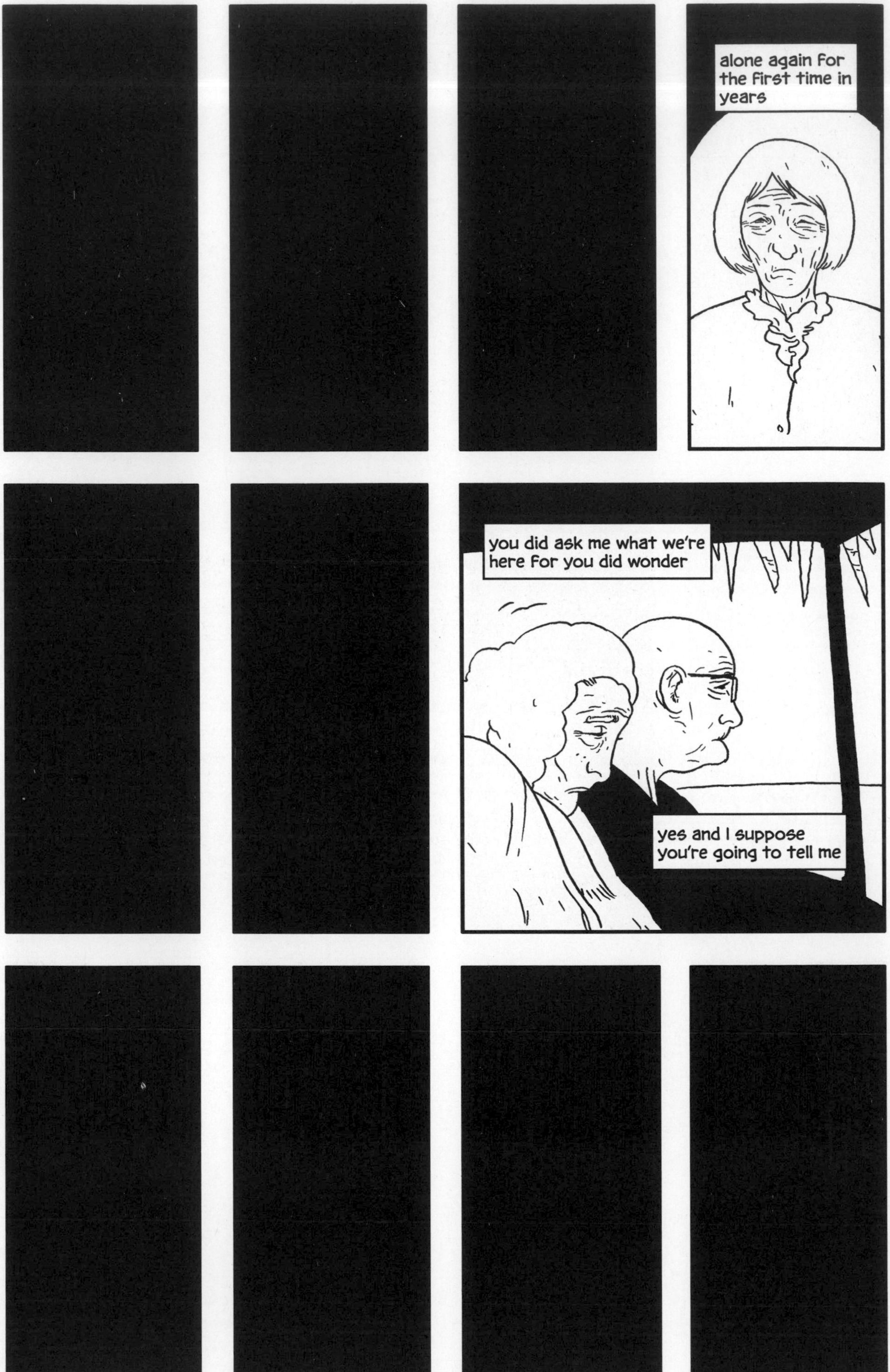
alone again for the first time in years
you did ask me what we're here for you did wonder
yes and I suppose you're going to tell me

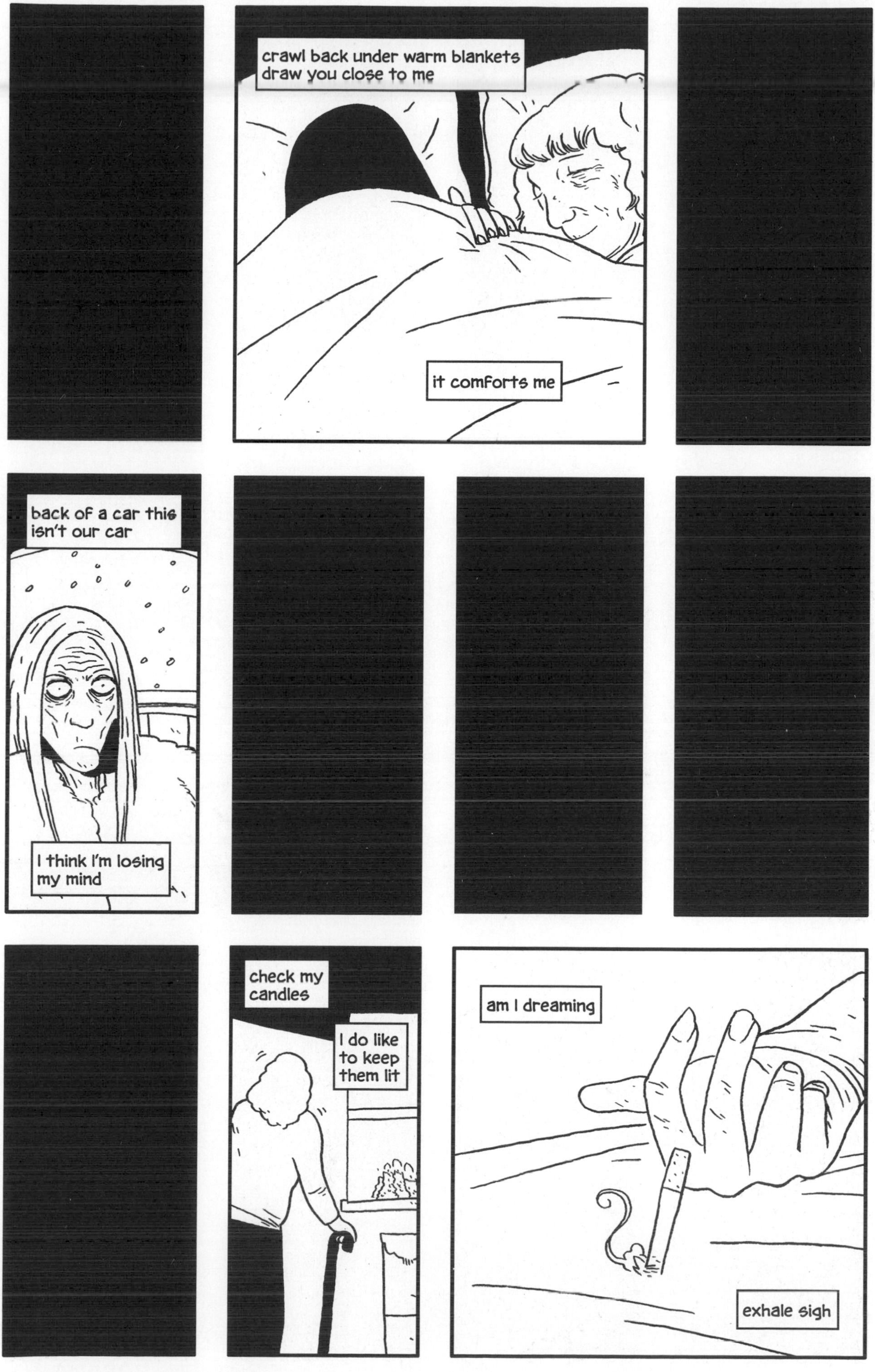
crawl back under warm blankets
draw you close to me
it comforts me
back of a car this
isn't our car
I think I'm losing
my mind
check my
candles
I do like
to keep
them lit
am I dreaming
exhale sigh

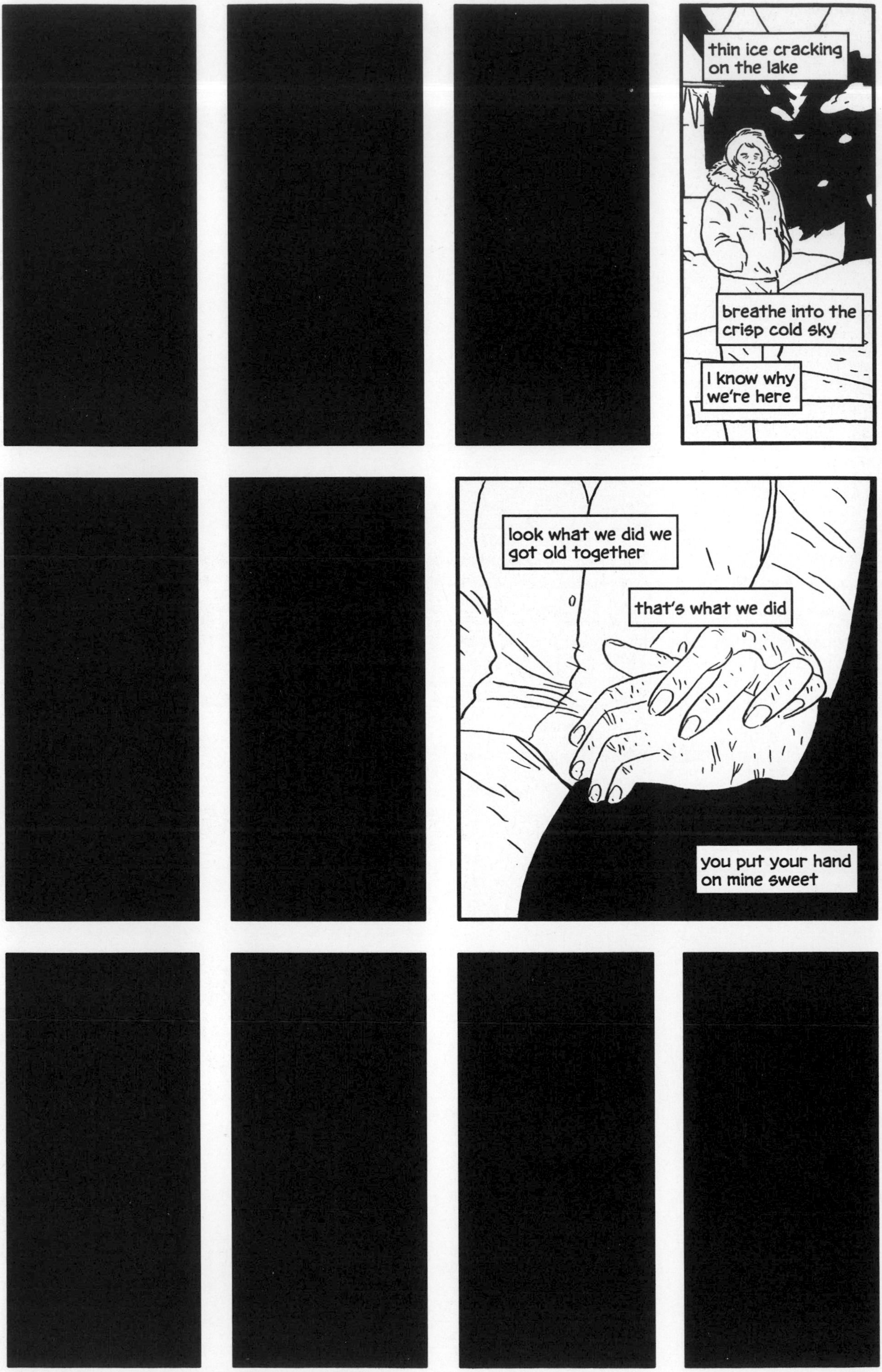
thin ice cracking on the lake
breathe into the crisp cold sky
I know why we're here
look what we did we got old together
that's what we did
you put your hand on mine sweet

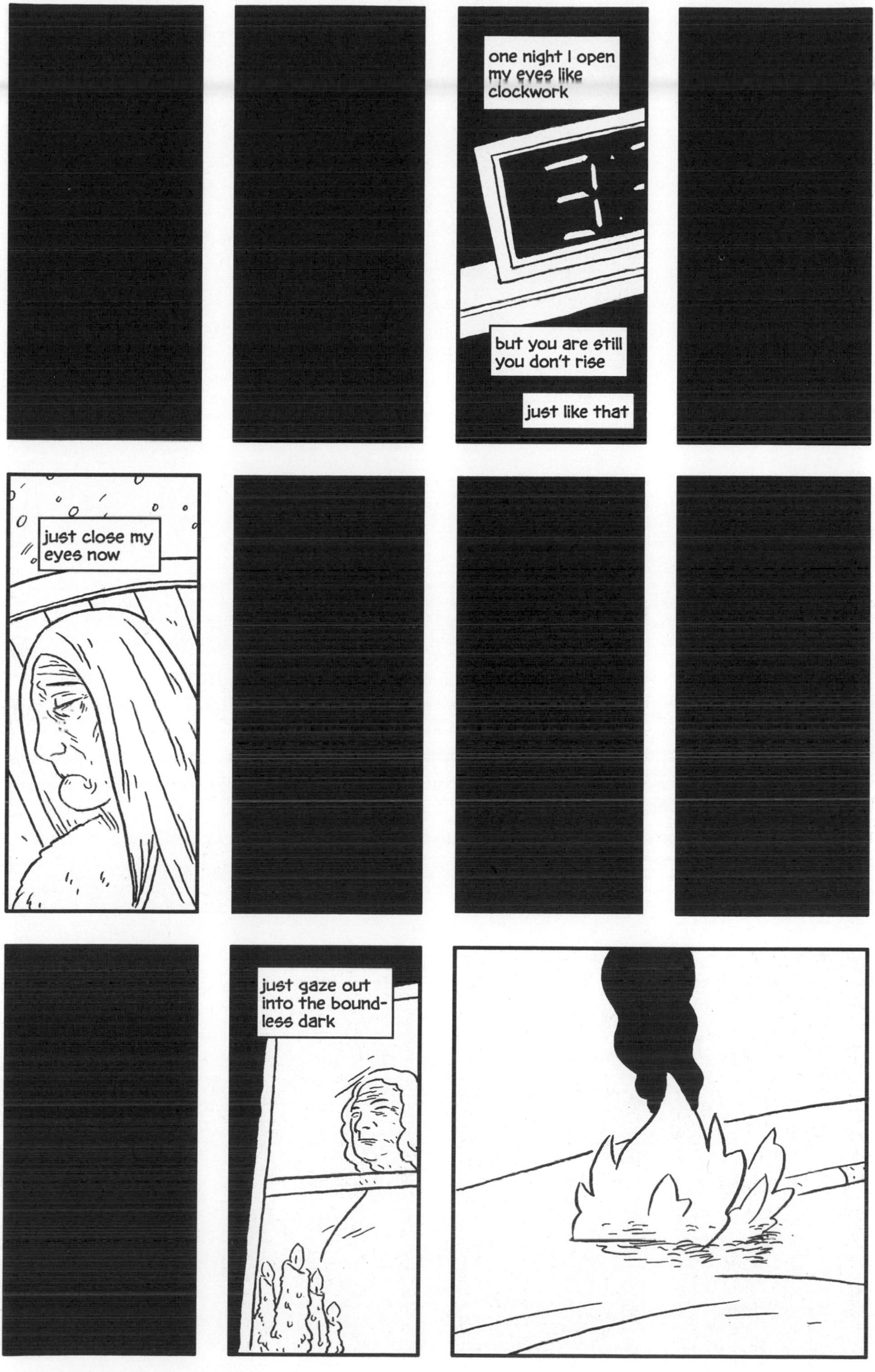
one night I open my eyes like clockwork
but you are still you don't rise
just like that
just close my eyes now
just gaze out into the bound-less dark

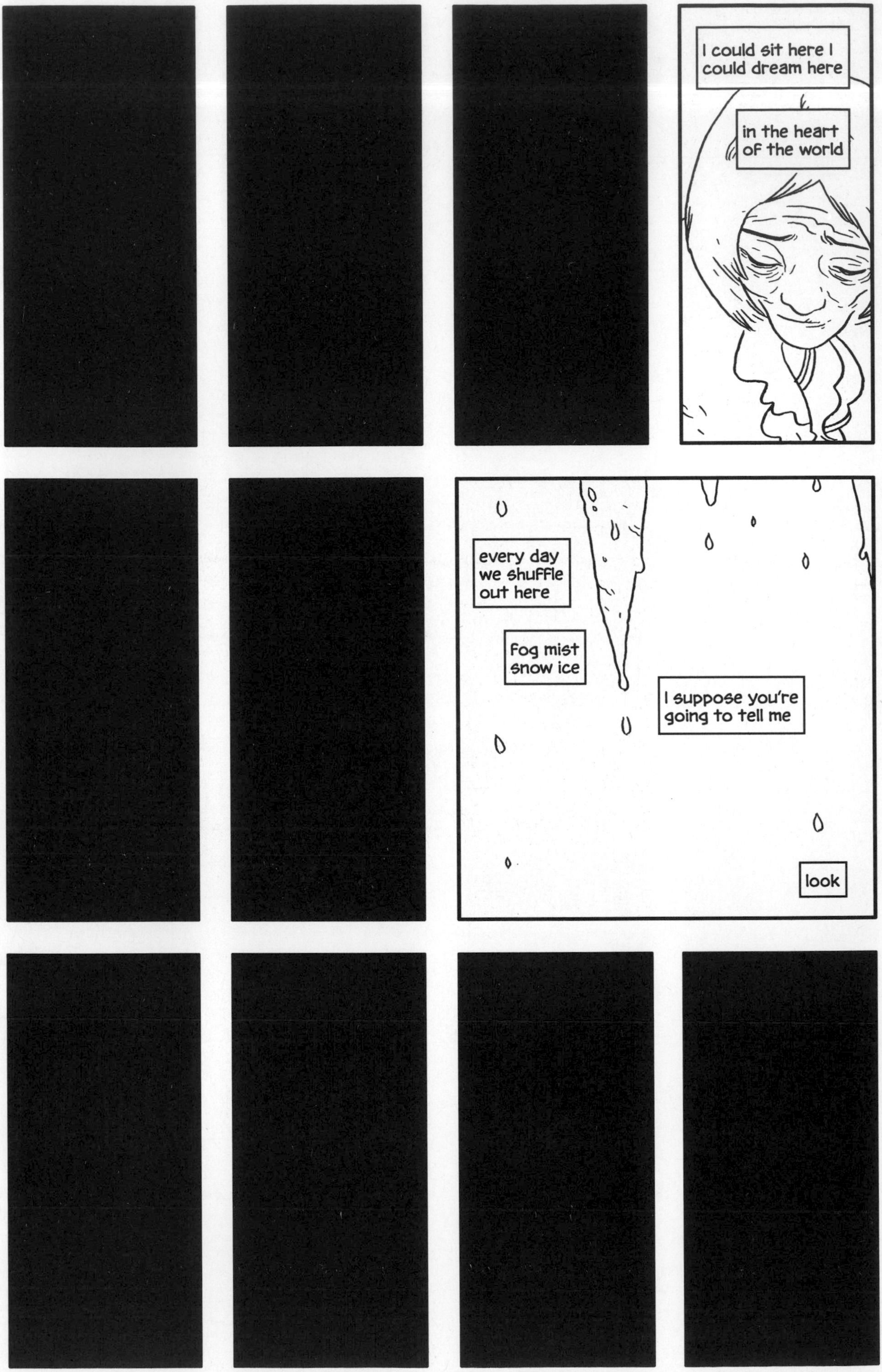
I could sit here I could dream here
in the heart of the world
every day we shuffle out here
fog mist snow ice
I suppose you're going to tell me
look

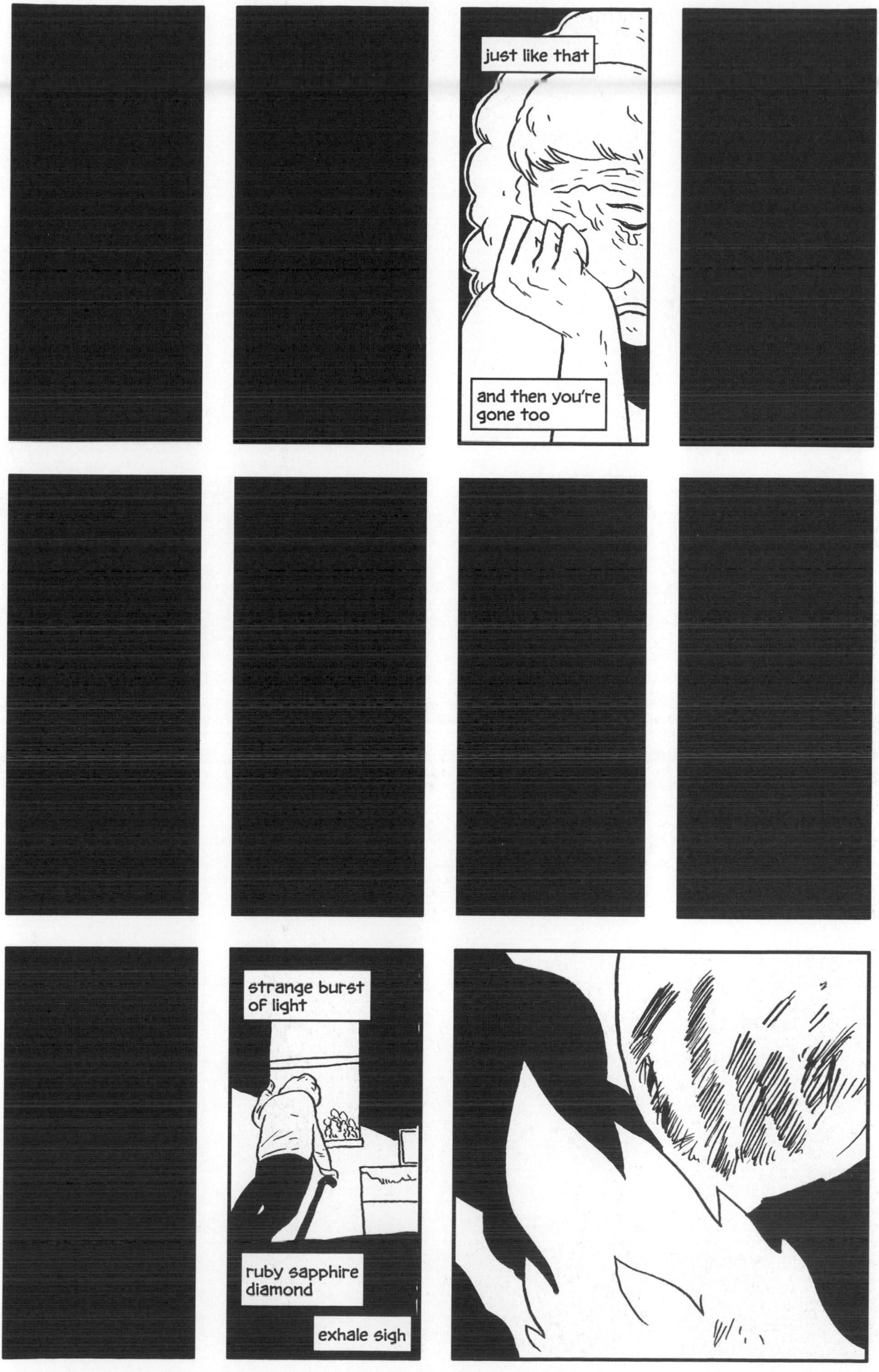
just like that
and then you're gone too
strange burst of light
ruby sapphire diamond
exhale sigh

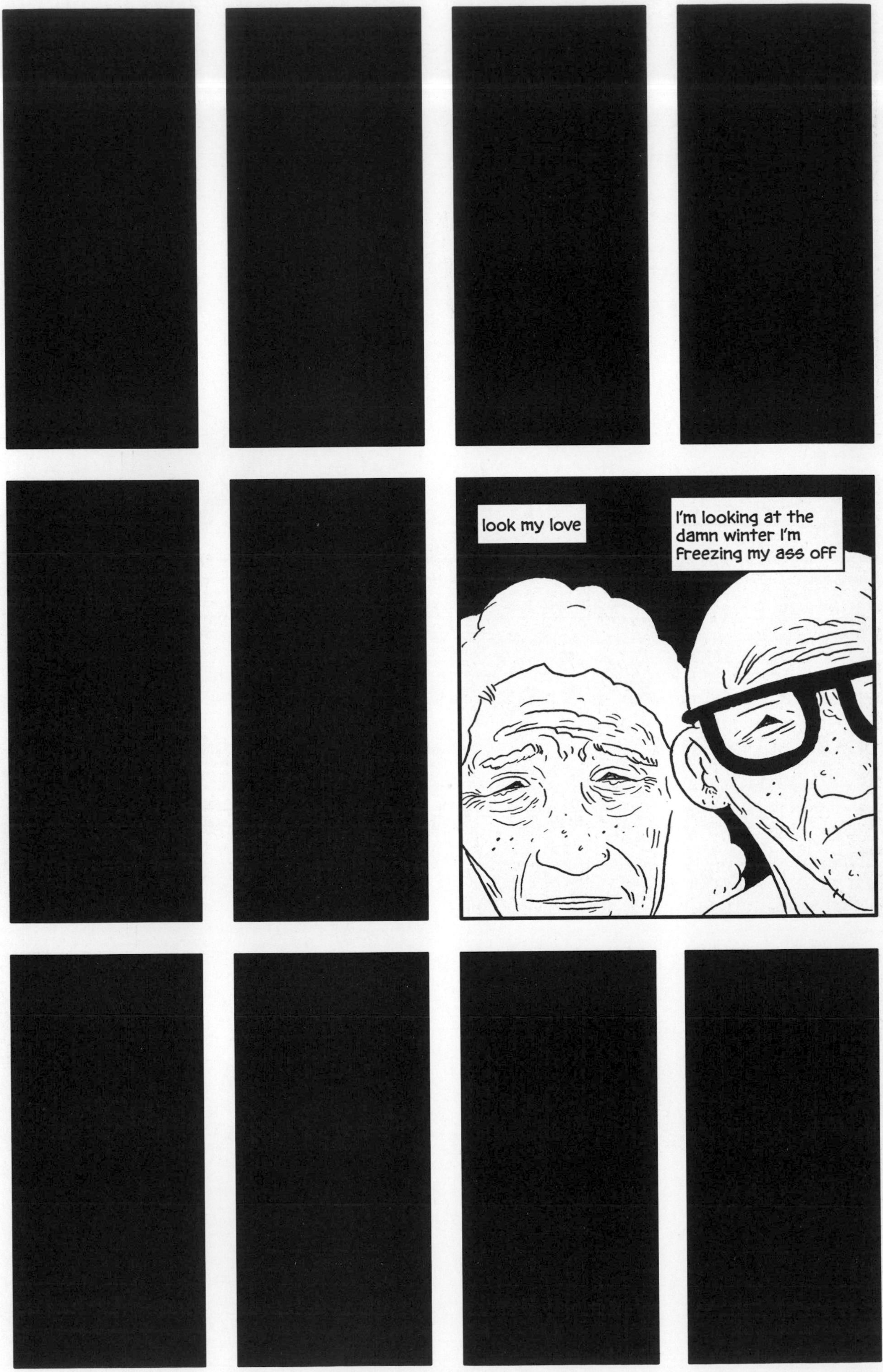
look my love
I'm looking at the damn winter I'm freezing my ass off

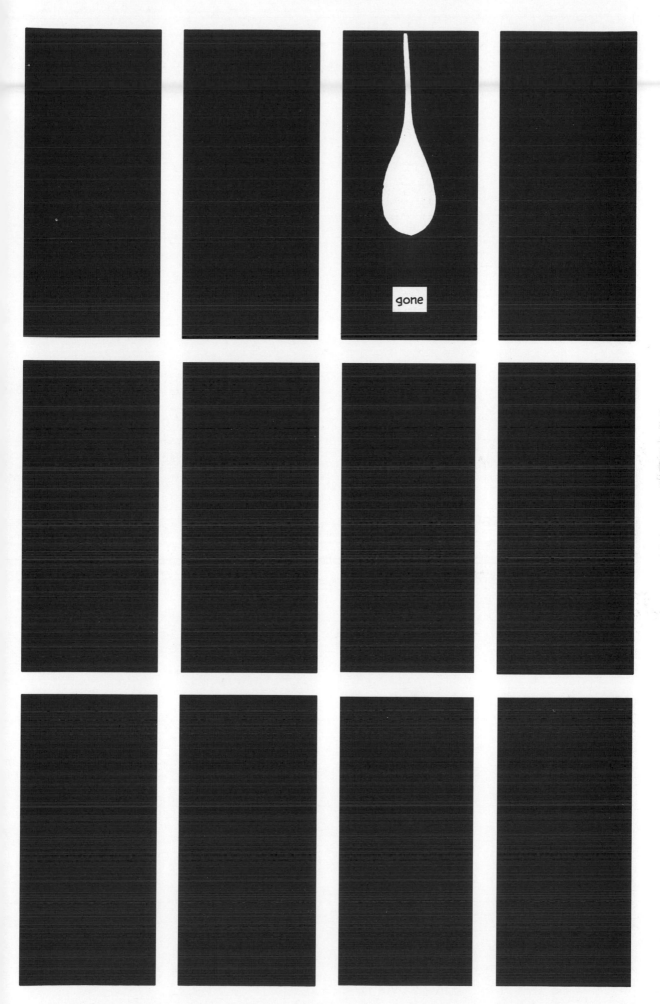

gone

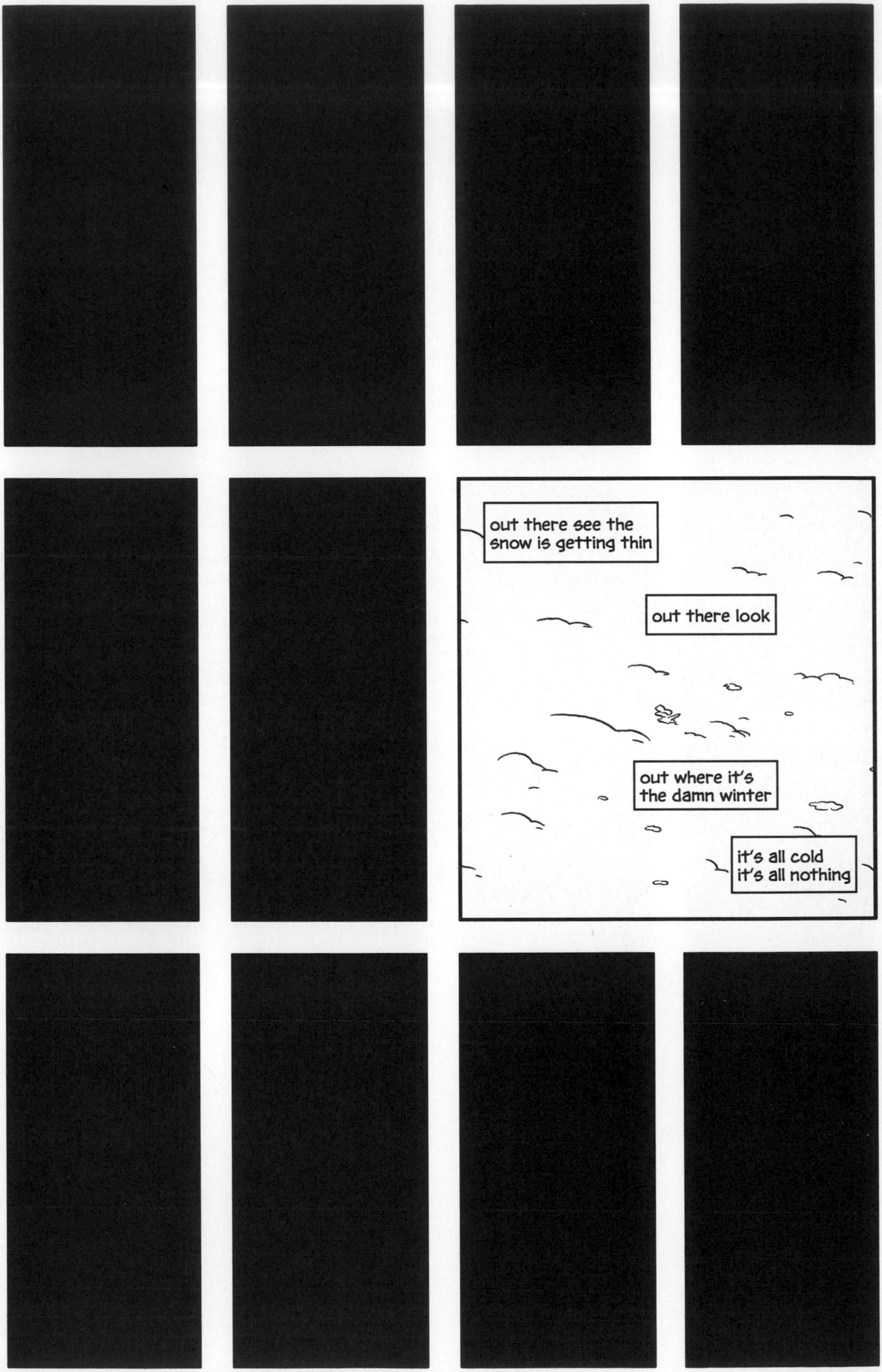
out there see the snow is getting thin
out there look
out where it's the damn winter
it's all cold it's all nothing

[redacted]

[redacted]

[redacted]

[redacted]

[redacted]

[redacted]

[redacted]

[redacted]

[redacted]

[redacted]

[redacted]

[redacted]

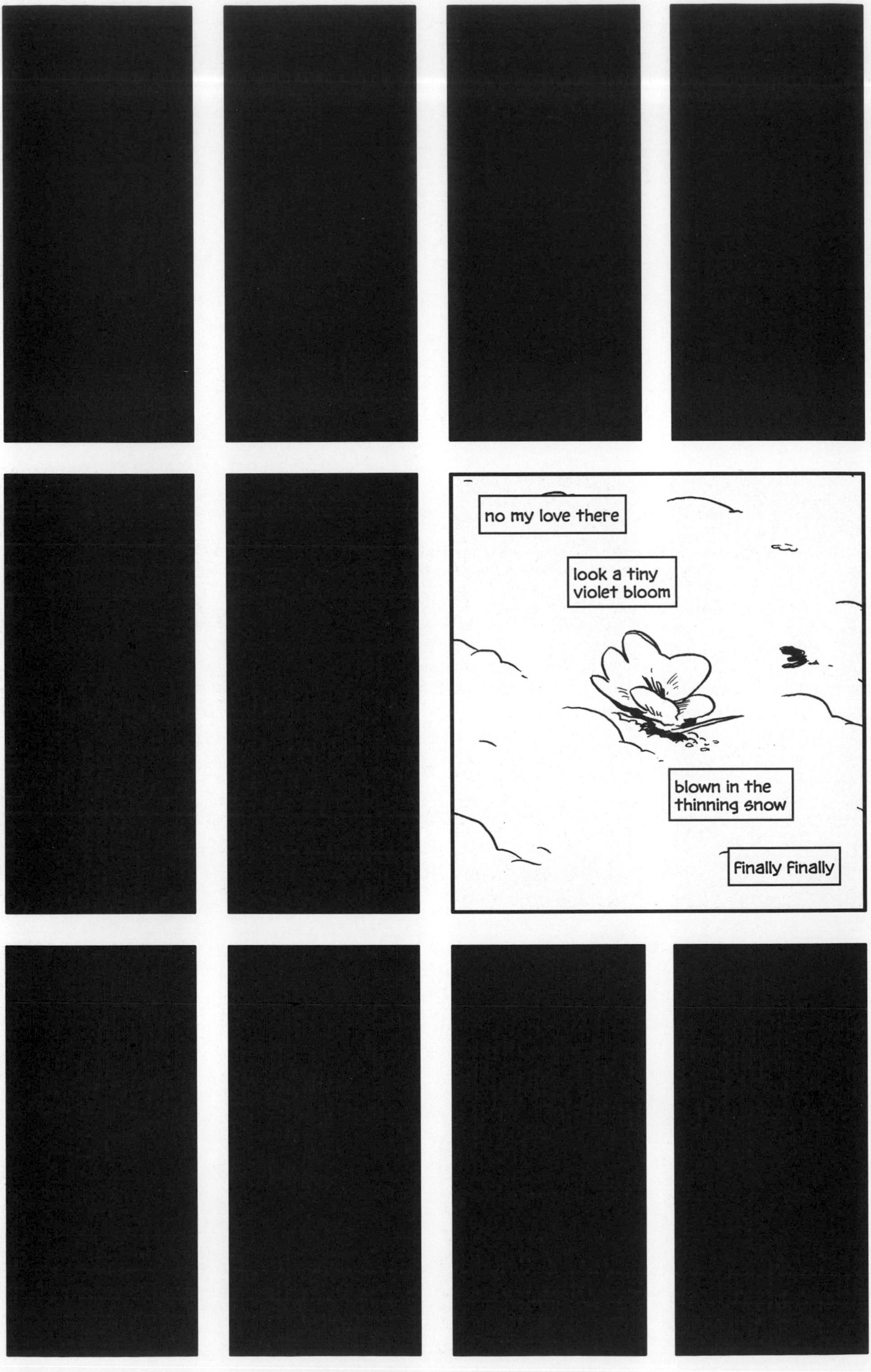
no my love there
look a tiny violet bloom
blown in the thinning snow
finally finally

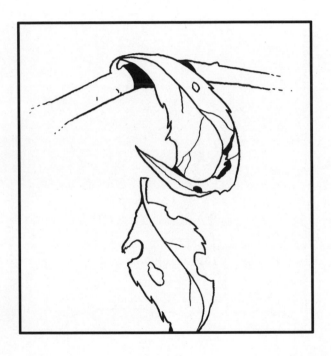

Published by
Oni Press, Inc.

*publisher*
Joe Nozemack

*editor in chief*
James Lucas Jones

*director of sales*
Cheyenne Allot

*director of publicity*
John Schork

*production manager*
Troy Look

*senior designer*
Jason Storey

*editor*
Charlie Chu

*associate editor*
Robin Herrera

*inventory coordinator*
Brad Rooks

*administrative assistant*
Ari Yarwood

*office assistant*
Jung Lee

*production assistant*
Jared Jones

ONI PRESS, INC.
1305 SE Martin Luther King Jr. Blvd.
Suite A
Portland, OR 97214
USA

onipress.com
facebook.com/onipress · twitter.com/onipress · onipress.tumblr.com

rayfawkes.com

First edition: August 2014
ISBN 978-1-62010-168-1 · eISBN 978-1-62010-169-8

Library of Congress Control Number:  2014932453

10 9 8 7 6 5 4 3 2 1

PRINTED IN CHINA.

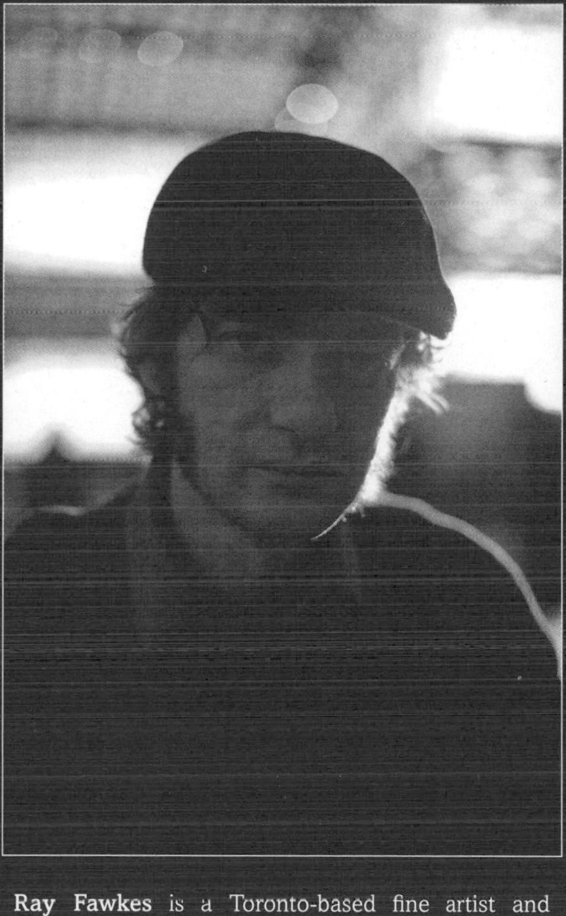
Photo by Charlie Cha

**Ray Fawkes** is a Toronto-based fine artist and writer of comics and graphic novels. He is an Eisner, Harvey, and three-time Shuster Award nominee, a CBC Radio "Bookie" award winner for *The Spectral Engine* and a YALSA award winner for *Possessions Book One: Unclean Getaway*.